S0-BDQ-500

WORK STRESS
Studies of the Context, Content and Outcomes of Stress
A Book of Readings

Edited by
Chris L. Peterson

POLICY, POLITICS, HEALTH AND MEDICINE SERIES
Vicente Navarro, Series Editor

Baywood Publishing Company, Inc.
Amityville, New York

Printed in the United States of America on acid-free recycled paper.

Baywood Publishing Company, Inc.
26 Austin Avenue
Amityville, NY 11701
(800) 638-7819
E-mail: baywood@baywood.com
Web site: baywood.com

Library of Congress Catalog Number: 2003048111
ISBN: 0-89503-280-5 (cloth)

Library of Congress Cataloging-in-Publication Data

Work stress : studies of the context, content, and outcomes of stress : a book of readings / edited by Chris L. Peterson.
p. cm. -- (Policy, politics, health, and medicine series)
Includes bibliographical references and index.
ISBN 0-89503-280-5 (cloth)
1. Job stress. 2. Work--Psychological aspects. I. Peterson, Chris L., 1949- II. Policy, politics, health, and medicine series (Unnumbered)

HF5548.85.W675 2003
158.7'2--dc21

2003048111

Work Stress

Contents

Foreword

I recently asked an elderly relative what the term "work stress" meant to him during his working life, from which he had retired more than 20 years ago. "Didn't exist when I was a lad," was his response. Likewise, "coping" was something to do with making a roof slope to deal with water. Yet entering "work stress" into my favorite Internet search engine generated nearly 3 million hits, and "coping" another 1.2 million. There can be little doubt that work stress and how it is dealt with has become one of the major issues of the day. At the academic research level, the occupational health and safety database OSHROM has more than 1,000 references on work stress.

As a concept, work stress is hotly contested. Does it exist? Is it a legitimate illness? What causes it? Should it be compensable? Do the causes lie more in the individual or in the work situation? What is the relative usefulness of stress management versus work reorganization? Are nonwork sources of stress relevant? There can be few areas of inquiry today (at both the academic and the policy level) that are as contentious.

Some aspects of the phenomenon cannot be denied: The organization of work has changed significantly in the general direction of the "speedup of the production line" in most workplaces. This "speed up" affects workers, and most of its effects are in some way deleterious to their health. And some stakeholders have a vested interest in denying these effects, as others likewise have a vested interest in revealing them.

This book represents a significant contribution to these debates, under the editorship of Dr. Chris Peterson, who has made a substantial contribution to the study of work stress in his various publications. The book brings together a range of expert authors and commentators to explore the issues, drawing on their own and others' meticulous research. In spite of attempts in the current neoliberal economic climate to define work stress as essentially a personal issue of lack of individual adaptation to a changing work environment, books such as this one ensure that work stress, its content and context, remains a lively and contested issue within the world of work and in society generally.

Evan Willis
Professor of Sociology and Head of Humanities and Social Sciences
La Trobe University, Albury-Wodonga Campus

Chapter 1

INTRODUCTION

Chris L. Peterson

Knowledge about stress at work has been with us for some time. Since the early writings of Walter Cannon (1) and the later works of Hans Selye (2, 3), stress has become an acknowledged component of medical science, particularly since Selye's summation (2) that stress is part of the etiology of all diseases. Yet stress has not necessarily become an acknowledged part of employees' experience at work, and there are still substantive groups who virtually deny the existence of work-related stress. For example, while many regions now compensate workers for this condition (e.g., the West Coast of the United States and Britain, Canada, and Australia), other regions (e.g., the East Coast of the United States) do not easily acknowledge the legitimacy of the condition. In addition, it is still relatively recently that compensation has been awarded in many countries.

However, both official figures on compensation and anecdotal stories attest to the experience of work-related stress. Work stress literature of the 1970s and 1980s focused on identifying the different stressors at work and the strength of their effects on employees, and it made important inroads into the psychophysiology of stress. However, in the late 1980s and 1990s the industrial and commercial landscape was changing, introducing a relatively new type of organizational and management style that was to spread rapidly through internationalization and globalization. There was a need in the stress literature to refocus on new and emerging issues, in particular the effects of managerialism on work organization and stress. In this developing world of work, principles of rational economic management had taken root and much of the emphasis of management and organization practice turned to emphasizing the fiscal role and accountability of management and professionals, downsizing and rationalizing work organizations, outsourcing work, and directing public administration towards privatization. Downsizing increased, and unions played a less predominant role.

In the context of these rapid changes in organizational management and the predominance of a managerial ethos, this book has a number of aims. First, it aims to provide readers with an international perspective on the causes of stress. Second, it provides perspectives on workload and work demand and stress and discusses their usefulness in analyzing the causes of stress. Third, it presents case studies that demonstrate the application of stress analyses in a number of different settings. Finally, few books on work stress have seriously examined stress in the context of older workers, transitions into retirement, and other important life roles. The experience of being a caregiver and decisions to retire are looked at within the framework of work stress.

As we show in the book, the major developed countries are facing many similar problems in relation to stress at work. Downsizing has had considerable effects on all occupational levels, yet more research needs to be conducted to determine appropriate methods for dealing with changing market demands other than simply shedding labor. Downsizing can have particularly stressful consequences and does not necessarily lead to increased productivity and market value for companies; it is one contributor to the wave of increased work intensification. Downsizing needs to be conducted carefully, in a planned and transparent manner, if it is to avoid posing longer-term health, morale, and productivity problems.

The moves towards privatization in the public sector in the United Kingdom, United States, and Australia, for example, have also had important effects on the way work is carried out, on job security, and on psychosocial and other health consequences. Privatization has brought with it downsizing and rationalization of work processes to fit the demands of an open marketplace and has overridden some of the protective work regulations previously in place.

It is the effects on stress of these types of work changes that require more study in order to determine the extent to which a changing environment itself precipitates high levels of stress. One commonly reads reports on employees citing too much effort required for the job, too many tasks to perform in short time periods, and an imbalance between work demands and domestic and rest-of-life responsibilities. These pressures and other economic exigencies have forced older employees in some industries to deal with increased stress in the workplace, exacerbated by the demands made by new, increasingly complex technologies. They have also led many employees to retire earlier and to face the relatively new phenomenon of dealing at a younger age with the stresses associated with retirement.

STAKEHOLDERS IN WORK STRESS

While there is still debate among individual employees, unions, management, and government over the extent to which stress needs to be prioritized, the issues have been quite focused in stress research. We have evidence of the causes of stress, the links between stress and psychological and physical ill-health, and some tested ways of best dealing with stress. Individual employees and unions face the issue of the degree to which employees are still blamed for being victims of stress, as well as important issues of personal health and well-being and the extent to which the individual pays for the consequences of stress through pressures on domestic and community relations. Increasing numbers of studies are now looking at the effects of work stress on the rest of life (e.g., 4, 5).

Management needs to acknowledge that stress is occurring and is a concern. Best-practice models are needed for reorganizing work and work relations to deal effectively with stress. The lack of available models poses a problem, although a large body of work focuses on issues such as lack of control as central to understanding causes of much stress. What is needed is a greater effort in developing and testing best-practice models for the management of stress (6). Additional focus needs to be given to the relationship between stress reduction and associated morale and productivity increases, both in the short and long term, and management's role in promoting healthy workplaces.

Government needs to increase its focus on national profiles on stress. Stress has identifiable morbidity and mortality consequences and as such is an important public health issue deserving of more attention by the State. There are hidden community costs of stress (7) in terms of medical service utilization and community service resources, and these need to be accounted for as costs of stress at work.

One important priority that is not well addressed is the extent to which current occupational health and safety programs provide a sufficient "safety net" for employees who experience stress. Employees who are stressed often find themselves in counseling programs or, worse, simply exiting the organization, as the resources to support them are not available. An important reform in dealing with stress at work would seek to provide effective support networks within the organization before employees with stress become victims. This may take the form of trained negotiators or the like who could provide that "safety net." In working towards these types of solutions, increased union, management, and government cooperation is essential.

ISSUES IN THE FUTURE

Developments in technology and positive economic conditions promised an easier worklife. In particular, proponents of new technology presented it as liberating workers from meaningless tasks and from many of the burdens of work. However, new technology, including information technology, the Internet, and other advanced technological developments, has failed to deliver on that promise. In many cases work has become much more difficult, with a reduction in job opportunities in some work sectors (notably blue-collar work).

Some of the challenges for the early 21st century are to provide continued work opportunities for those affected by technological developments and to provide a management style that accounts for human needs in the context of regular downsizing and privatization. The effects of work changes are starting to become evident in human and organizational costs. The sooner management, unions, and government come to terms with some of the complexities in dealing effectively with change in a rapidly altering work environment, the sooner emerging problems will be confronted. That is, the work experience can be more positive and productive, challenges for productivity better addressed, and the community, social, and personal costs of a rapidly changing work environment better dealt with.

ORGANIZATION OF THE BOOK

The book is divided into four sections. The first section investigates international perspectives and experiences in work-related stress, from the United Kingdom, United States, and Australia. Chris Peterson (Chapter 2) discusses the role that rational economic management practices and policies have played in workplace changes during the last decade and a half in Australia. He discusses the trends towards managerialism and work-intensification practices and outlines current practices and frameworks for researching stress and work, arguing that few studies have reported the effects of workplace change on stress experienced at work. He presents results from the 1995 Australian Workplace Industrial Relations Survey to show the nature of stress in Australia in the mid-1990s and looks at the effects of self-reports on changes that took place in the 12 months preceding the survey. Four types of change are important predictors of stress. Changes in influence and support, which are related to control, and changes in workpace and effort were the two strongest predictors of stress, more so than work factors measured at a static point in time, such as job security and effort expended on the job. As Peterson concludes, an understanding of the effects of changes in key work practices is important if we are to appreciate some of the stronger causes of work stress. This also has implications for change-management programs.

John Chandler, Elisabeth Berg, and Jim Barry (Chapter 3) present an overview of the major trends in stress experienced in the United Kingdom, adopting a sociological explanation for the emergence of stress in a number of different work areas across the country. Stress is prevalent to a high degree in the United Kingdom and recently has been especially affecting managerial employees. Although British workers have been seen as idle, they have the longest working week in the European Union. The U.K. labor market has changed in recent years, with part-time and casual work becoming more common, and there has been an increase in performance-based systems for work. This has had particular effects on management. Chandler and coauthors discuss the extent to which British managers are now working longer hours, and the reasons for this. They also discuss how work roles have been changing and the changed identity among many U.K. workers in terms of the work they perform. A section of the chapter is devoted to discussing how public sector work has changed throughout the United Kingdom; this also includes groups such as school teachers. The authors also pose a number of explanations for the relatively lower levels of stress found among U.K. part-time employees.

Lawrence Murphy and Lewis Pepper (Chapter 4) evaluate the effects of downsizing and restructuring on stress in North American companies. Much downsizing has taken place without accounting for the health costs to employees and companies or the organizational consequences. In fact, downsizing has been related to deteriorating health and well-being of employees. The authors conducted a study comparing the effects of downsizing on employees and organizations in two types of settings: an organization with repeated episodes of downsizing and an organizations with a single episode of downsizing. The study focused on outcomes such as survivor's syndrome and stress symptoms, as well as physical health. Significant downsizing outcomes were evident on stress, job security, health, and coping in both settings. Downsizing history affected health, stress, and job security, regardless of how downsizing was undertaken. Murphy and Pepper also found that positive changes in the work environment after downsizing can lead to beneficial effects for survivors. If downsizing is planned and implemented fairly with honest and open communication, the negative effects can be somewhat minimized.

Jane Ferrie (Chapter 5) examines the relationship between labor market change, job insecurity, and health, in investigating downsizing and privatization in the United Kingdom. In the last two decades, the U.K. labor market has undergone considerable change. Ferrie focuses on a civil service agency, the civil service traditionally being protected from marketplace pressures. Civil service privatization was introduced in 1984, and by the end of the century most private utilities had been privatized or opened to competition. Ferrie examines the privatization process and related job insecurity in the selected agency. Her study reports on the Whitehall II studies as applied to the selected civil service department. The outcome measures included self-rated health, longstanding illness, recent symptomatology, health problems in the last year, cardiovascular measures, and responses to a mental health questionnaire. Before privatization, job insecurity had some modest effects on poor health; after privatization, there was poorer health among those in less favorable employment. Also, morbidity was greater for those in insecure employment than for those securely reemployed. Ferrie found that the study supports the relationship between unemployment and health effects. She also found that social support at work, normally considered a buffer for stress and ill-health, suffered as a result of privatization, and that reemployment may be experienced as unsatisfactory.

Wendy Macdonald presents both chapters in the section on work demands. In Chapter 6 she examines the concept and measurement of workload and adopts an ergonomic perspective to argue for the efficacy of workload measurement. She associates a number of attempts to improve work performance with the intensification of work. Macdonald maintains that the relationship between workload and stress is not well understood, in that high workload on its own does not necessarily ensure high levels of stress. She presents a comprehensive picture of the ergonomics view of workload and examines its various aspects and determinants; she also presents a model of the multidimensional aspects of workload, from an ergonomic perspective. Macdonald then takes on the task of relating workload to work demand, presenting a number of different arguments to explain the relationships. She finally works with a comprehensive model to discuss the relationship between workload and stress and the types of stressors that are related to the determinants of workload. The chapter concludes with a helpful discussion on the utility of the workload construct as applied in practical situations.

In Chapter 7 Wendy Macdonald investigates the nature of work demands and stress in blue-collar work. The chapter focuses on workload as a contributing factor to work efficiency and work stress. It draws on data from a recent research project, which aimed to evaluate formal and informal methods of setting work rates in a sample of Australian companies, focusing on how much control employees had over pace as opposed to being paced by external factors. Production targets, external pacing by a production process, and having to meet deadlines and orders had a greater effect than whether formal or informal methods were used in setting work rates. In addition, stress scores were higher where the timing of the production process and operating time of the machine influenced the work rate. Employees engaged in difficult work were more likely to rate the task as too fast, but with simple work, working to deadlines appeared to be a challenge. Overall, stress was higher where general satisfaction scores were lower.

Beginning the section on occupational case studies, John McCormick (Chapter 8) reviews the experience of work-related stress among the professions. The serving professions are characterized by vocation or calling and can have some psychic rewards. However, the work may be associated with some violence in client/professional contact and some failure—for example, for doctors, when patients die. Dentists and teachers may not have that extreme of stress but nonetheless are subject to testing relationships with clients. Professionals also have a problematic relationship with the bureaucracies within which they work—bureaucratization, for example, can lead to work becoming deprofessionalized. McCormick discusses all these relationships, as well as the nature of social change vis-à-vis the changing status of professions and societal changes that affect a professional's work. He presents an "attribution for responsibility for stress" model for dealing with professional stress in bureaucratic organizations. For professionals, much stress and burnout can be associated with idealistic and unrealistic work expectations. One way of dealing with stress created in bureaucracies is to reduce the distance between professionals and the bureaucracies within which they work.

Chris Peterson (Chapter 9) discusses stress among blue-collar workers. He begins by outlining a significant reduction in the number of jobs, some of which is attributable to downsizing due to automation and technological change. In many studies conducted on this occupational group, control over work is a central feature. Peterson analyzes the 1995 Australian Workplace Industrial Relations

Survey and makes connections with some of the results presented in Chapter 2. Blue-collar workers reported being less secure than either white-collar workers or management and professional employees. However, fewer blue-collar workers reported changes in workplace organization and management, and while they put a lot of effort into their jobs, a smaller proportion did so than in white-collar and management/professional groups. As was found for the sample of employees reported in Chapter 2, changes at work were the most significant predictors of stress for blue-collar workers, with a change in influence and support (related to control) the most important determinant. Although stress levels for blue-collar employees do not seem to have risen at the same rate as for other occupational groups, these workers are also subject to the effects of work intensification and the rational economic style of management that dominated in the 1990s. Evidence from other studies shows the difficulty for blue-collar workers in coping with the demands of a stressful job and the effects, on family and the rest of life. In this sense, blue-collar workers continue to be disadvantaged in the workplace in relation to stress.

Claire Mayhew (Chapter 10) investigates the links between stress and precarious employment. She begins by describing the causes of stress and stress-related illnesses and demonstrates that a lack of control at work is an important cause of stress. The problems associated with precarious employment relate to financial hardships, unemployment, and threats of redundancy. Central to her argument on the relationship between precarious employment and stress is that economic insecurity, control at work, and work demands place undue pressure on employees. Mayhew examines ten Australian studies of precarious employment based on data collected through face-to-face interviews, for subjects ranging from long-haul transport drivers to precariously employed outworkers in the clothing industry. Most precariously employed workers spent long hours on the job and reported fatigue. They lacked control over their length of employment, their pay, and the work process, and distress for these workers is inevitable. For example, more than 15 percent of long-haul transport drivers reported clinically significant levels of a measure of psychiatric morbidity, and the most precariously employed truck drivers reported the highest morbidity scores. Mayhew concludes that precariously employed workers have a disproportionately high level of ill-health, injury, and economically induced stress.

The final section of the book addresses the relationship between stress and older workers, retirement, and the role of caregivers. David de Vaus and Yvonne Wells provide both chapters. Chapter 11 looks at the relationship between work and home and discusses work stress and caregiver stress. Recently, attention has been paid to the caregiving role at home for older workers—that is, to the extent that caregivers find the work and home interface produces stress. The authors use data from the Australian Healthy Retirement Project. More than 10 percent of the sample defined themselves as caregivers, providing for parents, spouses, or disabled children. Wells and de Vaus found that caregiving might interrupt performance at work, but caregivers were not likely to report higher work stress than noncaregivers. However, controlling for the effects of working long hours, caregivers were more likely to report higher job stress. There were no differences in job satisfaction, work commitment, or work ethic between caregivers and noncaregivers. Overall, caregivers were less likely to be happy and healthy, and this was true for both women and men. But work stress did not have a more negative effect on the nonwork activities of caregivers compared with noncaregivers.

In Chapter 12 de Vaus and Wells investigate stress and retirement. Little is known about the transition of older workers into retirement. This chapter focuses on the extent to which older workers find their work environment stressful; the degree to which retirement itself is stressful; and whether workers who experience work stress also have a stressful retirement. The authors again use data from the Australian Healthy Retirement Project. Men have been leaving the workforce earlier, and more women have been staying longer. However, policies have been developed to increase labor force participation; for older workers this means remaining in work that is often less secure. De Vaus and Wells provide models to explain the nature of stress for older workers. They find that only a minority of older workers found work highly stressful. However, a number of older workers felt they were not appreciated at work. High stress was related to low job satisfaction, a view of the workplace as unpleasant, and a feeling of lack of appreciation and support. Those who had retired from work thought all stages of retirement were fairly easy; relatively few found themselves more stressed following retirement. The authors conclude that more research is needed to identify the ways of best coping with retirement, rather than struggling: this will aid people to make successful transitions into their retirement years.

REFERENCES

1. Cannon, W. B. The interrelationships of emotions as suggested by recent physiological researchers. *Am. J. Psychol.* 25: 256–282, 1914.
2. Selye, H. A syndrome produced by diverse nocturnal agents. *Nature* 138: 32, 1936.
3. Selye, H. *The Stress of Life.* McGraw Hill, New York, 1956.
4. Chan, K. B., et al. Work stress amongst six professional groups: The Singapore experience. *Soc. Sci. Med.* 50(10): 1415–1432, 2000.
5. Grzywacz, J. G., Almeida, D. M., and McDonald, D. A. Work family spillover and daily reports of work and family stress in the adult labour force. *Fam. Relations Interdisciplinary J. Appl. Fam. Stud.* 51(1): 28–36, 2002.
6. Peterson, C. Dealing with stress-related disorders in the public sector. In *Occupational Health and Safety in Australia: Industry, Public Sector and Small Business,* edited by C. Mayhew and C. Peterson, pp. 174–186. Allen and Unwin, St. Leonards, 1999.
7. Industry Commission. *Work, Health and Safety: Inquiry into Occupational Health and Safety,* Vols. I and II. Report No. 47. AGPS, Canberra, 1995.

Section I

International Perspectives on Stress

Chapter 2

WORKPLACE CHANGES IN AUSTRALIA AND THEIR EFFECTS ON STRESS

Chris L. Peterson

Australia, like most developed countries in the global economy, has been experiencing significant changes in work practices since the late 1980s. Many of these changes have resulted from globalization, with its pressure to conform to worldwide economic changes and trends. In Australia the changes have been somewhat masked and have been couched as developments necessary to meet the demands of responsible government and business planning. The effects of these changes, however, have been evident through anecdotal reports and newspaper stories of the increasing toll of work on personal, family, and social life. The National Occupational Health and Safety Commission, formerly Worksafe, has reported increasing numbers of people making claims for compensation for stress (1), and the actual compensations have marginally increased. In addition, an increasing number of studies on the effects of management practices and work intensification have shown stress levels to be a major concern.

Economic rationalist policy has been associated with the growth of managerialism and economic downturn (2). While economic rationalism was introduced into the United States and United Kingdom in the early 1980s to reduce public sector debt, in Australia it began to have a significant impact from the mid to late 1980s under a Labor government. One of the key features of the open market competition that characterizes economic rationalism is increased economic competition and its associated high unemployment, albeit also due to global economic trends. Apart from market competition, the major features that became evident, according to Gardner (2), were increased privatization, the introduction of economic incentives, a focus on program budgeting, and an increase in management fiscal and budgetary accountability. While introduced under a Labor government, this paved the way for state and later federal Liberal governments to implement economic policy that reflected the Liberal philosophy of individualism and growth through open market competition. It also heralded a significant decline in the welfare state.

A number of studies have identified changes in Australian workplace practices during the 1990s (e.g., 3, 4). These have shown that work has intensified, as measured by increasing pace and increasing number of tasks, accompanied by a reduction in control. Many of these studies report changes in Australian practices as part of global changes in work intensification (4).

O'Donnell and coworkers (5) argue that three types of change have occurred in the way labor is utilized in Australia. First, work has intensified, with a greater requirement for work output. Second, job content has been expanded as workers take on more tasks with the increasing demand for output. Third, jobs have become less secure as management exercises a prerogative for flexibility. O'Donnell and colleagues report on national figures for hours of work and note that since 1995 employees are working on average two hours more per week than they did in the three previous decades. In the 1994-95 Workplace Bargaining Survey (Federal Department of Industrial Relations), 11,233 employees were asked to rate changes during the 12 months prior to the survey. More than half reported at least two types of change, labeled complex change and radical change; the latter referred to increasing functional flexibility, insecurity, and intensification.

In this chapter I discuss a number of relatively new issues in relation to stress and changing workplace practices. First, while stress was recognized as an important phenomenon, the causes and consequences of stress have to some extent been ignored by business and government. Second, more recent economic and workplace changes appear to be associated with increased stress in the workplace, yet there is relatively little research that identifies the effects of workplace change on stress. Third, Australian Workplace Industrial Relations Survey (AWIRS) study, as a national Australian sample, provides important evidence of the strength of workplace change as a factor increasing stress, beyond the traditional stress factors. This chapter investigates the hypothesis that certain types of recent work-practice change are strong predictors of increased stress at work, beyond the effects of traditional stressors.

STRESS AT WORK

There are many reasons for stress among employees at work. The role of negative work factors has proved to be important (e.g., 6). Other recent research has looked at the effects of noxious work demands on stress (7). The effects of negative work practices have been reported by many writers (e.g., 6, 8, 9). These studies show that a lack of control, too little variety, qualitative and quantitative overload, and a lack of utilizing skills are some of the factors accounting for increased stress (7, 10, 11). However, relatively few studies have examined the effects of work changes on stress. Perceived control is one factor that has been studied (e.g., 9, 12–14); decision-making power is another (10). There have been other studies on the effects of technology and of noxious or dangerous work environments, the under-utilization of skills (15, 16), and role-related problems (17, 18). Others have examined the effects of control by management on stress (e.g., 19). Studies on poor relationships at work (e.g., 17, 20, 21) have found that poor relationships with management can be a cause of stress. Other studies have found stress caused by organizational structure and negative climate of management attitudes (6, 22). Peterson and Wilson (23), for example, have argued for the effects of organizational culture on stress. More recent studies have investigated the role of power in stress, to identify and emphasize structural factors (e.g., 24).

Importantly, stress has been shown to occur at different rates for different occupational groups. Few studies, however, have compared occupational groups. Those that have done so have shown that lower-level (blue-collar) workers have higher levels of stress than white-collar and managerial groups (e.g., 6, 25–29).

WORKPLACE CHANGE AND STRESS

The vast majority of the literature on the effects of negative work factors measures their effects at a given time. A relatively small body of literature, however, reports on the effects of changes in work practices on stress.

The Department of Industrial Relations conducted two major workplace studies in Australia (1990 and 1995). The first, in 1989–90 (AWIRS90), was an attempt to collect national data on two workplace characteristics and the extent of workplace change, given the lack of available data (3). The study demonstrated (among other things) the extent of workplace changes that had occurred during the very early 1990s. One component of both surveys was a study of workplace characteristics and the types of changes that had taken place during the year before the survey. The 1994–95 survey (AWIRS95) represented a significant study of workplace changes taking place during a period when economic rationalist policy had been heightened in government planning, and the effects on workplace practices proved to be quite dramatic.

In an analysis of the occupational health and safety implications of the AWIRS95 study, Mitchell and Mandryk (30) maintain that the survey provided important additional data on occupational injury and illness incidence and resulting time-off to the National Data Set. Thus the study represents a particularly important national work-related data collection. They found overall that managers, clerks, and professional groups reported least injury and illness, while lower occupational groups such as tradespersons, apprentices, plant and machine operators, laborers, and related workers reported most. As had been reported in the National Data Set 1994–95 and in other sources (31), stress was one of the most frequently reported injury and illness experiences, together with dislocation/sprain/strain and bruising/crushing (30).

According to Rimmer (32), three major changes took place between 1990 and 1994–95. First, there was a significantly reduced union presence in the workforce. Second, the number of involuntary redundancies greatly increased, more so in places that were not unionized. Third, there was a marked increase in devolution of responsibilities down the organizational hierarchy. However, rather than representing an increased spread of the power base in organizations, it was increased responsibility without commensurate authority. In other words, lower-level workers started to take workplace planning problems and issues home, despite no corresponding pay to match the responsibility. In short, Australia had seen a significant shift in organizational structure and policy that was affecting a large number of workplaces and employees. At the time, the national press had occasionally published articles about increased frustration for employees, with the reduction of jobs, increased tasks and workloads, and a greater number of retrenchments.

However, not until 1998 was a national campaign organized by the Australian Council of Trade Unions (ACTU) to focus on stress in the workplace. The flagship of the campaign was the report of a study conduced by the ACTU on stress in the workplace and its health effects (33). The campaign, through a media launch and follow-up publicity on television and in state newspapers, increased awareness among unions, all employees, and the community of the extent of stress in the workplace and the denial of many employers that stress was a cause for concern. A day was set aside nationally for an organized stress-free break at work for employees to acknowledge and address the issue of stress at work. Later in 1998 the ACTU ran a national stress conference to highlight current stress-related problems in the workplace. A significant issue identified at the conference was the extent of stress linked to workplace changes during the 1990s.

How stress is portrayed in the media has important implications for the way it is dealt with in the community. Lewig and Dollard (34) conducted a study of stress as portrayed by the Australian media. The major contributor to media presentations was the union movement. The authors found that stress was portrayed as an epidemic with a large economic cost, as an outcome of negative work experience, but most of the media presentations suggested there were individual solutions. Media reports also associated stress mainly with public sector employees, possibly because this group receives greatest compensation for the condition. However, herein lies a problem in terms of the ideology of stress. There is scant recognition of its structural basis, and the emphasis on individual solutions does not grapple with some of the structural causes such as work intensification and longer working hours.

In a longitudinal study of workplace change and its effects on stress, Huuhtanen and colleagues (35) investigated several aspects of work content in 1981 and 1992 among the same Finnish sample. Workers responded that job demands had increased during that time, especially the extent of physical work and knowledge use. Women identified higher physical demands than did men, and knowledge use had increased more among women. The authors found that older workers perceived more demand and in fact worked at a higher rate than younger employees.

Fenwick and Tausig (36) found in a longitudinal study that macroeconomic effects influence job structures. Increases in stress were associated with higher unemployment rates and lower life satisfaction, particularly as a result of reduced control and increased job demands. These authors found that recession could affect job structure and expose workers to greater stress. In another study, the same authors report the effects of changes in the labor market on job structures and how these changes affect men and women (37). For men, increases in work demands and reductions in decision latitude provided significant explanations of stress; for women, reduced job security was significantly associated with stress. Consequently, women's and men's responses to labor market trends as manifest in changing work structure were different. This indicates that changes in economic planning and conditions that affect the way organizations are structured will have some important effects on stress. Brodsky (38) also found that work changes had effects through initiating negative sociopsychological states.

In a study of suicide among women, undertaken over a period of 14 years of follow-up, the risk of suicide was found to be eight times higher for nurses with high stress or diazepam use than for those reporting low stress and no diazepam use (39). In all phases of analysis, women in the high-stress category were more susceptible to risk of harm or illness.

METHODS IN THE STUDY OF WORKPLACE CHANGE

The data set used here is from AWIRS95, collected and compiled by the federal Department of Industrial Relations in Australia. The employee survey is a sample of 19,155 employees randomly selected from an initial sample of 2001 workplaces employing 20 employees or more. An analysis of the employee survey questionnaire forms the basis of this study. Results of the different surveys are reported, for example, by Moorhead and coworkers (3). The study provides an opportunity to look at a number of variables that may affect causes of perceived changes in stress in a national sample of Australian workers.

Of major interest in the study was that, despite significant changes in the way work is organized in Australia during the 1990s, relatively little is known of the extent to which these changes have contributed to employee and management stress. The AWIRS95 study was excellent for this purpose, as it records the extent to which a number of changes in workplace practices occurred in Australian workplaces in the mid-1990s. This was recorded through self-reports by employees in the sample, based on recall of those changes over the 12 months preceding the study. In particular, data collected in the study enabled the testing of the effects of these work changes on stress through a regression model.

A number of hypotheses were developed for testing in the study. The first hypothesis is that there will be some differences in the experience of stress between different occupational groups, but these differences may not be significant. During the 1970s and 1980s a number of studies compared stress differences between some occupational and professional groups; however, only a relatively small number of studies compared the experience of stress for the full range of occupational groups, from management to blue-collar and laboring workers. Many of these studies showed that blue-collar workers were significantly more stressed than workers in higher occupational groups, especially management (25–28). My study (6) also reported these differences. While there were fairly large differences in stress between blue-collar workers and white-collar workers and management, these differences were not statistically significant. However, the consistent trend was that blue-collar workers were more stressed than higher occupational groups.

The second hypothesis is that changes involving decision latitude and control will have the most important effects on stress. It is predicted that workplace change will be an important predictor of stress. A relatively small number of studies have investigated the effects of specific changes at work; however, these studies have shown changes to have important effects on stress. Studies of the effects of negative work practices (see 6) have shown that a lack of control has been a strong predictor of stress. Aronsson (9), Frankenhaeuser (11), Jackson (40), Karasek (12, 13), and others have shown that lack of control has important influences in increasing levels of stress. In this study I hypothesize that when these types of work changes take place they will have the most important effects on stress.

The third hypothesis is that effort put into the job will be a strong predictor of stress. Outcomes from work intensification studies reported early in this chapter highlight the extent to which employees have needed to increase effort on the job. O'Donnell and coworkers (5) have demonstrated a relationship between increased effort and stress. Karasek (12, 13) has also demonstrated that increased demand coupled with reduced control is a strong predictor of stress. It is expected that increases in demand will be a stronger predictor of stress than effort measured at a single point in time. Again, the few studies of changes at work show that increases in negative work practices have strong effects on stress.

The AWIRS95 questionnaire contained a large number of variables pertaining to the types of working conditions experienced by employees and to changes in working conditions and experiences. In this study, however, the only variables of interest are a small number of biographical variables, a series of questions reporting change experienced during the 12 months preceding the study, and a number of other negative work factors such as effort on the job.

Descriptive statistics are reported for each of these variables later in the chapter. Univariate, bivariate, and multivariate analyses; one-way ANOVA; and a multiple regression model are presented. Variables are analyzed in separate blocks, based on the time sequence when independent variables took place (Figure 2.1). For example, age and gender are in the first block, as these statuses are assigned at birth. Results are reported as standardized regression coefficients (beta) scores and total effects of independent variables on the dependent variable *stress*. The latter are the sum of direct effects (controlling for the effects of all other variables, but

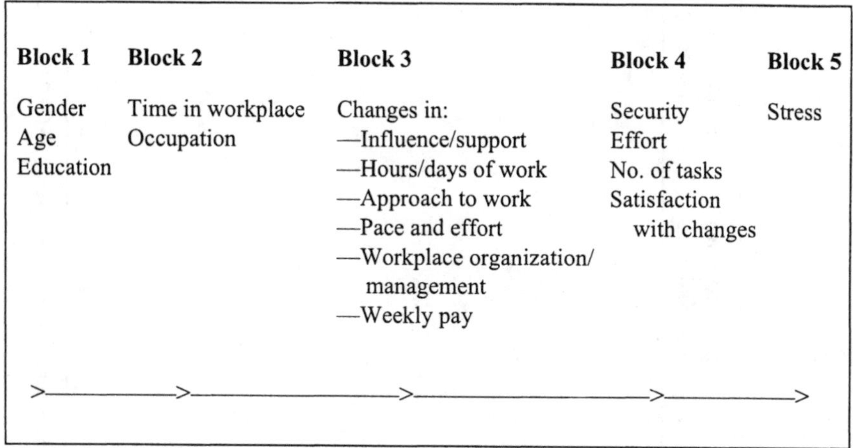

Figure 2.1 Block recursive model.

not accounted for by the variables in the model) and indirect effects (effects of independent variables accounting for the effects of mediating variables).

In addition, important information can be gained through examining the partial regression coefficient (*b* scores). A unit of change in the independent variable is shown as the *b* score change on the dependent variable. In the regression model, the dependent variable has been converted to a scale of 1 to 100. The unstandardized regression coefficients represent unit changes in stress scores from 1 to 100; these can also be read as percentage changes in stress.

Two dummy variables have been included in the regression model (i.e., education, occupation). The regression coefficient scores are read for these variables as compared with the omitted category: for education, years 10 and 11 of schooling; for occupation, clerks. Therefore, a tertiary-educated person's score is as compared with one who has achieved a year 10 or 11 education; and all other occupations are compared with clerks.

A factor analysis was undertaken of a number of variables, measuring change that had taken place in the preceding 12 months. The change measured was a self-report of whether the work factor had reduced (coded 1), remained the same (coded 2), or increased (coded 3).

Four different factors emerged using a Varimax rotation, which produced the strongest factor solution (Table 2.1). The first factor, *influence and support,* refers to a change in control, including satisfactions with work, changes in training, and satisfaction with the home/work interface, which can affect a feeling of support from the work environment. Six items in the scale achieved a moderate to strong reliability (Cronbach's alpha = .73) and .31 inter-item correlation. The second factor, *number of hours and days of work,* contains items

Table 2.1

Factor analysis of changes at work

	I	II	III	IV	Average inter-item correlation	Reliability (Cronbach's alpha)
I Influence and support						
1. Change in say in decisions	.75	–.09	–.04	.10		
2. Change in use of ideas	.73	–.08	–.08	–.18		
3. Change in promotion opportunity	.68	–.12	–.02	–.05		
4. Change in satisfaction	.74	–.05	.03	–.08		
5. Change in family balance satisfaction	.51	.26	.06	.25		
6. Change in amount of training	.48	–.05	–.12	–.06	.31	.73
II Number of hours and days of work						
1. Change in hours	–.01	.89	.05	.20		
2. Change in hours per day	.03	.80	.08	.26		
3. Change in number of days per week	–.01	.70	.03	–.09	.21	.79
III Type of work and approach to doing work						
1. Change in type of work	.14	–.10	.77	–.06		
2. Change in how you do your job	.09	–.06	.81	–.19	.54	.78
IV Work pace and effort						
1. Change in effort	–.17	.07	.13	.80		
2. Change in pace	.02	.13	.16	.79	.43	.60

Note: Factor loadings were obtained using Varimax rotation with unities in the main diagonal. Eigenvalues (percent explained variance) are 3.26 (21.73%), 2.35 (15.64%), 1.6 (10.75%), 1.08 (7.17%).

related to overall working hours, hours worked during the day, and days during the week. The scale has a strong reliability (.79) and .21 inter-item correlation. The third factor, *type of work and approach to doing work,* contains items related to changes in the type of work and changes in how you do your job. The scale has a strong reliability (.78) and an average inter-item correlation of .54. The final factor, *work pace and effort,* refers to change in effort and change in pace. Reliability is moderate (.60) and the inter-item correlation is .43.

RESULTS

Of the 19,155 employees in the study, 44.8 percent (8,550) were women and 55.2 percent (10,553) were men. The largest group in the sample were clerks (18.4 percent) and the smallest managers. The gender and occupational breakdown of the sample is shown in Table 2.2. The highest proportion of women and of all workers were clerks (31.8 and 18.4 percent, respectively); 14.9 percent of employees were under 25 years, and 15.9 percent were 50 years and older; average age was 37.5 years. The largest group of workers (27.7 percent) had completed year 10 or 11 of education, and 18.5 percent had completed secondary school. A small number (2.5 percent) had only a primary education; 23.7 percent had either an undergraduate or postgraduate degree or diploma. Employees, on average had spent more than six years at their current workplace (6.28 years).

Mean scores are presented for the major variables in the study (Table 2.3), with a high score representing a negative work factor or experience. Each variable representing a change refers to a change measured during the 12 months prior to the study. For example, a high score on the scale of 1 to 3 for amount of effort refers to having to expend more effort on the job than previously during the past 12 months. Employees were neither satisfied nor dissatisfied with the changes over the 12 months preceding the study (mean = 1.92). There had been a slight increase in the amount of influence and support at work (1.94). The number of hours and days worked had increased slightly (2.13), there had been relatively few changes in the type of work and approaches to doing work (1.55), and workpace and effort had increased dramatically (2.49).

As Table 2.4 shows, 31.4 percent felt insecure about their job, and 43.7 percent felt secure. Workplaces had undergone substantial change in the 12 months prior to the study: 58.3 percent had experienced changes in workplace organization. For most (60.8 percent), pay had gone up; for 5.6 percent it had gone down. There was a great deal of variety in employees' work, with 84 percent reporting they were doing lots of different tasks. Overwhelmingly, 88.9 percent felt they were required to put a lot of effort into their jobs. Employees generally felt things were better as a result of changes at work (1.92, where 2 refers to neither here nor there), with 32.2 percent saying they were better off and a relatively large group (24.3 percent) reporting they were worse off. Overall, employees reported quite a high level of stress (58.36 on a scale of 1 to 100).

Table 2.2

Sample composition

	Women		Men		Total	
Occupational group	No.	%	No.	%	No.	%
Laborers and related	1,169	13.8	1,514	14.4	2,683	14.3
Plant and machine operators	179	2.1	1,593	15.2	1,772	9.3
Sales and personal services	1,553	18.4	752	7.2	2,305	12.3
Clerks	2,694	31.8	797	7.6	3,491	18.4
Tradespersons and apprentices	87	1.0	1,516	14.5	1,603	8.5
Paraprofessionals	951	11.3	1,343	12.8	2,294	12.1
Professionals	1,391	16.4	1,682	16.1	3,073	16.2
Managers	383	4.5	1,180	11.3	1,563	8.3
Other	62	0.7	95	0.9	157	0.8
Total	8,469	100.0	10,472	100.0	18,941	100.0

Table 2.3

Means, medians, and standard deviations for each of the variables in the model

	Score			
	n	Mean	Median	S.D.
Length of time at workplace, years	19,046	6.28	4.00	6.89
Security, 1–3	17,407	2.12	2.00	.86
Tasks, 1–3	18,622	1.23	1.00	.56
Amount of effort, 1–3	18,672	1.13	1.00	.38
Satisfaction with changes, 1–3	17,021	1.92	2.00	.75
Change in influence and support	18,851	1.94	2.00	.41
Change in number of hours and days of work	18,612	2.13	2.00	.41
Change in type of work and approach to doing work	18,568	1.55	1.50	.44
Change in workpace and effort	17,930	2.49	2.50	.49
Change in workplace organization	18,323	1.58	2.00	.49
Change in pay	18,597	1.45	1.00	.60
Better due to changes	17,021	1.92	2.00	.75
Stressfulness, 1–100	18,420	58.36	50.00	39.34

Table 2.4

Selective aspects of working conditions and changes at work

	No.	%		No.	%
Job security			Lots of different tasks		
Feel secure	7,601	43.7	Agree	15,643	84.0
Neither here nor there	4,332	24.9	Neither agree nor disagree	1,729	9.3
Feel insecure	5,474	31.4	Disagree	1,250	6.7
Total	17,407	100.0	Total	18,622	100.0
Change in workplace organization			Effort into the job		
			Disagree	307	1.6
No	7,634	43.7	Neither here nor there	1,761	9.4
Yes	10,689	58.3	Agree	16,604	88.9
Total	18,323	100.0	Total	19,155	100.0
Change in pay			Better due to changes		
Gone up	11,307	60.8	Better off	5,484	32.2
Stayed the same	6,242	33.6	About the same	7,406	43.5
Gone down	1,048	5.6	Worse off	4,131	24.3
Total	18,597	100.0	Total	17,021	100.0

Table 2.5 shows that managers had the highest levels of stress (74 points on a scale of 1 to 100; a very high level of stress). Paraprofessionals (68.8) followed, with professionals (67.0) the next most highly stressed. Surprisingly, laborers reported the least stress (48.7). Tradespersons were the next least stressed (50.7). Differences between occupational groups were significant ($F = 133.3$, $df = 7$, $P = .00$). Scheffe post hoc tests were carried out to identify where differences between specific occupational groups were significant (.05). Managers were significantly more stressed than all other groups. Paraprofessionals and professionals were significantly more stressed than all other groups except managers. Plant operators and clerks were significantly more stressed than laborers.

For men, the same pattern was evident: managers most stressed (73.1 points) and laborers least stressed (49.2). Scheffe post hoc tests identified that paraprofessionals were significantly more stressed than all groups except professionals and managers. Professionals were significantly more stressed than all groups except paraprofessionals, and managers had higher stress than all groups except paraprofessionals. Plant operators and clerks were significantly more stressed than laborers. For women, managers were most highly stressed (77), followed by professionals (69.4) and then paraprofessionals (69.2). Female tradespersons

Table 2.5

Stressfulness of the job (score 1–100)

	Male	Female	Total
Laborer	49.2	47.9	48.7
Plant	54.7	50.9	54.3
Sales	53.1	52.0	52.4
Clerk	56.6	52.0	53.1
Trades	50.9	47.4	50.7
Paraprofessional	68.4	69.2	68.8
Professional	64.9	69.4	67.0
Manager	73.1	77.0	74.0
Total	59.1	57.4	58.4
F	67.5**	67.8**	133.3**

**$P < .01$

were least stressed (47.4), followed by laborers (47.9). A similar pattern of occupational differences emerged for women, as shown by the Scheffe post hoc test, except that there were no significant differences between paraprofessionals, professionals, and managers. For both women and men, there were significant occupational differences (women: $F = 67.5$, $df = 7$; men: $F = 67.8$, $df = 7$; $P < .01$).

The block recursive method provides a more substantial understanding of the effects of variables on the independent variable (changes in stress). This allows for a more accurate assessment of variable effects and is more consistent with the theory underlining the model being tested. Effects of variables are parceled into total, direct, and indirect effects. Presented in Table 2.6 are the block recursive model regression results showing total effects for partial regression coefficients and the unstandardized regression coefficients (*b* scores: the unit change in the dependent variable for each point in the independent variable). The variables are entered in four blocks (see Methods and Figure 2.1). In the first block, age and educational achievement have significant effects in predicting stress levels. As age increases, stress is likely to increase (beta = .08). In fact, for each additional year of age there is about a 1.5 percent increase in stress ($b = 1.46$ per year, on a scale of 1 to 100).

Employees with a completed secondary education (beta = –.04) are significantly less stressed than employees with year 10 or 11 education only. The latter are omitted from the analysis of education, and therefore the basis for comparison as education is a dummy variable). However, employees with a certificate level of education are significantly more stressed than those with

Table 2.6

Regression results for determinants of stressfulness of the job (dependent variable = stress)[a]

Independent variables (entered in blocks)	Total effects[b]	
	b	beta
Block 1		
Women (cf. men)	–1.18	–.02
Age	1.46	.08**
Primary	–2.45	–.01
Secondary	–3.34	–.04**
Certificate	4.25	.03*
Tertiary	0.42	.00
Adjusted R-squared		.01
Block 2		
Length of time in workplace	0.51	.09**
Occupational group:		
Laborers	–4.54	–.04**
Machine operators	–2.79	–.02
Sales	0.72	.01
Trades	–4.42	–.04*
Paraprofessionals	13.26	.11**
Professionals	11.96	.04**
Managers	19.19	.12**
Adjusted R-squared		.05
Block 3		
Change I	26.10	.28**
Change II	7.01	.07**
Change III	–5.69	–.06**
Change IV	16.90	.21**
Change in workplace organization/management	3.01	.04**
Change in weekly pay	1.81	.03*
Adjusted R-squared		.17
Block 4		
Security	4.50	.10**
Effort	6.49	.06**
Number of tasks	–3.88	–.05**
Satisfaction with changes	6.24	.12**
Adjusted R-squared		.20

[a]The stress scale has been recalculated between 1 and 100.
[b]b is the partial regression coefficient; beta, the standardized regression coefficient.
**$P < .01$; * $P < .05$

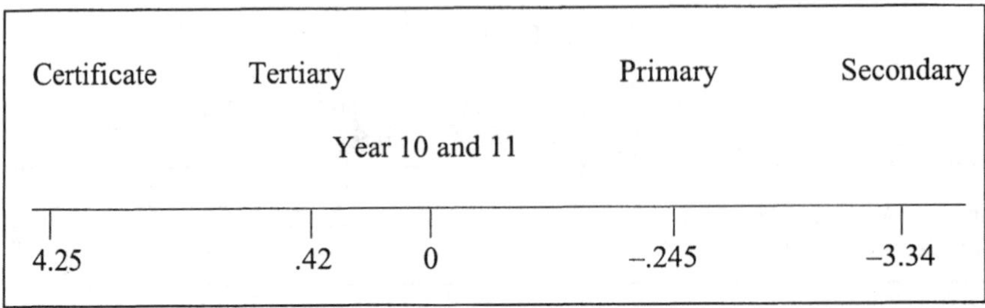

Figure 2.2. Stress by education (block 1).

year 10 or 11 education (.03). In fact, secondary-educated employees report 3.34 percent less stress than those with year 10 or 11 education, while certificate-educated employees report 4.25 percent more than employees with year 10 or 11 education (Figure 2.2).

The second block of variables shows that the longer employees are with the one organization, the higher the stress (beta = .09). Surprisingly, managers can be expected to have the highest level of stress (.12), followed by paraprofessionals (.11) and professionals (.04), compared with the omitted category, clerks. Laborers and tradespersons, however, are likely to have the least stress of all occupational groups (–.04). Managers have 19.19 percent more stress than clerks (Figure 2.3), as shown by the partial regression coefficients. Paraprofessionals and professionals have 13.26 and 11.96 percent more stress, respectively, while machine operators have 2.78 percent less stress than clerks. Tradespersons have 4.42 percent less stress and laborers have 4.54 percent less.

All the work change variables included in the study significantly predict changes in stress. In the third block of variables, *changes in influence and support* is shown to be the factor that predicts changes in stress most strongly (beta = .28). The difference between no change in influence and support and reduced influence and support (change I in Table 2.6) accounts for an increase of 26.10 percent of stress. *Changes in pace and effort on the job* (change IV) is the second highest predictor of stress (.21), with a movement from no change to an increase in pace and effort predicting an increase of 16.9 percent in stress. An *increase in the number of hours and days of work* (change II) accounts for a significant increase in stress (.07), with an increase, compared with no change in the past 12 months, predicting a 7.01 percent increase in stress. *Changes in type of work and approach to doing work* (change III) is also a significant predictor of stress (–.06), with an increase predicting a reduction of 5.69 percent in stress. *Changes in workplace organization and management practices* has a significant effect on stress (beta = .04), while *changes in weekly pay* has a small effect only (.03), with a reduction in pay (occurring for a small proportion of the sample) predicting a 1.81 percent increase in stress.

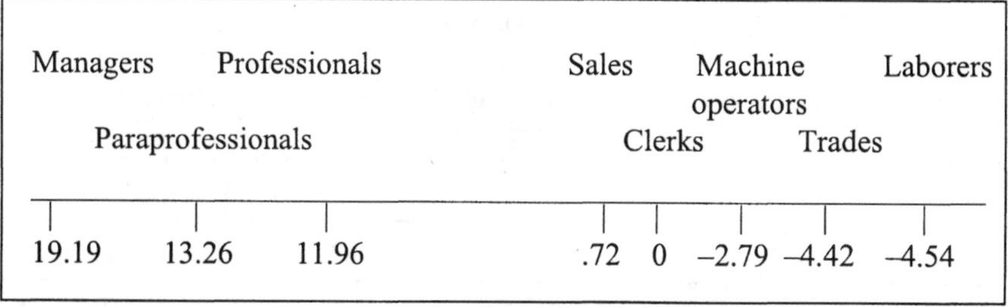

Figure 2.3. Stress by occupational groups (block 2).

Finally, block 4 reports work factors measured at a single point in time (whereas block 3 variables measure changes over the past 12 months). Satisfaction with changes over the past 12 months has a strong effect on stress levels (beta = .12), with dissatisfaction predicting a 6.24 percent increase compared with those who were satisfied with the changes. Being insecure in the job is likely to lead to a more than 4.5 percent increase in stress compared with those with security (.10), and those who have to put effort into the job compared with those who do not are likely to experience almost 6.49 percent more stress (.06). However, those who have more tasks can be expected to have more than 3.88 percent less stress than those with few tasks (–.05).

Only a small amount of variation in stress scores (1 percent adjusted *R*-square = .01) is accounted for by sociodemographics (block 1) and by occupational experience and position (4 percent, block 2). However, changes in work experience over the preceding 12 months (block 3) account for 12 percent of variability in stress scores, while certain work factors measured at a single point in time (block 4) account for 3 percent of variation. In all, the model shown in Table 2.6 explains 20 percent of variability in stress scores, with 80 percent of stress experienced by employees not accounted for by the model.

Table 2.7 shows the total, direct, and indirect effects of variables in the block recursive regression model; this can be a useful way of detecting the influence of mediating variables on the effects on stress of specific sociodemographic and work factors. The influence of mediating variables is measured on the independent variable of interest. That is, stress is likely to occur partly due to the effect of intervening variables in subsequent blocks (e.g., blocks 2, 3, and 4). Further analyses on the specific effects of these variables through intervening variables can be undertaken by separating out the effects of variables through each of the mediating variables on the dependent variable (see 41).

That older workers are likely to experience greatest stress (total effect = .08) is explained almost entirely by the effects of age on mediating variables (.07) (Table 2.7). In the case of age, the major indirect effect is that older workers are more likely to be employed in lower occupational groups, and this is likely to lead

Table 2.7

Total, direct, and indirect effects of selective sociodemographic and change variables

	Beta		
Variables	Total	Direct	Indirect
Block 1			
Age	.08	.01	.07
Block 2			
Length of time in workplace	.09	.05	.04
Block 3			
Change in influence and support (change I)	.28	.19	.09

to less control and influence and thus to stress. The effect of length of service for one organization (.09) is almost half explained by mediating variables (.04); a little more than half of the effect is unexplained (.05). Half of the indirect effect on stress is due to the fact that the longer employees spent in one organization, the more likely they were to perceive control and support during the past 12 months as diminished. Consequently, the increased stress was due to a perceived reduction in control and support.

Finally, the other variable with a large effect explained indirectly is changes in influence and support. About one-third of the effect of increased influence and support on reducing stress is through its effects on mediating variables (.09), and about two-thirds (.19) is unexplained by the model. Two-thirds of the indirect effect is due to the fact that employees experiencing little control and support feel they were worse off because of changes during the past 12 months.

DISCUSSION

Differences in stress among occupational groups is of particular interest in this study. A number of studies have been conducted on differences in stress in a whole range of occupational groups (from blue-collar through management; see 6, 25, 26, 28), showing that stress was greater for lower-level employees. However, in the study presented here, the highest stress was reported by managers, followed by professional and paraprofessional workers. While lower-level workers experienced less stress, it was nonetheless quite high. Other studies have shown that for professional and managerial workers, factors related to work intensification and overload, such as performance targets and an unsatisfying balance between work and homelife, particularly affect this group of employees (see 42).

One possible explanation is that the change in patterns of stress among occupational groups was due to the "rebound" effect of rational economic planning and management. That is, as management assumed more control and influence and extended the managerial prerogative, this process forced management into greater accountability, particularly budgetary accountability. The changes heralded by rational economic management therefore set the scene for and perpetuated larger increases in stress for higher occupational groups. In addition, there has been the trend of increasing competition in cost-containment practices, leading to increased accountability of professional and paraprofessional groups. As shown in the early part of this chapter, rational economic management has had a pervasive effect and has strongly influenced stress among higher-level occupational groups. Consequently, the first hypothesis, that differences between occupational groups will not be significant, is not verified.

The second hypothesis, that changes in influence and support are likely to affect stress more than other changes, is verified. In the regression model, the standardized regression coefficient of .28 (significant at <.01) is greater for this change variable than for any others. There is a large literature on the negative effects of a lack of control at work (see 9) and a lack of support by management (6), as well as on the need to improve management practice (4, 33). The results of this study confirm the importance of influence and control by employees but, importantly, also show that changes in control and influence are particularly strong predictors of stress.

The third hypothesis, that effort put into the job is likely to be a strong predictor of stress, is also verified. In the regression model, the (standardized regression coefficient for the effect of stress is .06 (significant at <.01). The difference between no effort and a lot of effort is a nearly 9 percent increase in stress. Much of the recent literature on changes in Australian workplace practices has shown effort to be a significant factor in the work that people do (e.g., 4, 33). In the regression model, it is a less strong predictor of stress than lack of job security and satisfaction with changes in the way work is done over the past 12 months.

The study also found that change in workplace pace and effort is likely to be a stronger predictor of stress than effort measured at a single point in time: standardized regression coefficients of .21 and .06, respectively. This is an important finding in that, at least on one dimension of the job, changes in workplace practices are shown to have stronger effects than the same negative work practice measured at a single point in time. The regression model presented in Table 2.6 was run again, this time including change in effort instead of change in pace and effort. The effect of a change in effort over the past 12 months was very much greater than the effect of effort per se: a standardized regression coefficient of 16.79 for changes in effort and workload compared with 6.5 for effort measured at a single point in time. This represents more than twice the effect on stress.

Further research is required on the relationship between changes in negative practices and negative practices measured at a single point in time, but the preliminary results indicate that change itself may be an important precursor of stress.

In all, in the regression model, changes at work generally had stronger effects than static negative work factors, indicating the need for more research into the effects of workplace change. As I noted in the review of literature earlier in the chapter, relatively few studies have been conducted into the effects of work practice changes on stress, compared with the large number focusing on negative workplace practices. More research needs to focus on these issues.

IMPLICATIONS FOR STUDIES ON STRESS

The findings on the effects of changes in negative workplace practices are important in the field of stress at work, given the paucity of research in this area. The last decade in Australia has seen unprecedented changes in negative practices, with the reduction of unionism in the workplace and a system that is based on enterprise agreements. Further, work contracts have shortened, work has become less secure for many employees, and the system of award restructuring undertaken by the federal Liberal government has undermined the basis for bargaining in much of industry. In fact, deregulation of the workplace has led to the reduction of security and to employers having more power to dictate conditions and terms of employment.

A finding of this study consistent with past stress research is that control in the workplace is a major predictor of stress. However, the extent to which *changes* in control and influence affect stress means that this is an important change to focus on in analyzing and understanding variations in stress. With work-change programs being commonplace in industry, the ramifications and consequences of changes in control and influence must not be underestimated, and this study may help unravel the often negative latent consequences of change programs. As the effects on stress become better understood, positive ways of affecting control and influence may help change-program outcomes—but this requires a management keen to invest in workforce capacity and resources through change programs, rather than simply introducing change as a way of responding to environmental demand or using the change process as a control mechanism.

Measures of the effects of negative work factors at a single point in time are extremely important in understanding the conditions under which stress occurs, as well as the management practices conducive to a stressful working environment. In fact, there are strong arguments for measuring the effects of government policy and management practice via changes in workplace practices. The findings on the potent effects of changes in effort, a far stronger predictor of increased stress than effort measured at a single point in time (even though that itself has a strong influence on stress), are an argument for more change-focused stress research. We need qualitative data collections for employees engaged in workplace change, over time, to understand the specific influences, although before-and-after studies and self-reports will also yield useful results.

CONCLUSION

The trend over the past decade of increased managerialism, shortened contracts for employment, reduced union involvement, and increased job insecurity has shifted the focus of stress research in important ways. Control over work and the role of management control have been important foci of stress research, particularly since the work of Braverman (43), but have assumed an even more important significance in unpacking the effects of workplace change on stress. These concepts continue to be the most fruitful basis of analysis for interpreting the effects of workplace relations, particularly in a time when rational economic planning and managerialism have become so prominent.

Importantly, the study of the effects of actual changes in workplace practices will provide a focus on the outcomes of a relatively new period of workplace relations, dominated more significantly by the managerial prerogative. It gives an opportunity to investigate the consequences of rational economic management practices and government deregulation practices through their effects on changing work practices.

The study reported here has shown that workplace change is an important predictor of stress, in some cases more potent than negative work practices at a single point in time. The findings on the effects of change in control and support, change in effort and workplace, and the comparative strength of the effect of change in effort, compared with effort expended on the job, encourage the development of more intensive studies on the effects of workplace change. These studies need to account for the broader social, cultural, and management attitude context, as well as the nature of work relations, in order to provide more detailed evaluations of the impact of workplace change on stress.

A fuller understanding of the effects of workplace change will be gained by identifying the nature and effects of the managerialism, and the hegemony, that encourages employees and the community to adopt a management perspective. In addition, the context of government deregulation that advantages a managerial perspective over that of employees and the community must be taken into account—for example, through an acceptance of workplace practices that disadvantage employees but yield high levels of profitability for corporations.

REFERENCES

1. Mayhew, C., and Peterson, C. Introduction: Occupational health and safety in Australia. In *Occupational Health and Safety in Australia: Industry, Small Business and the Public Sector,* edited by C. Mayhew and C. L. Peterson, pp. 1–10. Allen and Unwin, St. Leonards, 1999.
2. Gardner, H. (ed.). *Health Policy in Australia.* Oxford, Melbourne, 1997.
3. Moorhead, A., et al. *Changes at Work: The 1995 Australian Workplace Industrial Relations Survey.* Longman, South Melbourne, 1997.
4. Weeks, K., Peterson, C. L., and Stanton, P. Stress and the workplace: The medical scientists' experience. *Labor Ind.* 11(3): 95–120, 2001.
5. O'Donnell, M., Peetz, D., and Allan, C. *What's Happening at Work? More Tasks, Less Job Security and Work Intensification.* School of Industrial Relations and Organisational Behaviour, University of New South Wales, Sydney, 1998.
6. Peterson, C. L. *Stress at Work: A Sociological Perspective.* Baywood, Amityville, N.Y., 1999.
7. Peterson, C. L. Stress at work: A critical review. *Int. J. Health Serv.* 24(3): 495-519, 1994.
8. Cooper, C. L., and Marshall, J. Success of managerial and white collar stress. In *Stress at Work,* edited by C. L. Cooper and R. Payne, pp. 81–105.Wiley, Chichester, U.K., 1974.
9. Aronsson, G. Dimension of control as related to work organisation, stress, and health. *Int. J. Health Serv.* 19(3): 459-469, 1989.
10. Levi, L. *Stress in industry: Causes, effects, and prevention. Occupational Safety and Health* Series No. 51. International Labor Organization, Geneva, 1984.
11. Frankenhaeuser, M. Coping with job stress—A psychobiological approach. In *Working Life: A Social Science Contribution to Work Reform,* edited by B. Gardell and G. Johansson, pp. 213–234, Wiley, New York, 1981.
12. Karasek, R. A. Job demands, job decision latitude and mental strain: Implications for job redesign. *Adm. Sci. Q.* 24: 285–308, 1979.
13. Karasek, R. A. Job socialisation and job strain: The implications of two related psychosocial mechanisms for job design. In *Working Life: A Social Science Contribution to Work Reform,* edited by B. Gardell and G. Johansson, pp. 75–94, Wiley, New York, 1981.
14. Israel, B. A., et al. The relationship of personal resources, participation, influence and interpersonal relationships and coping strategies to occupational stress, job strain and health. A multivariate analysis. *Work Stress* 3(2): 163–194, 1989.
15. O'Brien, G. E., Dowling, P., and Kabinoff, B. *Health, Work and Leisure.* Working Paper No. 28, National Institute of Labour Series, Adelaide, 1976.
16. Lowe, G. S., and Northcott, H. C. The impact of working conditions, social roles, and personal characteristics on gender differences in distress. *Work Occup.* 15(1): 55–77, 1988.
17. French, J. R. P., and Caplan, R. D. Organisation stress and individual strain. In *Failure of Success,* edited by A. J. Murrow, pp. 30–66. American Management Association, New York, 1973.
18. Sutherland, V. J., and Cooper, C. L. Identifying stress among general practitioners: Predictors of psychological ill-health and job dissatisfaction. *Soc. Sci. Med.* 37(5): 575–581, 1993.

19. Leigh, J. H., Lucas, G. H., and Woodman, R. W. Effects of perceived organisational factors on the role stress–job attitude relationships. *J. Manage.* 14(1): 41–58, 1988.
20. Guppy, A., and Gutheridge, T. Job satisfaction and occupational stress in UK general hospital nursing staff. *Work Stress* 5(4): 315–323, 1991.
21. Van Dijkhuizen, N. Towards organisational coping with stress. In *Coping with Stress at Work: Case Studies from Industry,* edited by J. Marshall and C. L. Cooper, pp. 203–220. Gower, London, 1981.
22. Kircaldy, B. D., and Cooper, C. L. Cross cultural differences in occupational stress amongst British and German managers. *Work Stress* 6(2): 177–190, 1992.
23. Peterson, M., and Wilson, J. F. The culture-work-health model and work stress. *Am. J. Health Behav* 26(1): 16–24, 2002.
24. Brooker, A. S., and Eakin, J. M. Gender, class, work-related stress and health: Towards a power-centered approach. *J. Community Appl. Soc. Psychol.,* 11(2): 97–109, 2001.
25. Kohn, M. L., et al. Position in the class structure and psychological functioning in the United States, Japan and Poland. *Am. J. Sociol.* 95(4): 964–1008, 1989.
26. Caplan, R., et al. *Job Demands and Worker Health.* Survey Research Centre, Institute for Social Research, University of Michigan, Ann Arbor, 1980.
27. Schwalbe, M. L., and Staples, C. L. Class position, work experience and health. *Int. J. Health Serv.* 16(4): 583–602, 1986.
28. Otto, R. Patterns of Stress, Medical Help Seeking amongst Women and Men in Selected Occupations. Ph.D. dissertation, La Trobe University, Bundoora Campus, Melbourne, 1976.
29. Barney, J. A., et al. An analysis of social class and certain attitudinal and personality variables: A comparison. *Coll. Student J.* 21(1): 13–18, 1987.
30. Mitchell, R., and Mandryk, J. *The 1995 Australian Workplace and Industrial Relations Survey (AWIRS95): An OHS Perspective*. National Occupational Health and Safety Commission, Commonwealth of Australia, Canberra, 1998.
31. Driscoll, T., and Mayhew, C. Extent and cost of occupational illness and injury. In *Occupational Health and Safety in Australia: Industry, Small Business, and the Public Sector,* edited by C. Mayhew and C. L. Peterson, pp. 28–51. Allen and Unwin, St. Leonards, 1999.
32. Rimmer, M. Opening address to the National Stress Conference, ACTU, Melbourne, 1998.
33. ACTU Occupational Health and Safety Unit. *Stress at Work: Not What We Bargained For.* Report of the 1997 Survey into Stress at Work. ACTU, Melbourne, 1998.
34. Lewig, K. A., and Dollard, M. F. Social construction of work stress: Australian newsprint media portrayal of stress at work. *Work Stress* 15(2):179–190, 2001.
35. Huuhtanen, P., et al. Changes in stress symptoms and their relationship to changes at work in 1981–1992 among elderly workers in municipal occupations. *Scand. J. Work Environ. Health* 23(Suppl. 1): 36–48, 1997.
36. Fenwick, R., and Tausig, M. The macroeconomic context of job stress. *J. Health Soc. Behav.* 35(3): 266–282, 1994.
37. Fenwick, R., and Tausig, M. Recession, Gender and Stress. Paper presented to the American Sociological Association, 1997.
38. Brodsky, C. M. Suicide attributed to work. *Suicide Life Threat. Behav.* 7(4): 216–229, 1997.

39. Feskanich, D., et al. Stress and suicide in the Nurses' Health Study. *J. Epidemiol. Community Health* 56(2): 95–98, 2002.
40. Jackson, S. E. Participation and decision making as a strategy for reducing job related strain. *J. Appl. Psychol.* 68: 3–19, 1983.
41. Pedhauser, E. *Multiple Regression in Behavioural Research: Explanation and Prediction,* Holt, Reinhart and Winston, New York, 1982.
42. Chan, K. B., et al. Work stress amongst six professional groups: The Singapore experience. *Soc. Sci. Med.* 50(10): 1415–1432, 2000.
43. Braverman, H. *Labour and Monopoly Capital: The Degradation of Work in the Twentieth Century.* Monthly Review Press, New York, 1974.

Chapter 3

WORKPLACE STRESS IN THE UNITED KINGDOM: CONTEXTUALIZING DIFFERENCE

John Chandler, Elisabeth Berg, and Jim Barry

At the risk of stereotyping, workplace stress would seem to have joined the weather and sports failure as a fairly standard topic of conversation for "whinging poms." This chapter does not examine whether these complaints are valid or whether workers in the United Kingdom experience more workplace stress than those in other nations, but it does seek to explore the extent of "stress" among particular groups of employees in the United Kingdom, using a variety of secondary sources. In doing so it demonstrates the use of a sociological analysis that sets "stress" in its social and institutional context.[1]

Sociological alternatives to the dominant psychological and social psychological literature on stress can, of course, take a number of forms. There is considerable merit in examining, for example, the origins of "stress" in capitalist social relations in general (cf. 1) or in other sets of relations such as those of gender (2). In this chapter, however, we set out to show that other possibilities exist too, and we examine how stress can be experienced differently by different groups of workers within a particular country—with our focus being the United Kingdom.[2] In doing so we are acutely conscious of the problematic nature of the term "stress" and its relationship to other similar concepts such as "anxiety," but here "stress" is to be used as a synonym for psychological strain, in keeping with much of the literature and its use in everyday life (cf. 3, pp. 31–32).

[1] Here we do not focus on the institutional isomorphism associated with the "New Institutionalism" (53). Instead we concentrate on a particular national institutional context. As such, our approach has more in common with studies that draw attention to national systems of labor regulation or employee relations (e.g., 54, 55).

[2] Of course, the United Kingdom can be seen—and should perhaps increasingly be seen—as several countries rather than one, but for the purpose of this chapter we ignore differences between the constituent parts of the United Kingdom.

PREVALENCE OF WORKPLACE STRESS AND STRAIN IN THE UNITED KINGDOM

A number of recent studies point to stress being prevalent in the U.K. workplace. A major study for the U.K. Health and Safety Executive, designed to investigate the extent of stress and to assess the impact on health, surveyed 17,000 people in one major (and reasonably representative) city in England—Bristol. The study found that 20 percent of respondents could be described as "highly stressed," although it also found much variation: 8.8 percent not stressed and 29.3 percent mildly, 43.4 percent moderately, 15.8 percent very, and 2.7 percent extremely stressed (4).

Another relevant study set out to chart the experience of work in the context of the "employment relationship" (5). This was based on interviews conducted in 1992 with nearly 4,000 employed people and a further 1,000 unemployed from across the whole of Britain. One of the questions posed to employed respondents was a measure of what the study refers to as "work strain." The respondents were asked, "Thinking of the past few weeks, how much of the time has your job made you feel each of the following?

- After I leave my work I keep worrying about job problems.
- I find it difficult to unwind at the end of a workday.
- I feel used up at the end of a workday
- My job makes me feel quite exhausted by the end of the workday" (5, p. 219).

The respondents were asked to rate themselves on each of these items on a six-point scale ranging from "never" to "all of the time"—thus emphasizing duration of symptoms. The results showed that "31 percent of all employees experienced a high level of work strain" (5, p. 220), although the findings reveal a fairly even distribution across the range of possible responses (Table 3.1).

Table 3.1

Employee perceptions of work strain

	Percent of responses			
	Much of the time	Some of the time	Occasionally	Never
Worries about job after work	11	22	39	28
Finds it difficult to unwind	13	23	34	30
Feels used up at end of workday	21	27	37	15
Feels exhausted at end of workday	22	29	36	13

Source: Gallie et al. (5, p. 220).

The researchers also asked respondents whether the stress involved in the job had increased, stayed the same, or decreased over the past five years. Overall, 53 percent said it had increased, 34 percent said it had stayed the same, and 12 percent said it had decreased.

The findings of this study would seem to gain support from a number of others. Burchell and colleagues (6), for example, found that more than 60 percent of the employees they surveyed thought there had been an increase in the speed of work and in the effort they had to put into their job, while only about 5 percent thought these had decreased. Another large-scale national study in the United Kingdom, the 1998 Workplace Employee Relations Survey (7), was based on a survey of 2,191 workplaces and more than 28,000 responses from employees (complementing the survey of managers with responsibility for personnel matters and worker representatives). The findings are not directly comparable with those of the study by Gallie and coworkers (5), but some of the questions were similar. In particular, employees were presented with three statements seen as indicators of work intensity and work-related stress: "my job requires I work very hard"; "[there is] never enough time to get work done"; and "I worry about work outside working hours." Again, there was a fair spread of opinion (Table 3.2). As has also often been noted in the United Kingdom, working hours seem to have increased in recent years to the point where they are, on average, the highest in Europe for full-time employees (8) (Table 3.3).

Taken together, these findings suggest a challenge to more than a century of concern about the British worker as idle, represented in popular stereotypes

Table 3.2

Perceptions of work intensity

	Percent of responses				
	Strongly agree	Agree	Neither agree nor disagree	Disagree	Strongly disagree
My job requires that I work very hard	26	50	19	4	0
Never enough time to get work done	14	26	32	25	3
Worry about work outside working hours	5	18	22	36	18

Source: adapted from Cully et al. (7, p. 171).

Table 3.3

Average hours usually worked per week[a] by full-time employees, by gender

	Hours per week			Hours per week	
	Men	Women		Men	Women
United Kingdom	45.7	40.7	Sweden	40.2	40.0
Portugal	42.1	39.6	Finland	40.1	38.2
Greece	41.7	39.3	Italy	39.7	36.3
Spain	41.2	39.6	Denmark	39.3	37.7
Germany	40.4	39.3	Netherlands	39.2	38.5
Luxembourg	40.3	37.4	Belgium	39.1	37.5
France	40.3	38.7	E.U. average[b]	41.3	39.0
Austria	40.2	39.8			

Source: Office for National Statistics (8, p. 74).
[a]Excludes meal breaks but includes regularly worked paid and unpaid overtime.
[b]Average calculated with 1997 data for Irish Republic.

as well as numerous pieces of 20th century popular culture as more concerned with tea breaks than with work. Allen portrayed this as labor taking "a substantial part of its wages not in money but in leisure, most particularly the leisure that is taken at the place of employment" (quoted in 9, p. 13). Yet now the concern seems to have shifted to the psychological and physical health of the "stressed" British worker.

We might hypothesize that these expressions of "private troubles" (10) in various surveys, as well as the figures for working hours, are reactions to, or symptoms of, a change in the nature of work in the United Kingdom or in the U.K. labor market. These changes are, of course, very complex and we suggest that the findings outlined above may stem from at least two sources, which may be combined in any one individual case of a "stressed worker": the reconfiguration of the labor market and the reconfiguration of particular occupational roles. These two sets of institutional factors cannot be examined in any detail in the space of a single chapter, but some of the most significant changes may be outlined and their impact discussed in relation to particular categories of workers. Just three such groups are selected for analysis: managers in the private sector, public sector employees, and part-time workers. We have chosen these not because together they constitute a representative cross-section of U.K. employees but rather because they illustrate different institutional pressures at work and different experiences of stress.

INSTITUTIONAL CHANGE IN THE UNITED KINGDOM

The Labor Market

There has been much discussion in recent years, in the United Kingdom as elsewhere, of a tendency towards increasing "flexibility" within the labor market. There are numerous competing conceptualizations of such change, but rather than summarizing these debates here we will make just two points. The first, descriptive point is that the changes have been associated with the growth of what is sometimes labeled "atypical" employment at the expense of more conventional forms. These atypical forms that have seen recent growth are temporary and contract work, part-time work, and self-employment. The second, analytical and inevitably rather more controversial point is that while such changes are connected with processes of global economic and technological change, they are also subject to institutional mediation at national and organizational levels. Thus government policies, labor market regulation, and national "systems" of employee relations can be seen as influencing the form and extent of "flexibility" in particular countries, with managerial policies also influencing their take-up in particular organizations (for further description and justification of this approach, see, e.g., 11).

A number of critics have pointed to a variety of institutional factors in the United Kingdom leading to the prevalence of "financial engineering" and a resulting decline in manufacturing, with that which is left being concentrated in the low value-added areas (12–14). This has been associated with U.K. firms tending to emphasize certain forms of flexibility—particularly those providing numerical and temporal flexibility rather than relying on "functional" flexibility through multiskilling or more flexible production or marketing systems (14).

Reconfiguration of Particular Occupational Roles

Probably very few occupations have been immune from change in recent years—in the United Kingdom as elsewhere. No doubt each occupation is subject to a different set of pressures and opportunities, but most occupations have faced change as a result of technological factors, managerial change, or regulatory change—or as often as not some combination of these. Little will be said about technological change here, beyond noting the ubiquitous nature of information technology–related modifications to work practices. On managerial change, however, we may note several significant trends identified within the United Kingdom. The first is the decline of joint regulation of employment relations through collective bargaining (7). This decline is, of course, uneven and has been accomplished in different ways in different industries and organizations, but it is a significant change. Related to this is the rise of performance management systems (5) and implementation of techniques such as "culture change," total quality management, business process reengineering, and just in time. Nevertheless, U.K. management might still best be described as reactive and pragmatic, with no one approach being dominant: some of the rhetoric of human resource management and the like is in evidence, but various studies point to a wide variety of practices and the lack of a consistent and coherent "model" of management finding widespread favor (15). In short, we might characterize British management as highly varied and subject to fads and fashion that render change within particular organizations the norm rather than the exception.

Regulatory change is also something that has affected many occupations. While different regulatory bodies and policies—some of them European Union inspired—have affected sectors as diverse as financial services, retailing, and manufacturing, these regulations (and modifications of them) have brought about the need for changes in work practices as well as a need for monitoring.

With these necessarily brief pointers to aspects of the changing institutional context, we now turn to particular groups of employees and their experiences of stress. This will take us a little way beyond the averages presented in most of the stress-related statistics dealt with so far, which may, of course, conceal great variety in the experiences of different categories of U.K. workers.

Managers in the Private Sector

A number of studies have pointed to U.K. managers having a hard time in recent years. Of course, we should not be too sorry for them, since in many ways they remain a privileged group with relatively high pay, interesting work, task discretion, and opportunities to increase skill and secure career advancement. Nevertheless recent studies have pointed to long hours, job insecurity, and changes in role that are often viewed in negative ways. Each of these will be examined in turn.

Working Hours. According to Cully and colleagues (7), 32 percent of employees in their category of "managers and administrators" worked more than 48 hours per week. A telephone survey by the Institute of Personnel and Development (IPD) (16) conducted in 1998, found rather less than this, but still a considerable proportion: 22 percent in the "managerial and administrator" category claimed to be working more than this. Meanwhile, two separate surveys of Institute of Management members provide other indications: one gives an average (mean) of 48 working hours for private sector managers (17); the other found 40 percent claiming to work more than 51 hours per week, with 50 percent of public limited company (PLC) managers claiming to work more than two hours per day over contract (18). If these findings portray a rather inconsistent picture, they nevertheless point to a high proportion of managers working beyond normal contractual hours.

Of course, there is no necessary link between working hours and even perceived stress. Indeed, according to the IPD survey, 41 percent of those working more than 48 hours claimed that it was "totally their own choice" (16, p. 1), while 2 percent gave their main reason as "work enjoyment—love the job." Others gave very different reasons; however: according to Worrall and Cooper (18), the top four reasons for working long hours were: "it's the only way to deal with the workload"; "the only time available for thinking/planning"; "being part of the organization's culture"; and "employer expectations." All of which point to a higher degree of perceived constraint, even compulsion.

We must be cautious about taking self-reports of working hours at face value, and the reasons people give for them. It is likely that they are subject to the operation of selective memory, social approval seeking, attribution errors, and psychological defense mechanisms. Nevertheless, there does seem to be an association between reports of working long hours and self-reports of stress (4).

Insecurity. The same survey sources also point to an increasing sense of insecurity among managers in the private sector. Cully and colleagues (7) found managers exhibiting the least security of all occupational groups, with only 56 percent saying they felt secure in their jobs; Poole and colleagues (17) found job security declining over a 20-year period. Perhaps this is not surprising, given the prevalence of changes in organizations that affect management. According to Worrall and Cooper (18), 58 percent of PLC managers witnessed redundancy programs and 32 percent delayering (removing layers of middle management) in their own organizations in the last year alone. These authors also found a pronounced association between organizational change and perceived job insecurity (19). Another significant finding, perhaps, is that 84 percent of PLC managers agreed with the statement "my career development has become increasingly down to me" (18).

Role Changes and Identity Work. Changes in the role of managers can be discussed in terms of relations with superiors as well as in terms of skill and task variety. Here the research points to a rather complex picture of change. Gallie and coauthors (5) suggest that more managers and professionals experienced decreased "tightness of supervision" in the last five years than experienced an increase (42 percent as opposed to 24 percent). Worrall and Cooper (18) also found more managers agreeing than disagreeing with the statement that "my level of empowerment has increased"—but responses were variable and the authors commented that it is "perhaps disappointing . . . that more managers do not feel empowered" (18, p. 44). What this seems to represent is an uneven trend towards an increase in "responsible autonomy." Gallie and coauthors (5) point to managers and professionals having the highest exposure to bureaucratic control, by which they mean internal progression rules, appraisal systems, and merit and pay performance. Perhaps this is the explanation for Poole and colleagues' finding (17, p. 34) of a trend towards an increasing but small proportion of managers agreeing with the statement that "top management no longer treats middle managers as individuals." Another finding from the same source is that an increasing proportion agreed that "in recent years my job has become more routine and lacks scope for managerial initiative and action" (17, p. 35). This is consistent with Gallie and coauthors' argument (5) that managers and professionals "appear to have seen increased constraints on their ability to take everyday decisions," while Worrall and Cooper report that the "strongest positive score of the effects of organisational change we have measured is the 'accountability at work has increased' item" (18, p. 30).

Clearly, the three factors—working hours, insecurity, and changing roles—are interrelated. Working long hours may be a demonstration of organizational commitment and a way individuals prove—perhaps as much to themselves as to the employer—how valuable they are to the organization. It is equally likely to stem from changes in role as new responsibilities or tasks are added or complexity increases. And all may be compounded by other factors both inside and outside the workplace. Fewer managers are, for example, able to rely on a "housewife" to insulate them from demands in the domestic sphere—partly because more of them are women, and partly because an increasing proportion are in two-job households. This does not seem to have ushered in an era of egalitarian distribution of unpaid domestic work, but according to one study, "higher levels of the men's social class are associated with their partners spending less time on household work and an increasing level of sharing" (20, p. 244). While the burgeoning market in paid domestic labor is a source of solutions to shortage of time, it is also likely to lead to new problems and stresses. The increase in divorce is likely to be both a symptom and a cause of strain as employees strive to reconcile the competing demands of home and work. The survey by Smith and colleagues (21) supports this, finding those who were divorced, separated, or widowed reporting significantly higher levels of stress than those who were either single, married, or cohabiting.

Within the workplace, too, there have been some changes in the occupation of management that have potentially stressful implications. For example, the increasing proportion of the managerial group that is female is likely to be important in several ways. First, if women managers tend to face greater sources of stress than their male counterparts, then this implies that stress is likely to increase as the numbers of women in managerial positions increase. And while the evidence does not all point in the same direction,[3] a recent review did conclude that "the evidence undeniably shows that women managers are faced with substantially greater sources of stress than their male counterparts" (22, p. 5). If these sources of stress stem in part from many such women still being primarily responsible for providing or organizing childcare and housework within their households, they would also seem to originate in the ways women are in large part led to "manage like a man" (23) or to adapt to "rules of the game" that tend to favor men (2, pp. 24–26; 24–26).

For a variety of reasons, then, the U.K. manager might be considered relatively highly stressed. It is tempting to employ the much-used categories of role ambiguity, role conflict, and role overload to make sense of the above brief discussion. But the notion of role is too static for our purposes, failing to capture the fluidity of the self in late modernity (27). Instead we prefer to point to three kinds of "identity work" (28) operating here, sometimes simultaneously. These draw attention not so much to the origins of stress as to the variable nature of responses or adaptations (cf. 29). They are identity switching, extending, and reshaping.

Identity switching implies shape-shifting or metamorphosis. This is where managers might learn to become different people at different times or in different contexts. The stress and anxiety in this stem from possible threats to ontological security—knowing who they are or having to deny their "real self." Some of the dilemmas inherent in this are eloquently captured in Marshall's study (30) of women managers "moving on," in which the reasons for moving (often out of management altogether) are found in difficulties in reconciling these different identities. The idea of *extending,* on the other hand, is that of doing more of the same. This might be seen as approximating to the "universal" or "abstract" worker (25), where the gendered substructure or understructure (26) places demands on individuals to give their all to the organization at the expense of responsibility and interests outside. But the strains of doing this may be great. *Reshaping,* the third type of identity work, can be seen as reconfiguring one's identities, either by altering one's behavior within a given role or rebalancing various demands.

While the literature points to the existence of all these adaptations, Britain's "long hours culture" points to extending as the most visible type of identity work.

[3] Findings from the survey by Smith and colleagues (21) suggest that in socioeconomic categories 1 and 2 (i.e., professional and managerial categories), a higher proportion of women than men are in the high-stress group. This pattern is reversed for all other occupational groups, although the differences by gender are not very great and are statistically significant only in the case of socioeconomic group 1. Similarly, while they report "no significant differences between males and females" for any of their job categories, the proportion of women reporting high stress levels is greater than for men in their category that contains the managerial occupations (21, p. 22).

If this does in fact dominate over reshaping, perhaps this is connected with other institutional factors—particularly the lack of a well-established training and development ethos within the United Kingdom in general and among managers in particular (31), which might inform reshaping.

Public Sector Employees

The United Kingdom's public sector has witnessed significant change in recent years, with a number of commentators suggesting the impact of a managerial reform movement or the adoption of what is called the new public management (NPM). Hood has identified NPM as associated with the use of mechanisms such as disaggregation, greater hands-on management, emphasis on "discipline and parsimony" in use of resources, increasing measurement of performance and use of "pre-set output measures" (32, pp. 95–97). All these have been in evidence in the United Kingdom over the last 20 years, leading commentators such as Clarke and Newman (33) to talk of managerial colonization. This was initially associated with the so-called New Right, or Thatcherism, and with policies designed to roll back the frontiers of the state and to deal with a perceived fiscal crisis. But the post-Thatcher era and that of "New Labour" under Prime Minister Blair have, if anything, seen the entrenchment of managerialism, even if there are some differences in approach and emphasis (34).

Not surprisingly, such managerialism would seem to have had an effect on public sector workers. The survey by Smith and colleagues (21) found that teachers and nurses (both predominantly although not exclusively found in the public sector) were the most likely to report high stress levels among all occupational groups in the study. And, according to Cully and colleagues' survey, public sector workers were more likely to agree with all three measures of job intensity than were private sector workers: "my job requires I work very hard"; "never enough time to get work done"; and "worry about work outside work hours" (7, p. 171). Cully and colleagues found that 49 percent of public sector workers agreed that there was never enough time to get work done, as opposed to 36 precent in the private sector. Of course, we cannot take such statements at face value, and these attitudes appear to be at odds with Worrall and Cooper's survey (18) finding that public sector managers seem to be working shorter hours on average than their private sector counterparts, although many do seem to be working considerably longer than their contractual hours. Thus 37 percent of the public sector managers in the Worrall and Cooper survey claimed to be working in excess of two hours per day over contract, as opposed to 50 percent of PLC managers. However, Poole and coworkers (17) put the average hours for public sector managers at 55, in contrast to 48 for managers in the private sector, so there seems to be some grounds for uncertainty about any public-private comparison. Perhaps the difference in survey results are related to Cully and coauthors' finding (7) of considerable variation within the public sector—with 15 percent in education working more than 48 hours, but only 4 percent in health and 8 percent in public administration.

In any event, public sector jobs are seen as stereotypically secure, and this finds support in Gallie and coworkers' finding (5) of significant differences in the perceptions of public sector and private sector employees concerning ease of dismissal. However, they also found that "It is notable that people's satisfaction with their job security was not simply a reflection of dismissal procedures" (5, p. 142). And according to Cully and colleagues, "There was no difference at all between employees in workplaces with a guaranteed security policy and those without: but where there had been workforce reductions job security was lower" (7, p. 169). A relatively high proportion of public sector workers have witnessed such workforce reductions—37 percent of public sector managers in Worrall and Cooper's survey (18) had experienced redundancies in their organization in the last year.

Perhaps, though, it is the reconfiguration of roles that is most significant. Here there seem to be many similarities with the private sector, with Worrall and Cooper (18) finding culture change, cost reduction programs, delayering, and the use of temporary and contract staff all in evidence in the public sector at levels similar to those in the private sector. But what seems to have made a particular impact on reconfiguring the occupational roles of public sector employees is the attempt to impose systems of performance management and regulation on the public sector as the United Kingdom has moved to what Power (35) describes as the Audit Society. This is perhaps illustrated at its starkest in schools. Here we have seen the introduction of a national curriculum (in England and Wales at least) together with testing of students at the ages of 5, 7, and 14 against national "targets." The performance of individual schools is now monitored against these targets, and the results published in "league tables." These in turn affect parents' perceptions and thus local demand for places in particular schools—something that has serious consequences for some schools, as funding is related to enrollments. The monitoring of performance is also conducted through a rigorous system of school inspections.

Perhaps not surprisingly, as far as schoolteachers are concerned, there is a growing body of literature charting the incidence and growth of stress in the U.K. education sector. As an issue, it has been taken up by teachers' unions, pressing for action to address the problem. For example, in one report the National Union of Teachers says, "Stress is one of the biggest problems facing teachers today. . . . 36 percent of teachers told a 1999 NUT study that they felt the effects of stress all or most of the time. . . . For many teachers, the major contributing factors to problems of stress (although not the only ones) are the current levels of workload and bureaucracy in the education system" (36, p. 1).

Teachers' responses, however, need to be set in the context of their expectations, which are shaped in part by general normative expectations about what constitutes a "fair day's work," as well as occupationally specific expectations built up from the individual and collective experience of teaching. But the language of stress provides a convenient foil in arguing against any change that threatens a group's interests, even if, as Hepburn and Brown (37) argue, employing such a subjective and individualizing concept may lead to token measures rather than substantial changes in employee relations and conditions.

Nor should the changes that have occurred within the public sector be seen as gender neutral. A number of authors have pointed to the presence of macho styles of management (cf. 38, 39) for local government, and much of the change would seem to be predicated on the assumption that employees can be nongendered "universal" workers (25, 26). However this may be, in the terms introduced earlier, we might see public sector workers as unable to respond to the changes around them entirely through extending, for while the changes no doubt often do require simply more of the same (e.g., more grading, as student-staff ratios have increased in universities), they also imply a reconfiguration of occupational roles. This, we would argue, frequently involves public sector workers engaged in identity switching—for example, between "professional" and "managerial" identities—but also in reshaping. This is evident in attempts to reconfigure professional autonomy into responsible autonomy in order to bring professionals under greater managerial control, as Dent (40) has argued is the case for hospital doctors in the United Kingdom.

Part-Time Employees

The number of part-time workers in the United Kingdom has risen significantly in recent decades. Since 1984 the number of male part-time workers has doubled and the number of females has increased by 25 percent (8). Part-time workers now represent about a quarter of those in employment—within the European Union, only the Netherlands has a higher percentage (41). This increase can of course be seen as the product of a complex set of influences. One significant factor would seem to be the sectoral shift in the U.K. labor market, with the relative decline of manufacturing and the rise of services. Some commentators also see it as associated with a developing international division of labor, with institutional factors within the United Kingdom pushing the economy in the direction of concentration on price-competitive and low value-added markets (11). But there are also supply-side influences. One such influence, although able to explain only a relatively small proportion of the total increase, is the growth in numbers of students working part-time: in 2001 they represented approximately 16 percent of all part-time employees (42). But of greater significance is the number of women seeking part-time work, since women make up about 80 percent of the part-time labor force (42). The degree to which part-time work is a freely made choice for women rather than a choice made under conditions of constraint has been the subject of a sometimes heated debate (see 43–45). But what is undeniable is the increase in the number of women working part-time.

While commentators on labor market flexibility have often expressed concern, as we might expect, at the insecurity, stress, and intensification that come in its wake (11, 46), a number of studies have pointed to relatively low levels of stress among part-time workers. Smith and colleagues (4) found only 8.8 percent of part-time workers in the high work stress category, compared with 21.8 percent of full-time workers. Similarly, Gallie and colleagues found part-time workers "less likely to experience work strain than any of the categories of full-time workers," and "perhaps the most notable feature of the data is the strong linearity of the relationship between work hours and strain within both the part-time and full-time groups" (5, p. 225). This might seem surprising if such workers are seen as a "marginal" group subject to greater exploitation than full-timers. Moreover, with many of these part-timers being women with dependent children, one might hypothesize they are subject to higher levels of stress emerging from pressures outside work and perhaps are less able as a result to meet workplace demands.

Four explanations might be suggested for these findings. The first is that the high proportion of the part-time workforce that is women may account for the difference: perhaps women have better coping strategies or are less prone to stress for some reason. However, this seems unsatisfactory as an explanation, since Cully and coauthors (7) found women more likely to claim work strain than men doing similar hours, and Smith and coauthors (21) found women full-timers *and* part-timers more likely to report high stress levels than men. These findings are consistent with the hypothesis that having responsibility for dependents increases stress, as Cully and colleagues (7) found parents were more likely to report intense and stressful jobs than those without dependents. Nevertheless, a relatively high proportion of part-timers having dependents may not explain all the variation between the two groups.

A second possible explanation is that part-timers are less committed either to the job or to the organization so that, frankly, they care less. This is consistent with Hakim's controversial characterization of many women part-timers as being less committed to work than full-timers—as putting their family and domestic responsibilities before job or career (47; but see 45 for a rather different analysis based on Australian data). However, Cully and colleagues actually found part-timers to have higher organizational commitment than full-timers, as well as showing higher levels of job satisfaction; this difference was found in all occupational groups except assembly workers (7, p. 187). In this case they measured organizational commitment based on how far respondents agreed or disagreed with the following statements: "I share many of the values of my organization"; "I feel loyal to my organization"; "I am proud to tell people who I work for" (7, p. 185). Whether survey responses to such questions really tell us much about what are likely to be complex attitudes may be doubtful, but some association between such measures of organizational commitment and commitment to the job seems likely particularly if we take into account the findings in relation to job satisfaction. Certainly, whatever their shortcomings, the findings do not support the hypothesis that part-timers' lack of commitment explains their lower expressed levels of stress.

A third explanation for the relatively low levels of perceived stress among part-time workers is related to job characteristics. Perhaps the difference between the two groups arises from the differences in the kinds of work done or the demands placed upon workers in the two categories. For example, part-time workers were concentrated in certain kinds of job—particularly administrative and secretarial, sales, and customer services—together accounting for 36 percent of the total, while only 11 percent were in managerial or professional occupations, compared with 25 percent of full-timers (40). But although some of the jobs in which part-timers are concentrated are among those where workers seem to report relatively low levels of stress, such as catering, clerical work, care work, and cleaning (21), others are in jobs that appear in the "high reported stress category"—including teaching and nursing. In fact, according to the analysis by Smith and coworkers (21), full-timers are more likely to report high stress levels than part-timers in all socioeconomic and occupational categories. This seems surprising, if we consider one of the most influential models of job strain (48–50). The Karasek model relates the degree of strain to the combined effects of job demands and decision latitude (the higher the degree of demand and the lower the degree of decision latitude, the greater the strain). It seems unlikely that part-timers would have greater decision latitude than their full-time counterparts, and it is not obvious why demands upon them would be less (at least on a pro rata basis). Nor does the addition of the variable of social support from colleagues or supervisors seem to explain any difference, since we might hypothesize that both kinds of support are likely to be less in evidence for part-timers, as there is less scope, or at least less time available, for social interaction. Similarly for job security: if anything we would expect part-timers to have less job security, in line with their "peripheral" status in the labor market. If existing models of job strain can be used to explain the difference between part-timers and full-timers, therefore, there would seem to be a need to examine how job demands vary between the two groups, since this seems the likeliest area of difference. Perhaps less is expected of part-timers; or part-timers may be better insulated from extensions to their role, or have less responsibility, or be less involved in the conflicts involved in "office politics" (51, p. 30). But to date there seems little research evidence to decide between these alternatives—indeed, surprisingly little research seems to have been done on part-time workers.

The fourth explanation, and possibly the most straightforward, for part-timers experiencing less stress is that working fewer hours makes it easier to meet the demands of the domestic sphere and to recuperate from any strain experienced at work. This latter point seems to find support from a number of studies that have established a link between working long hours and various kinds of ill-health (52).

Of course, Hakim's position (47) on the "voluntary" nature of part-time work and the "preference" many women have for it has attracted much critical comment, as noted previously. But much of the heat generated in this debate can be removed if we see any such "preferences" or choices as arising within a field of experience and opportunities (27) in which men and women tend to make different "choices" according to their respective positions within gendered organizational and domestic (or "family") spheres. Such choices are best seen as the product of explicit or implicit negotiation between partners as well as arising from processes of "identity work." It is these processes of negotiation and identity formation that seem to have been little explored in the case of part-time workers in the United Kingdom—a rather surprising and regrettable gap in the research literature. But if this deficiency is to be remedied, there will need to be a move beyond considering the part-time category as homogeneous. Commentators such as Walsh (45) have, rightly in our view, pointed to the diverse nature of the part-time category. Certainly as far as reported stress is concerned, while there seems to be a consistent difference between part-time and full-time workers, there also seems to be a significant difference among different categories of part-timer: according to Smith and colleagues' survey (21), those in socioeconomic groups 1 and 2 (managerial and professional workers) are more than twice as likely to report high levels of stress as those in any other group.

CONCLUSION

This brief examination of three categories of workers in the United Kingdom suggests varying degrees of stress in evidence. It also points to a variety of institutional factors operating at different levels to influence the degree and type of stress experienced, as well as the responses to it, and these are summarized in Table 3.4. At a national and supranational level, certain institutional contexts can shape the degree to which jobs of particular types (e.g., full- or part-time) are available and thus the likelihood of stress. They also shape the experience within particular types of job and organization as they determine the degree of intensification, reorganization, and insecurity that prevails. In the United Kingdom at least, the trends may point not in the direction simply of increasing stress but to a more complex picture of stress as being more significant for some groups than others. This brief investigation of three such groups also points to considerable variation within them, as cross-cutting differences of gender, sector, hours worked, and occupational characteristics weave their way through each category—and to these differences could be added many others, including age, ethnicity, and industry.

The findings discussed in this chapter also point to stress of different kinds. For private sector managers, the pressures imposed by financial engineering and competitive pressures, as well as the perceived imperative to follow the latest management fashions, seem to result in the need both to extend the working

Table 3.4

Summary: Category of worker, institutional context, and stress

Group	Institutional context	Degree of stress	Response to stress
Private sector managers	Financial engineering; managerial "fads and fashions"	Relatively high	Identity switching and extending?
Public sector employees	New public management	Relatively high	Identity switching, extending, and reshaping?
Part-time workers	Drive for numerical and temporal flexibility	Relatively low	N.A.

day and to switch between different roles. For private sector managers and public sector employees alike, pressures emanating from reorganization and reconfiguration of occupational identities can lead to insecurity and what might be seen as anomic forms of stress, as old certainties and norms are set aside with uncertain consequences. These pressures might be seen as forms of intensification of the labor process, but if this is the case it stems not just from a simple quantitative increase in work of a given type in a given time but from a complex set of qualitative and quantitative changes.

We have also drawn attention to various ways in which employees respond to the pressures they face. In the United Kingdom there would seem to be a tendency to cope with pressure by simply trying to do "more of the same," or to approximate to Acker's universal worker (25, 26), at least among certain groups. In particular, this often takes the form of extending the working day—perhaps more extensification than intensification. However, the possibility of resistance and a reshaping of occupational roles remains, but responses and choices take place within a field of opportunities and constraints provided by a set of institutional contexts. And these in turn are shaped by global forces that are also subject to national and local mediation, suggesting complexity and diversity in stress and adaptation.

We hope this chapter has provided an illustration of one particular sociological approach to stress that is alive to its institutionally mediated nature. Perhaps it also shows that, for stress as for the weather and sports failure, it is not that those in the United Kingdom have more of it than those elsewhere, just that the rich variety of explanations, forms, and responses makes this a fruitful topic for everyday conversation as well as for research.

REFERENCES

1. Eyer, J., and Sterling, P. Stress-related mortality and social organization. *Rev. Radical Polit. Econ.* 9(1): 1–44, 1977.
2. Clark, H. *Women, Work, and Stress: New Directions.* Occasional Papers in Business, Economy and Society, No. 3. University of East London, London, 1991.
3. Lazarus, L. S. *Stress and Emotion: A New Synthesis.* Free Association Books, London, 1999.
4. Smith, A., et al. *The Scale of Occupational Stress: The Bristol Stress and Health at Work Study.* HSE Books, Sudbury, U.K., 2000.
5. Gallie, D., et al. *Restructuring the Employment Relationship.* Clarendon Press, Oxford, 1998.
6. Burchell, J. B., et al. *Job Insecurity and Work Intensification: Flexibility and the Changing Boundaries of Work.* Joseph Rowntree Foundation, York, U.K., 1999.
7. Cully, M., et al. *Britain at Work: As Depicted by the 1998 Workplace Employee Relations Survey.* Routledge, London, 1999.
8. Office for National Statistics. *Social Trends 30.* Stationery Office, London, 2000.
9. Nichols, T. *The British Worker Question: A New Look at Productivity in Manufacturing.* Routledge and Kegan Paul, London, 1986.
10. Mills, C. W. *The Sociological Imagination.* Penguin, Harmondsworth, U.K., 1959.
11. Murton, A. Labour markets and flexibility: Current debates and the European dimension. In *Organization and Management: A Critical Text*, edited by J. Barry et al., pp. 147–170. Thomson Learning, London, 2000.
12. Williams, K., Williams, J., and Haslam, C. The hollowing out of British manufacturing. *Econ. Soc.* 19(4): 456–490, 1990.
13. Armstrong, P. Accountancy and HRM. In *Human Resource Management: A Critical Text,* edited by J. Storey. Routledge, London, 1995.
14. Ackroyd, S., and Proctor, S. British manufacturing organization and workplace industrial relations: Some attributes of the new flexible firm. *Br. J. Ind. Relations* 36(2): 163–183, 1998.
15. Fenwick, P., and Murton, A. Human resource management and industrial relations. In *Organization and Management: A Critical Text*, edited by J. Barry et al., pp. 119–146, Thomson Learning, London, 2000.
16. Institute of Personnel and Development. *Living to Work?* London, 1999.
17. Poole, M., Mansfield, R., and Mendes, P. *Two Decades of Management: A Survey of the Attitudes and Behaviour of Managers over a 20-Year Period.* Institute of Management, London, 2001.
18. Worrall, L., and Cooper, C. L. *The Quality of Working Life: 2000 Survey of Managers' Changing Experiences.* Institute of Management, London, 2001.
19. Worrall, L., Cooper, C. L, and Campbell, F. The new reality for UK managers: Perpetual change and employment instability. *Work Employment Soc.* 14(4): 647–668, 2000.
20. Bond, S., and Sales, J. Household work in the UK: An analysis of the British Household Panel Survey 1994. *Work Employment Soc.* 15(2): 233–250, 2001.
21. Smith, A., et al. *The Scale of Occupational Stress: A Further Analysis of the Impact of Demographic Factors and Type of Job.* Stationery Office, Norwich, U.K., 2000.

22. Fielden, S. L., and Cooper, C. L. Women managers and stress: A critical analysis. *Equal Opportunities Int.* 20(1–2): 3–16, 2001.
23. Wajcman, J. *Managing Like a Man: Women and Men in Corporate Management.* Polity Press, Cambridge, 1998.
24. Billing, Y. D., and Alvesson, M. *Gender, Managers, and Organisation.* Walter de Gruyter, Berlin, 1993.
25. Acker, J. Hierarchies, jobs, bodies: A theory of gendered organisations. *Gender Soc.* 4(2): 139–158, 1990.
26. Acker, J. The future of 'gender and organisations': Connections and boundaries. *Gender, Work Organ.* 5(2): 195–206, 1998.
27. Melucci, A. Identity and difference in a globalized world. In *Debating Cultural Hybridity: Multi-Cultural Identities and the Politics of Anti-Racism*, edited by P. Werbner and T. Modood, pp. 58–69. Zed Books, London, 1997.
28. Thompson, P., and McHugh, D. *Work Organizations: A Critical Introduction, Ed. 2.* Macmillan, Basingstoke, U.K., 1995.
29. Jack, D., and Jack, R. Women lawyers: Archetype and alternatives. In *Mapping the Moral Domain*, edited by C. Gilligan et al., pp. 263–288, Harvard University Press, Cambridge, 1988.
30. Marshall, J. *Women Managers Moving On: Exploring Careers and Life-Choices.* Routledge, London, 1995.
31. Handy, C., et al. *Making Managers.* Pitman, London, 1988.
32. Hood, C. The 'New Public Management' in the 1980s: Variations on a theme. *Accounting Organ. Soc.* 20(3): 93–109, 1995.
33. Clarke, J., and Newman, J. *The Managerial State.* Sage, London, 1997.
34. Clarke, J., Gewirtz, S., and McLaughlin, E. *New Managerialism, New Welfare?* Sage, London, 2000.
35. Power, M. *The Audit Society: Rituals of Verification.* Oxford University Press, Oxford, 1997.
36. National Union of Teachers. *Workload, Stress, and Workplace Bullying.* December 2001. [Available online from URL: http://www.data.teachers.org.ulc.]
37. Hepburn, A., and Brown, S. D. Teacher stress and the management of accountability. *Hum. Relations* 54(6): 691–715, 2001.
38. Keen, L., and Scase, R. Middle managers and the new managerialism. *Local Government Stud.* 22(4): 167–186, 1996.
39. Lowndes, V. We are learning to accommodate mess: Four propositions about management change in local governance. *Public Policy Adm.* 12(2): 80–94, 1997.
40. Dent, M. Professionalism, educated labour and the state: Hospital medicine and the new managerialism. *Sociol. Rev.* 41(2): 244–273, 1993.
41. Eurostat. *European Social Statistics—Labour Force Survey Results 1999.* Office for the Official Publications of the European Community, Luxembourg, 2000.
42. Office for National Statistics. *Labour Force Survey: Quarterly Supplement November 2001.* Stationery Office, London, 2001.
43. Crompton, R., and Harris, F. E. Reply to Hakim. *Br. J. Sociol.* 49(1): 144–149, 1998.
44. Hakim, C. Developing a sociology for the twenty-first century: Preference theory. *Br. J. Sociol.* 49(1): 137–143, 1998.

45. Walsh, J. Myths and counter-myths: An analysis of part-time female employees and their orientations to work and working hours. *Work Employment Soc.* 13(2): 179–203, 1999.
46. Henry, M., and Franzway, S. Gender, unions and the new workplace: Realising the promise? In *Pink Collar Blues*, edited by B. Probert and B. R. Wilson. Melbourne University Press, Melbourne, 1993.
47. Hakim, C. *Key Issues in Women's Work: Female Heterogeneity and the Polarisation of Women's Employment.* Athlone Press, London, 1996.
48. Karasek, R. A. Job demands, job decision latitude and mental strain: Implications for job redesign. *Adm. Sci. Q.* 24: 285–308, 1979.
49. Karasek, R. A. The political implications of pyschosocial work redesign: A model of the psychosocial class structure. *Int. J. Health Serv.* 19(3): 481–508, 1989.
50. Karasek, R. A., and Theorell, T. *Healthy Work: Stress, Productivity, and the Reconstruction of Working Life.* Basic Books, New York, 1990.
51. Edworthy, A. *Managing Stress.* Open University Press, Buckingham, U.K., 2000.
52. Sparks, K., and Cooper, C. L. The effects of hours of work on health: A meta-analysis. *J. Occup.Organ. Psychol.* 70: 391–408, 1997.
53. Powell, W., and Di Maggio, P. (eds.). *The New Institutionalism in Organisational Analysis.* University of Chicago Press, Chicago, 1991.
54. Smith, M. R., Masi, A. C., and van den Berg, A. External flexibility in Sweden and Canada: A three industry comparison. *Work Employment Soc.* 9(4):689–718, 1995.
55. Walsh, J. Employment systems in transition? A comparative analysis of Britain and Australia. *Work Employment Soc.* 11(1): 1–25, 1997.

Chapter 4

EFFECTS OF ORGANIZATIONAL DOWNSIZING ON WORKER STRESS AND HEALTH IN THE UNITED STATES

Lawrence R. Murphy and Lewis D. Pepper

Downsizing and restructuring, involving large-scale layoffs, have been adopted over the last decade as a management tool with the purported aim of strengthening a company or agency by reducing budgets and personnel. During 2001, 21,345 mass layoff events occurred in the United States, resulting in 2,496,784 initial claims filings for unemployment insurance. The Mass Layoff Statistics program, maintained by the U.S. Department of Labor's Bureau of Labor Statistics, reports on mass layoff actions that result in workers being separated from their jobs. Both the number of events and the number of initial claimants in 2001 were the highest in the nearly seven-year history of the program. Manufacturing accounted for 42 percent of all mass layoff events and 49 percent of initial claims filed during 2001, the largest annual shares to date (1).

Sometimes downsizing is associated with a partial or complete restructuring, while at other times it is simply a reduction in the number of employees. Much downsizing has been implemented without information about the health impacts on remaining employees and the organizational and productivity costs. Often, corporate executives are rewarded financially after a downsizing event, and stock prices increase. But these stock increases are often temporary. For instance, stock prices of firms that downsized during the 1980s fell short of industry averages in the 1990s (2), and two-thirds of companies that downsize will downsize again within a year (3). In a study of more than 300 companies that downsized employees by more than 3 percent annually from 1980 to 1990, Cascio (4) found that downsizing did not lead to an improvement in company financial performance. Finally, Cascio and coworkers (5) examined the financial performance of firms that engaged in employment downsizing during the period 1981–92 and found no significant increase in profitability due to downsizing, when compared with industry averages. Taken together, these findings question whether downsizing is an effective tool for improving financial performance or creating a more efficient and competitive organization.

In addition, there is growing evidence of significant organizational consequences of downsizing. In a study by the American Management Association, 40 percent of organizations responding reported that productivity had sagged after downsizing, and nearly one-fifth reported that quality had suffered. This study also documented a decline in morale (reported by 58 percent of companies) and greater employee turnover (6). Likewise, Sommer and Luthans (7) found a decrease in organizational commitment, in trust among coworkers, and in job satisfaction following a downsizing event at a health care organization. Other studies have documented decreases in job security, organizational commitment, trust among coworkers, and job satisfaction, and increases in workplace conflict after downsizing (7).

Most research has focused on the effects of downsizing on workers' health and well-being. Noer (8) examined individual responses to downsizing and identified common symptoms of fear, insecurity, frustration and anger, sadness, and sense of unfairness as well as reduced risk-taking and lowered productivity. Noer named this compilation of symptoms "survivor syndrome," a syndrome that was originally identified in studies of survivors of Hiroshima/Nagasaki and the Holocaust. A follow-up study of organizations implementing layoffs found that many of these symptoms persisted for five years, although employees had become resigned to the outcomes (8). Still other studies have reported that the threat of downsizing can lead to deteriorated health, increased work demands, and tension in the workplace (9–11). A few studies (summarized in 7) found negative personal and job outcomes associated with downsizing. Cameron and colleagues (12), for instance, found significant associations between downsizing and decreased morale and increased conflict in the workplace. In an early review of the literature, Kozlowski and colleagues (13) noted the impacts of downsizing on interpersonal relationships, physical health, and emotional health. A recent study found that the effects of downsizing on employees' attitudes decrease over time and that one year later, their attitudes began returning to pre-downsizing levels (14). The implication for organizations that engage in repeated episodes of downsizing is clear: employees' attitudes will not have a chance to recover over time, and so will remain low.

Aside from the effects of downsizing per se, other research has established the importance of the process of downsizing, that is, *how* downsizing is accomplished. Brockner and colleagues (15–17) report that employees' perceptions of fairness, openness, and justice moderate the effects of downsizing on health and productivity. In addition, a literature is emerging about workers' perceptions of fairness in how decisions are made and implemented. Research to date shows that perceptions of fairness are important in the workplace and should be considered as an independent variable when analyzing organizational functioning and employees' health (18–21).

Likewise, Parker and coworkers (22), studying a company that had introduced planned employment changes (strategic downsizing), followed employees over a four-year period after downsizing. Although job demands increased after downsizing, employees' well-being and job satisfaction did not decrease. The authors concluded that the managed, strategic downsizing actually improved employees' sense of control, because of new work characteristics introduced as part of the reorganization. The authors suggested that when downsizing is planned or strategic, not reactive, and when it fosters employees' involvement, adverse outcomes do not necessarily occur.

This chapter examines the effects of downsizing on worker stress, coping, survivor syndrome health, and job security in two sites that represent extremes of downsizing. One site (site B) had been engaged in repeated episodes of downsizing since 1992; the other site (site A) had a single downsizing episode the year before the data were collected. The two sites also differed in the type of layoffs that occurred. In site A, all the layoffs were voluntary (e.g., early retirement), while at site B, about half of the workers lost their jobs through involuntary layoffs.

We proposed two hypotheses. The first is that survivor syndrome, job stress, and health symptoms will be higher, and coping and job security will be lower, at a site with multiple episodes of downsizing (site B, high downsizing) than at a site with a single episode of downsizing (site A, low downsizing). The second hypothesis is that the correlation between site and measures of survivor syndrome, job stress, coping, and job security will be minimized after adjusting for downsizing process variables (i.e., *fairness* of procedures, *openness* of communication, and *opportunities* for more creative and interesting work).

METHOD

Background

Following the dissolution of the Soviet Union and the end of the nuclear arms race, the U.S. Department of Energy (DOE) and the nuclear defense industry embarked on a process of changing the agency's mission and determining appropriate staffing levels reflecting this change. Anticipating future layoffs, Section 3161 of the National Defense Authorization Act for Fiscal Year 1993 outlined an approach to planning and implementing workforce layoffs consistently across the nuclear weapons industry. Section 3161 also identified objectives that each plan should address; these included minimizing social and economic impacts; giving workers adequate notice of impending changes; minimizing involuntary separations; offering preference-in-hiring to the extent practicable to those employees involuntarily separated; providing relocation assistance under certain conditions; providing retraining, educational, and outplacement assistance; and providing local impact assistance to affected communities.

In 1994 the DOE introduced the Strategic Alignment Initiative, a planning process that shifted core DOE missions from defense production to environmental management and the cleanup of radioactive and hazardous waste at 15 major locations in 13 states. The planning process involved a variety of changes, including reductions in the workforce, restructuring of contractor organizations, and the planned closure of certain facilities. Although the shift from arms production to environmental management was expected to produce a one-time major reduction in the workforce, layoffs continued into 1995 and beyond, driven by budget reductions and the realization that the number of retained production workers exceeded actual demand.

Study Sites

Site A. This site was located in the southwestern United States. Its principal mission was assembling and disassembling nuclear weapons. The mission has included fabricating chemical explosives for nuclear weapons, assembling nuclear weapons for the nation's stockpile, maintaining and evaluating nuclear weapons in the stockpile, and disassembling nuclear weapons retired from the stockpile. In response to the funding cutbacks, site A created and implemented a three-phase restructuring plan. Part I included a hiring freeze and preparation of the workforce layoff plan; phase II consisted of a voluntary separation incentive program (VSIP); and phase III consisted of allowing approved VSIPs to use the career transition center and preparing for an involuntary reduction in force.

The hiring freeze was instituted in April 1996. A workforce transition team—chaired by the human resources manager and consisting of managers of other divisions, including the equal employment opportunity/affirmative action department and the union leadership—was formed in March 1996 to oversee the process and contribute to the DOE workforce restructuring plan. The workforce planning team and division managers identified affected positions by (*a*) determining the functions required to accomplish plant missions, (*b*) determining the number of employees required to carry out those functions and the necessary skill level, and (*c*) grouping employees with similar skill levels within specific plant functions into peer groups. Affected positions were identified among various peer groups.

In December 1996, it was announced that 350 positions were to be eliminated and offered a VSIP, which included a cash incentive, extended medical benefits, educational assistance, and outplacement services. No involuntary downsizing was required, since the number of voluntary separations was sufficient. Leaders from the Metal Trades Council and the International Guards Union of America were invited to all meetings of the workforce transition team and approved the process for granting VSIPs to bargaining unit employees. Letters from the general manager discussing the planning process were printed on the front page of the employee newsletter. Between December 1996 and February 1997, at least 11 written communications were distributed on impending deadlines, answers to commonly asked questions, and updates on numbers of employees who had applied for the VSIP or for internal transfers. The written communications, video, and employee packet each described aspects of the process.

A career transition center was opened in 1997; it offered a full range of services, including free workshops on networking, resume writing, interviewing, and financial planning. Computers, phones, and copiers were made available to individuals for job searches. Career counselors were available for individual sessions.

Site B. This site was located in the Midwestern United States. It had traditionally produced highly enriched uranium and other components for nuclear weapons, but its new mission included dismantling nuclear weapons, manufacturing weapons components, warehousing nuclear materials for defense capabilities, and transferring technology. Reorganization and downsizing had been fairly constant at this site since 1992. Reduction-in-force (RIF) events occurred nearly every year to adjust to budget reductions. In 1993, the rationale for downsizing expanded to include changing missions and the need to decrease the workforce while maintaining "unique and critical positions." Reduced budgets continued to drive the downsizing over the entire study period, with particularly large cuts in funding environmental management work in 1996. While the defense mission remained throughout this period, production capacity needed to be reduced. Management determined that a RIF was again necessary and reviewed eight possible reduction plans. It offered an early retirement incentive plan to attract enough employees and not lose those with needed skills. By 1998, when a voluntary RIF was offered (with severance pay), management had adopted the term of "surplus positions" to identify those eligible to apply.

Downsizing plans at the site were reviewed by the director of equal employment opportunity/affirmative action and reviewed and approved by the vice president for human resources. Monetary incentives for voluntary and involuntary layoffs included severance pay (usually one week of salary per year of service); educational assistance (usually $10,000 over four years, starting within one year of RIF); extended medical insurance, with the employee paying increasing amounts; and relocation assistance. Involuntary reductions of bargaining unit employees were carried out based on seniority and contract provisions. Involuntary reductions of salaried employees included several distinct actions: (*a*) business managers determined the number of full-time employees that could be supported by the site budget, and allocated those positions by division; (*b*) division leaders identified positions subject to the RIF and openings available for internal placement; and, (*c*) managers ranked individuals in targeted areas or job categories.

Management developed a list of stakeholders in the workforce reduction process, including union representatives; all stakeholders received announcements about reduction plans, and a forum was established to discuss workforce reductions and to initiate mitigation activities in April 1992. Finally, a placement center was opened in 1993 to assist with a variety of testing (interest, aptitude), counseling (psychological, job), skill workshops, and job search efforts. The workforce restructuring task group worked with human resources to reduce the impact of the RIFs. Activities included area needs analyses, internal placements, measures to mitigate the impact on community, and retraining programs for separated workers.

Training was viewed as a key long-term strategy to reduce both layoffs and the impact of layoffs. The program helped RIFed workers to find new jobs, and sought to make "survivors" or retained workers more versatile and to fill in where skills had been depleted by the layoffs. Training courses were offered in areas where new missions were developing and a job was likely at the end of the training.

Table 4.1 presents a summary of the downsizing events experienced at the two study sites from January 1991 through June 1998.

Sampling

At site A, 1,179 employees were randomly invited to participate in the study (41.2 percent of the total workforce in 1998). This site had 11 divisions, ranging in size from 27 to 152 employees, with three divisions having fewer than 100 employees. Each division was a sampling unit and approximately 40 percent of employees in each sampling unit were randomly included in the survey sample. At site B, 2,442 employees were randomly invited to participate in the study (43 percent of the total workforce in 1998). There were 46 divisions at the site, ranging in size from 1 to 178 employees, with 29 divisions having fewer than

Table 4.1

Descriptive information on downsizing events at the two study sites

	Site A	Site B
No. of annual downsizing/restructuring episodes since 1991	1	5
Total no. of workers affected by downsizing since 1991	321	4,270
Total no. expressed as percent of original workforce in 1991	15%	52%
Percent of layoffs that were voluntary (early retirement, etc.)	100%	74%
Year of most recent layoffs	1997	1997
Percent voluntary layoffs in most recent downsize (1997)	100%	45%

100 employees. Twelve divisions had fewer than 20 employees (2 to 18 people), and we combined them, based on functional and hierarchical similarity, into three groups for the purpose of sampling. This resulted in a total of 36 sampling units. Approximately 40 percent of employees in each sampling unit were randomly included in the survey sample for site B.

Data-Collection Procedure

Surveys were first mailed to sampled employees in August 1998. One researcher visited the site to encourage participation and was available for questions and to collect completed surveys. Thank-you letters were sent two weeks after the survey to all sampled employees. Employees were asked to return the anonymous survey and a separate postcard with their name to indicate completion of the survey. Two additional reminder mailings were sent to all those who did not return a postcard.

Survey Development

Interviews with employees, focus group discussions, and reviews of relevant literature were used to identify important themes or constructs to include in the employee survey. Where possible, we used existing scales or individual items, but a number of new items and scales were used in this study, including scales to measure three downsizing process variables: *fairness* of the downsizing rules and procedures, *openness* of communication, and *opportunities* for more interesting and creative work as a result of the downsizing. The opportunities scale was developed as a result of comments received during focus group discussions about the absence of any measures of positive effects of downsizing.

The draft survey was pilot-tested at the study sites in 1997 and was revised based on workers' comments solicited during debriefing sessions. The final survey took about 30 minutes to complete and was divided into six major sections (demographic information—age group, race, marital status, education level, tenure at the site, and income; job characteristics; health and health behavior information; assessment of organizational change; and organizational climate). In this report, only a portion of the items and scales are analyzed.

Independent Variables

Three scales were developed for this study to measure downsizing process variables, that is, how downsizing was accomplished at the site. The response format for all three scales was a five-point, "strongly agree" to "strongly disagree" scale (unless otherwise noted, all scales in this study used this five-point format).

Fairness was measured with four items: "during the restructuring process, consistent rules and procedures were followed"; "the rules and procedures for restructuring were fair"; "decisions about who to layoff were made fairly"; and "during the restructuring process, employees were treated fairly." The alpha coefficient for both sites A and B was 0.86. *Open communication* was measured using five items: 'the reasons for restructuring were clearly explained to me by my supervisor"; "during the restructuring process, I had the chance to express my views to management"; "employees were included in making decisions about restructuring"; "employees were given enough notice about the restructuring"; and "my supervisor dealt with me in a truthful manner during the restructuring process." The alpha coefficients for sites A and B were 0.75 and 0.76, respectively. *Opportunity at work* was measured using seven items: "as a result of the restructuring that took place, I now have the opportunity to make better decisions"; ". . . to make quicker decisions"; ". . . to learn new things"; ". . . for more interesting work"; ". . . to be more creative"; ". . . to eliminate unnecessary work"; ". . . for better career growth and development." The alpha coefficient for both sites A and B was 0.91.

Dependent Variables

Downsizing *survivor syndrome* was measured using five items developed for this study. The items tapped the major elements of the syndrome that are commonly present as a result of downsizing: "as a result of the downsizing at this facility, I have been feeling frustrated"; "I have been feeling guilty"; "I have been feeling sad"; "I tend to blame others when things do not go well"; "I like to be left alone"; "I have no desire to get involved with additional work activities." The response format was a five-point, "much less often" to "much more often" scale. The alpha coefficients for sites A and B were 0.79 and 0.69, respectively.

Stress symptoms were measured using four items taken from Cohen and coauthors' perceived stress scale (23), which used a five-point "never" to "very often" response format. The items were "during the past month, how often have you: (*a*) felt you were unable to control the important things in your life, (*b*) felt confident about your ability to handle personal problems, (*c*) felt that things were going your way, (*d*) felt that difficulties were piling up so high that you could not overcome them?" The alpha coefficient for both sites A and B was 0.67.

Work stress was measured using a single item: "during the past month, I have experienced a lot of stress at work." *Coping* was measured using two items: "I deal effectively with the stress at this site" and "I am able to maintain a healthy balance between my work life and my home life." The alpha coefficients for sites A and B were 0.66 and 0.72, respectively.

Physical health symptoms was measured using a "yes" or "no" checklist containing seven items: "Have any of the following problems been bothering you in the past 30 days: headaches, rapid breathing, difficulty breathing, racing heart, irregular heartbeats or flutters, chest pain, backache?" The alpha coefficients for sites A and B were 0.77 and 0.74, respectively.

Job security was measured using a single item: "my job security is good" on a four-point "not at all true" to "very true" response scale.

RESULTS

Table 4.2 shows demographic data for the two study sites. Site A (single episode of downsizing, voluntary layoffs) had more workers in the younger age groups and fewer workers in the 50 to 59 age group than at site B (multiple downsizing, involuntary and voluntary layoffs). Likewise, more workers at site A were in the lower tenure groups than at site B and a higher percentage of the workforce was white. The two sites were similar with respect to sex, education, marital status, and income group.

Table 4.3 shows mean scores and univariate F tests for all study variables. Significant differences between sites are evident for age group, race, and tenure group ($P \leq .001$) but not for the remaining demographics. However, the two sites differed significantly on all independent and dependent variables (P ≤ .001), with site B having poorer scores than site A. The results support our first hypothesis.

Table 4.4 shows correlations among all study variables. The pattern of correlations is very similar between the two sites. The demographic variables do not correlate highly with any of the independent or dependent variables. The largest correlation is between income group and worker ratings of open communication during downsizing (site A, $r = .12$; site B, $r = .11$).

Correlations among the dependent variables are small to moderate, ranging from r = 0.10 to 0.42. However, coping and stress symptom scales correlate at 0.53 and 0.51, for sites A and B, respectively, and work stress correlates with coping at –0.42 and –0.36. Three downsizing process variables correlate moderately (range, 0.35 to 0.40), except for the fairness and openness scales, which correlate at 0.70 in site A and 0.71 in site B. Apparently, these two aspects of the downsizing process are very closely linked and may not be distinct constructs, at least for the two sites in this study.

We tested our second hypothesis using hierarchical stepwise multiple regression for the six outcome variables; the results are shown in Table 4.5. Separate regressions were run for each outcome variable, and each regression followed the same hierarchical procedure. At step 1, the site variable was entered into the model (site was dummy coded: site A = 0, site B = 1). At step 2, the demographic variables were entered in stepwise fashion and the model R^2 calculated. Only variables that were significant remained in the model for the next step. Fairness was entered at step 3, openness at step 4, and opportunity at step 5. In this approach, changes in the regression coefficient for site reveal progressive removal of non-unique variance. At the last step, the standardized regression coefficient for site reflects site differences in the outcome variable adjusted for all other factors. After adjustment, the site variable carries information about downsizing history (single episode, voluntary layoffs vs. multiple episodes, some

Table 4.2

Means, standard deviations, and results of univariate *F* test

	Percent of sample	
	Site A (N = 779) (single episode, all voluntary layoffs)	Site B (N = 1,162) (multiple episodes, with involuntary layoffs)
Age group		
20–29	5	1
30–39	24	16
40–49	39	40
50–59	25	37
60+	7	6
Sex		
Male	70	70
Race		
White	85	92
Black	5	6
Hispanic	7	1
Other	3	1
Education		
High school	25	26
Some college	20	27
Bachelor's degree	37	29
Advanced degree	18	18
Marital status		
Married	80	81
Single	5	5
Separated	1	1
Divorced	13	12
Widowed	1	1
Tenure at site		
0–4 yrs	21	6
5–9 yrs	25	15
10–14 yrs	12	15
15-19 yrs	20	21
20–24 yrs	10	22
25 or more yrs	12	21
Income		
$30,000–$60,000	51	52
$60,001–$90,000	34	31
$90,001 and above	15	17

Note: Percentages may not add to 100% due to missing values.

Table 4.3

Means, standard deviations, and results of univariate *F* test

	Site A (N = 779)		Site B (N = 1,170)		
	Mean	S.D.	Mean	S.D.	Sig.
Age group	3.05	0.98	3.31	0.84	.001
Race (white = 1; other = 0)	0.85	0.36	0.92	0.26	.001
Sex (male = 1; female = 0)	0.70	0.46	0.70	0.46	N.S.
Education	2.37	0.96	2.39	1.06	N.S.
Marital status (married = 1; other = 0)	0.80	0.40	0.81	0.39	N.S.
Income group	3.64	0.73	3.66	0.76	N.S.
Tenure group	3.09	1.66	3.99	1.54	.001
Stress symptoms	2.06	0.73	2.27	0.73	.001
Work stress	2.99	1.13	3.28	1.14	.001
Good coping	3.86	0.68	3.66	0.76	.001
Survivor syndrome	2.92	0.56	3.10	0.54	.001
Perceived job security	2.70	0.88	2.35	0.94	.001
Health symptoms	0.40	0.18	0.45	0.20	.001
Fairness	2.92	0.86	2.61	0.82	.001
Openness of communication	2.88	0.69	2.64	0.7	.001
Post-downsizing opportunities at work	2.81	0.59	2.62	0.65	.001

involuntary layoffs). One can also see the relative strength of each variable in the final model by directly comparing the standardized regression coefficients shown in the last column in Table 4.5.

For example, the first row of Table 4.5 shows the results for the downsizing survivor syndrome scale. The unadjusted regression coefficient for site is 0.17, indicating that site B (dummy code = 1) has higher scores on survivor symptoms than site A (dummy code = 0). The size of the coefficient for site remains unchanged when the demographics are entered, but drops to 0.12 when the fairness scale is entered. The R^2 increases from .06 to .12 when fairness is added to the model. In step 5, the coefficient for site drops to .11 and the model R^2 increases to .16. Across steps 1 through 5, the model R^2 increases from .03 to .16. Thus, the unique contribution of site to survivor syndrome is reduced as the downsizing process variables are entered into the model, but remains significant in the model. The final column of Table 4.5 shows the variables that remain statistically significant in the final model, with standardized regression coefficients shown in parentheses. Opportunity is the strongest predictor of survivor symptoms (–.22), followed by fairness (–.16), education (.16), site (.11), and race (.06).

Table 4.4

Correlations (r) among the variables—site A below the diagonal; site B above the diagonal

		1	2	3	4	5	6	7	8	9	10	11	12	13	14	15	16
1	Age group	—	–0.01	0.18	–0.09	0.00	0.05	0.45	–0.08	–0.13	0.01	–0.03	0.12	–0.10	0.04	0.03	0.00
2	Race	0.05	—	0.05	–0.08	0.10	0.01	0.00	0.02	0.03	0.00	0.01	0.10	–0.01	0.06	0.06	0.02
3	Sex	0.15	0.00	—	–0.01	0.25	0.03	0.19	–0.10	–0.08	0.02	–0.01	0.09	–0.16	0.03	0.01	–0.03
4	Education	–0.04	0.14	0.08	—	0.05	0.31	0.12	0.11	0.15	–0.07	0.13	–0.06	–0.09	0.02	0.08	0.01
5	Marital status	0.08	0.05	0.23	0.06	—	0.27	0.04	–0.01	–0.01	0.01	0.04	0.03	–0.04	0.02	0.02	0.02
6	Income group	0.10	0.09	–0.05	0.31	0.39	—	0.05	0.04	0.05	–0.03	0.11	–0.01	–0.04	0.08	0.11	0.00
7	Tenure group	0.47	–0.07	0.10	–0.11	0.05	0.07	—	0.01	–0.05	–0.04	–0.01	0.12	–0.02	0.05	0.03	–0.06
8	Stress symptoms	–0.13	0.02	–0.08	0.11	–0.01	–0.05	0.04	—	0.34	–0.51	0.25	–0.18	0.20	–0.17	–0.12	–0.18
9	Work stress	–0.08	0.07	–0.01	0.15	0.01	–0.08	0.00	0.36	—	–0.36	0.22	–0.17	0.17	–0.18	–0.15	–0.24
10	Good coping	0.03	–0.02	–0.06	–0.07	0.05	0.02	0.04	–0.53	–0.42	—	–0.26	0.21	–0.22	0.19	0.20	0.23
11	Survivor syndrome	–0.01	0.11	0.06	0.13	0.05	0.08	0.02	0.26	0.29	–0.31	—	–0.18	0.10	0.27	0.22	–0.29
12	Job security	0.05	0.04	–0.04	–0.06	–0.01	0.08	0.13	–0.12	–0.19	0.16	–0.16	—	–0.12	0.24	0.24	0.22
13	Health symptoms	0.01	–0.01	–0.12	0.01	–0.08	–0.04	–0.04	0.16	0.11	–0.15	0.08	–0.02	—	–0.18	–0.14	–0.13
14	Fairness	0.02	–0.02	0.02	–0.02	0.00	0.04	0.06	–0.15	–0.25	0.22	–0.21	0.26	–0.10	—	0.71	0.40
15	Openness	–0.04	0.04	–0.06	0.08	0.03	0.12	0.12	–0.11	–0.18	0.18	–0.19	0.24	–0.07	0.70	—	0.42
16	Opportunity	–0.08	0.01	–0.08	0.01	–0.05	0.04	0.06	–0.18	–0.20	0.28	–0.28	0.22	–0.06	0.35	0.37	—

Note: Coding: sex (male = 1, female = 0); race (white = 1, other = 0); marital (married = 1, other = 0).

A similar pattern is evident for coping, the stress symptom scale, and health status. In each case, the addition of the downsizing process variables decreases the coefficient for site and increases the model R^2. In each model, *opportunity* (for better and quicker decision-making, to learn new things, to do more interesting work, and to be more creative) and *fairness* of the downsizing process are the best predictors of each outcome, with site and education level remaining significant in the final regression models.

The regression model for job security shows a slightly different pattern. The addition of demographics to the model increases the coefficient for site, and the site variable has the largest regression coefficient in the final model, followed by tenure, opportunity, and fairness. Similar to other outcome measures, the addition of downsizing process variables reduces the size of the regression coefficient for site and increases the model R^2. Since the site variable carries information about downsizing history (after adjusting for demographics and downsizing process variables), this finding suggests that perceptions of job security are most influenced by the downsizing history of a site and by worker tenure, and somewhat less so by process variables such as fairness, openness, and opportunity.

The results provide partial support for our second hypothesis, which predicted that the site differences would be minimized after controlling for downsizing process variables. While the downsizing process variables do reduce the differences between the high and low downsizing sites, the site differences are still significant in the final regression models. This indicates that the downsizing process variables do not fully moderate the effects of site.

DISCUSSION

This study found significant effects of downsizing/restructuring on worker stress, health, coping, and job security in the two study sites. Site A had undergone a single episode of downsizing in the year before the study, and all the layoffs were voluntary. Site B had undergone multiple episodes of downsizing over a five-year period, and these included involuntary as well as voluntary layoffs. In a downsizing episode at site B that occurred the year before the study, about half of the layoffs were involuntary.

Site B, with a history of more downsizing episodes and involuntary layoffs, had significantly higher mean scores on all dependent and independent variables than site A, which had a single episode of downsizing. These differences remain statistically significant after adjustment for age, sex, race, education, income, and tenure. Regression analyses of each dependent variable separately reveal that downsizing process variables (opportunity and fairness) and site are significant factors in all the final models. In all models except health symptoms, education level also is significant in the final regression models, indicating that employees

Table 4.5

Hierarchical, stepwise multiple regression results

	Step 1 Unadjusted regression coefficient	**Step 2** Adjusted for demographics	**Step 3** Adjusted for demographics + fairness	**Step 4** Adjusted for demographics + fairness + openness	**Step 5** Adjusted for demographics + fairness + openness + opportunity	**Final model** All variables in final regression model (standardized regression coefficients)
Survivor syndrome						Site (.11), race (.06), education (.16), fairness (–.16), opportunity (–.22)
Coefficient for site	.17	.17	.12	.12	.11	
Adjusted model R^2	.03	.06	.12	.12	.16	
Work stress						Site (.09), age (–.10), education (.15), fairness (–.14), opportunity (–.17)
Coefficient for site	.12	.14	.10	.10	.09	
Adjusted model R^2	.02	.05	.09	.09	.11	

Cope						Site (–.08), education (–.06),
Coefficient for site	–.14	–.14	–.10	–.09	–.08	fairness (.13), opportunity (.19)
Adjusted model R^2	.02	.02	.06	.07	.09	
Stress symptoms						Site (.11), sex (–.09), age (–.13),
Coefficient for site	.16	.15	.12	.12	.11	education (.12), tenure (.10),
Adjusted model R^2	.03	.06	.08	.08	.09	fairness (–.10), opportunity (–.13)
Health symptoms						Site (.10), sex (–.14), fairness (–.14),
Coefficient for site	.13	.13	.10	.10	.10	opportunity (–.07)
Adjusted model R^2	.02	.04	.06	.06	.07	
Job security						Site (–.17), race (.06), tenure (.15),
Coefficient for site	–.18	–.23	–.19	–.18	–.17	fairness (.13), openness (.10),
Adjusted model R^2	.03	.05	.11	.12	.14	opportunity (.14)

with more education had higher scores on survivor syndrome, stress symptoms, and perceived job security, and lower scores on coping.

We assessed the relative effects of downsizing history and downsizing process variables by entering the site variable in the first step of each regression model and then examining how its regression coefficient changes as the downsizing process variables are entered. In most cases, the regression coefficient for site becomes lower, but still statistically significant, when fairness, openness, and opportunity are entered into the models. This indicates that the effects of the process variables on stress, health, coping, and job security are significant but do not explain all the variance due to site. Once the effects of demographic and process variables are removed in the regressions, the Site variable reflects downsizing history, so the results indicate that downsizing history per se has important effects on worker stress, health, and job security, regardless of how the downsizing was accomplished.

Our study focused on symptoms, not actual health outcomes. However, a recent study indicates how such symptoms can initiate a chain reaction leading to long-term sickness absence. Kivimaki and colleagues (24) demonstrated that downsizing resulted in changes in work, social relationships, and health-related behaviors, and that these changes contributed to increased rates of long-term sickness absence. For instance, sickness absence was twice as likely in job groups that had experienced major downsizing (>18 percent) as in those with minor downsizing (<8 percent). Moreover, the role of change in work characteristics after downsizing was assessed by adjusting the relationship between downsizing and sickness absence. After adjustment for changes in work characteristics (e.g., demands, control), the relationship between downsizing and sickness absence was reduced by nearly 50 percent.

Parker and colleagues (22) studied the effect of strategic or planned downsizing on employees' job satisfaction and job-related strain. Employees in a company that had introduced planned employment changes were followed over a four-year period. Although measured job demand increased, well-being and job satisfaction did not decrease. The authors concluded that the managed strategic downsizing actually improved employees' sense of control, because of new work characteristics introduced as part of the reorganization. Although our results do not entirely comport with Parker and coworkers' findings, the inclusion of downsizing process variables mitigated the effect of site and hence downsizing on the array of outcome measures.

Potential limitations of the present study include the use of workers from a single industry and reliance on self-report data. However, although both study sites were in the nuclear industry, there were many different contractors and a good range of different occupations within each site. Moreover, the pattern of results and agreement with prior downsizing studies suggest that the findings would generalize well to other industries. We used a cross-sectional design, and statements of causality are not possible with such data. This is not a problem with the comparisons between high and low downsizing sites, but the direction of causality can be an issue with the regression models. It is noteworthy that longitudinal studies of downsizing and restructuring have produced data that agree with our results (24, 25), and the direction of the causal arrow appears to be unambiguous. Finally, the exclusive use of self-report data, while entirely appropriate for measuring perceived worker stress and well-being, raises concerns about common method variance. Some have suggested that common method variance is not a great problem in this type of research (26), but future studies should balance self-report measures with more objective indicators such as absenteeism records, injury statistics, and the like.

CONCLUSION

The implications of our results for organizations that expect downsizing in the near future are straightforward. Downsizing episodes will be associated with measurable effects on survivors' stress and well-being. In the present study, the differences between high and low downsizing sites became smaller when the downsizing process factors were added to the regression models but site differences were still significant. Having said that, our results also clearly demonstrate that the effects of downsizing on worker stress, health, coping, and job insecurity can be reduced if organizations make efforts to conduct layoffs fairly and with open and honest communication.

Perhaps most importantly, the effects on worker stress and health can be further minimized if the post-downsizing work environment provides new opportunities for creative and interesting work, more worker involvement in decision-making, and more opportunities to learn new skills. This finding agrees with reports by Parker and coauthors (22), Kivimaki and coauthors (24), Preitzer and Mishra (27), and Burke (25) that changes to the work environment after downsizing can have important effects on workers' responses. Positive changes to the work environment after downsizing can reduce employees' negative responses to the downsizing event and can also reduce health and well-being consequences.

There are signs that research on the adverse health effects of downsizing on job survivors may be influencing corporate policies. A recent survey of 572 human resource professionals, conducted by the Society for Human Resource Management, found that most organizations in 2001 took preventive steps before resorting to layoffs (28). The top four pre-layoff steps were attrition (63 percent), hiring freeze (49 percent), not renewing contract workers (21 percent), and encouraging employees to take vacations (20 percent). If these steps are not enough to avoid layoffs, most organizations try to be sensitive to employees' needs. Forty-one percent of organizations said they had one-on-one discussions with employees that included the manager and a human resources representative, and more than half of the organizations indicated that they tried to enhance communication with employees about layoffs.

REFERENCES

1. U.S. Bureau of Labor Statistics. *Mass Layoffs Statistics.* Washington, D.C., December, 2001.
2. Pearlstein, S. Down with the organizational chart. *Washington Post National Weekly Edition,* 1993.
3. Cascio, W., and Young, C. *Corporate Downsizing: A Look at the Last 15 Years.* U.S. Department of Labor, Washington, D.C., 1996.
4. Cascio, W. Learning from outcomes: Financial experiences of 300 firms that have downsized. In *The New Organizational Reality: Downsizing, Restructuring, and Revitalization,* edited by M. Gowling, J. Kraft, and J. C. Quick, pp. 55–70. American Psychological Association, Washington, D.C., 1998.
5. Cascio, W., Young, C., and Morris, J. R. Financial consequences of employment-change decisions in major U.S. corporations. *Acad. Manage. J.* 40:1175–1189, 1997.
6. American Management Association. *Workforce Growth Slows: AMA's 13th Annual Workforce Survey Shows More Hiring, More Firing, More Companies Doing Both at Once.* October 26, 1999.
7. Sommer, S., and Luthans, B. The impact of downsizing on workplace attitudes: Differing reactions of managers and staff in a healthcare organization. *Group Organ. Manage.* 24: 46–70, 1999.
8. Noer, D. N. *Healing the Wound: Overcoming the Trauma of Layoffs and Revitalizing Downsized Organizations.* Jossey-Bass, San Francisco, 1993.
9. Ferrie, J. E., et al. An uncertain future: The health effects of threats to employment security in white-collar men and women. *Am. J. Public Health* 88: 1030–1036, 1998.
10. Woodward, C. A., et. al. The impact of re-engineering and other cost reduction strategies on the staff of a large teaching hospital. *Med. Care* 37: 556–569, 1999.
11. Woodward, C. A., et al. Changes in general health and musculoskeletal outcomes in the workforce of a hospital undergoing rapid change: A longitudinal study. *J. Occup. Health Psychol.* 6: 556–569, 2001.
12. Cameron, K. S., Freeman, S. J., and Mishra, A. K. Downsizing and redesigning organizations. *Organ. Change Redesign* 19–63, 1993.
13. Kozlowski, S., et al. Organizational downsizing: strategies, interventions, and research implications. In *International Review of Industrial and Organizational Psychology,* edited by C. L. Cooper and I. Robertson, pp. 263–372. Wiley, Chichester, U.K., 1993.
14. Allen, T. D., et al. Survivor reactions to organizational downsizing: Does time ease the pain? J. Occup. Organ. Psychol. 74: 145–164, 2001.
15. Brockner, J., et al. Survivors' reactions to layoffs: We get by with a little help from our friends. *Adm. Sci. Q.* 32: 526–541, 1987.
16. Brockner, J. The effects of work layoffs on survivors: Research, theory, and practice. In *Research in Organizational Behavior,* edited by B. Straw and L. L. Cummings, pp. 213–255. JAI Press, Greenwich, Conn., 1988.
17. Brockner, J., Wiesenfeld, B., and Martin, C. Procedural justice and survivors' reactions to job layoffs. *Organ. Behav. Hum. Decis. Process* 63: 59–68, 1995.
18. Alexander, S., and Ruderman, M. The role of procedural and distributive justice in organizational behavior. *Soc. Justice Res.* 1: 177–198, 1987.
19. Folger, R. Distributive and procedural justice in the workplace. *Soc. Justice Res.* 1: 143–159, 1987.

20. Fryxell, G. E. Perceptions of justice afforded by formal grievance systems as predictors of a belief in a just workplace. *J. Bus. Ethics* 11: 635–647, 1992.
21. Greenberg, J. Organizational justice: Yesterday, today and tomorrow. *J. Manage.* 16: 399–432, 1990.
22. Parker, K. P., Chmiel, N., and Wall, T. D. Work characteristics and employee well-being within a context of strategic downsizing. *J. Occup. Health Psychol.* 2: 289–303, 1997.
23. Cohen, S., Kamarck, T., and Mermelstein, R. A global measure of perceived stress. *J. Health Soc. Behav.* 24: 385–396, 1983.
24. Kivimaki, et al. Factors underlying the effect of organizational downsizing on health of employees: Longitudinal cohort study. *BMJ* 320: 971–975, 2000.
25. Burke, R. J. Nursing staff survivor responses to hospital restructuring and downsizing. *Stress Health* 17: 195–205, 2001.
26. Spector, P. E. Method variance as an artifact in self-reported affect and perceptions at work: Myth or significant problem? *J. Appl. Psychol.* 72: 438–443, 1987.
27. Preitzer, G. M., and Mishra, A. K. An empirical examination of a stress-based framework of survivor responses to downsizing. In *The Organization in Crisis: Downsizing, Restructuring, and Privatization,* edited by R. J. Burke and C. L. Cooper, pp. 97–118. Blackwell, London, 2000.
28. Society for Human Resource Management. *Layoffs and Job Security Survey.* 2001.

Chapter 5

PRIVATIZATION AND DOWNSIZING IN THE U.K. PUBLIC SECTOR: LABOR MARKET CHANGE, JOB INSECURITY, AND HEALTH

Jane Ferrie

Over the past two decades the structure of the labor market in the United Kingdom has undergone considerable change. As in all advanced industrialized societies (1, 2), four factors have made major contributions to this restructuring: deindustrialization, technological innovation, globalization, and a commitment to a free market economy, including the privatization of public services.

Deindustrialization and technological change have been accompanied in many countries by a strengthening of the role of market forces. In the United Kingdom, 1979 saw the election of a government that led the way in its commitment to the free market and the development of a competitive, efficient, and flexible labor force (3). Taken together, these changes mean that the labor markets and job security associated with the social order since the Second World War have undergone major change (4). The informal social contract governing employment relations has also changed. A tranche of legislation has weakened trade unions (5), and a climate has been created that has facilitated the erosion of employment rights and the casualization of labor (6, 7). Simultaneous cuts in public spending have had two effects on job security: cuts in public expenditure have led to job losses in the state sector, while cuts in welfare and unemployment benefits have made unemployment even less attractive (8), exacerbating feelings of insecurity.

Traditionally, the brunt of labor market changes has been borne by blue-collar workers. However, increasingly during the last decade of the 20th century, downsizing, mass layoffs, long-term unemployment, and downward mobility affected white-collar workers. The result was that these comparatively well-educated workers, traditionally accustomed to long-term, secure employment, came to experience degrees of employment instability largely unknown to them in the past (9–11). However, job insecurity was not the only effect generated by these processes. Downsizing can be achieved only if the survivors take on the work previously covered by their coworkers. The result is an intensification of work pressure, with the burden of greater efficiency at lower cost falling on the workforce (12).

The public sector and the civil service in the United Kingdom were for a long time immune from the pressures of the marketplace. Among the main attractions of public sector employment were the offer of job security, a career, and good conditions of service. However, much of this changed during the 1980s, when the United Kingdom led the way among industrialized countries in moves toward privatization and away from planned public ownership and provision (6). Privatization of the first public service came in 1984, with the sale of British Telecommunications. By the end of the century, the remaining public utilities and many of the executive functions of central government had been privatized or opened to private sector competition. The 21st century has seen no change in government policy, with privatization increasingly introduced into education, health care, and local government.

An early casualty of the privatization process was the Property Services Agency, a civil service department, sold in its entirety to the private sector. In this chapter, I describe the effects of this process on the health and well-being of the white-collar workers employed by that organization. The emphasis is on the job insecurity generated by the process, and explanations for observed effects on health and well-being are sought in changes in other characteristics of the psychosocial work environment, health-related behaviors and individual differences.

PROPERTY SERVICES AGENCY

The Property Services Agency (PSA) was the civil service department responsible for the design, construction, and maintenance of all government buildings (13). PSA had a long and illustrious history, stretching back 600 years to the formation in 1378 of the Office of the King's Works (14). By the late 1980s, the workforce had been reduced to 24,500 (15), but PSA remained the largest single construction business in the United Kingdom.

In 1986 a government report recommended the examination of civil service functions to determine which could be abolished or transferred to the private sector (16). Few civil servants were aware of the long-term implications of this report, and its recommendations were not initiated until August 1988. For PSA, however, restructuring along these lines was being debated somewhat before this. Early in 1988 its future was envisaged in terms of a trading fund, a plan jettisoned in favor of privatization by December of the same year (17). Between April 1990 and July 1991, PSA was split into six stand-alone businesses, of which PSA Projects covered the design and construction side (18). Many civil servants in PSA Projects were construction industry professionals or technicians. PSA Projects was hived off to the private sector in December 1992, and the five remaining maintenance companies had all been sold by October 1993 (18). In this way, thousands of public sector construction industry professionals and building workers came onto the labor market between 1992 and 1993, when the U.K. construction industry was in deep recession (15).

DOWNSIZING, PRIVATIZATION, AND FACTORY CLOSURE: THE PROCESS

The privatization of PSA followed a process that is common to many cases of workplace closure, privatization, or downsizing (Figure 5.1). At baseline the workers are in *secure employment,* unaware of future organizational change. This is followed by a period of uncertainty and rumor, the *anticipation phase,* which may be protracted: members of the workforce realize that change is likely to happen but are not sure how, or if, they may be affected. This phase is followed either by the removal of the threat and continued employment or by the *pre-termination phase:* the period immediately prior to the redundancies. By this time, some workers have already left, and future job change or job loss for most others is certain. In cases where the whole process is very rapid, both the anticipation and pre-termination phases may be very brief. After closure or privatization, workers undergo job transfer or job change or experience non-employment in the form of early retirement, retirement, or unemployment. Subsequently, nonemployment continues or workers become reemployed (19).

JOB INSECURITY

Social attitudes surveys and studies of job characteristics suggest that security is of major importance to workers (20, 21). Much work on the concept of job insecurity has been carried out by Hartley and colleagues (22), who define it, in general terms, as the discrepancy between the level of security a person experiences and the level she or he prefers. There are two categories of job insecurity: attributed and self-reported. Attributed job insecurity relates to threats external to the individual, while self-reported job insecurity represents the individual's appraisal of the threat: they are significantly associated in the expected direction. Most studies that set out to examine the effects of job insecurity have self-reported job insecurity as their exposure measure; while workplace closure studies and studies of privatization or downsizing tend to have attributed job insecurity as their exposure (Box 5.1). The level of stress engendered by job insecurity has been shown to depend on the perceived probability and perceived severity of job loss (22–24). For this reason, self-reported job insecurity is likely to be the more potent stressor, as groups to whom job insecurity has been externally attributed will include participants who do not perceive themselves to be under threat. This

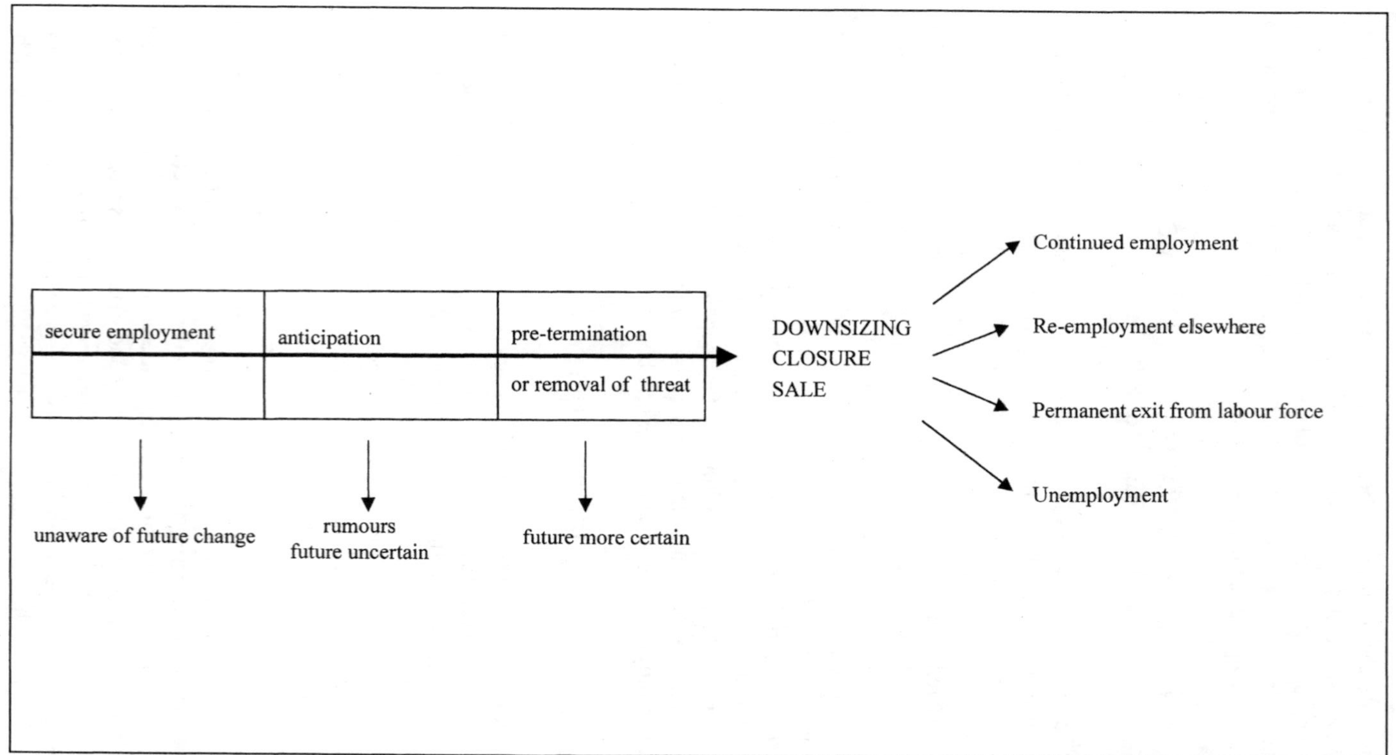

Figure 5.1. Stages of a typical workplace downsizing, closure, or sale. Adapted from Joelson and Wahlquist, *Soc. Sci. Med.* 25: 179–182, 1987.

Box 5.1
Studies of Job Insecurity

Attributed job insecurity
Studies examine closure, privatization, or downsizing.
Subject group contains participants who do not perceive themselves to be at risk.
Associations are likely to be minimum estimates.

Self-report job insecurity
All participants in the subject group are insecure.
Associations are likely to be maximum estimates.

means that studies of attributed job insecurity are likely to produce minimum estimates of effects.

When the investigation of PSA started, the effects of job insecurity on health had attracted limited research interest. Workplace closure studies and studies in the psychological and sociological literature documented consistent adverse effects on mental health, and there was some evidence, albeit weak and inconsistent, of adverse effects on physical health and cardiovascular risk factors. However, well-designed longitudinal studies of both attributed and self-reported job insecurity remained scarce (25).[1] In addition, most previous studies had been unable to address the issue of reverse causality, that is, whether job insecurity and job loss cause ill-health or ill-health leads to feelings of insecurity and eventual job loss. The only way this problem can be resolved is to obtain data from a period of secure employment, before even the rumor of future workforce reductions. The Whitehall II study, a longitudinal cohort of mainly white-collar civil servants set up for other purposes in 1985, when a job in the U.K. civil service was known as a "job for life," provided the ideal vehicle for such as study.

THE WHITEHALL II STUDY

Whitehall II followed on from the first Whitehall study, set up in 1967 to examine 18,403 male office-based civil servants (26). Findings from the first Whitehall study showed that after ten years of follow-up, men in the lowest employment grade had nearly three times the mortality of men in the highest grade (27). These mortality differences were only partly explained by differences in traditional risk factors, such as smoking, obesity, physical activity, blood pressure, and

[1] Reference 25 is a full review of the effects of job insecurity on health, including more recent data.

plasma cholesterol level (27–29). The Whitehall II study was set up to investigate additional factors that might explain this gradient in mortality, to study the degree and causes of the social gradient in morbidity, and to include women. In particular, Whitehall II has developed a specific interest in psychosocial causes of disease and the mechanisms through which these operate.

One reason the civil service was chosen for such studies was that the security of tenure enjoyed by civil servants meant study participants were easy to trace and follow up over long periods. However, the privatization of PSA and changes in the organization and structure of the civil service, which later affected all departments, were to change that. As similar changes were taking place at the time in many other large organizations, both public and private, we decided to use the opportunity to examine effects of these labor market changes on health. In addition to reflecting a general trend, the Whitehall II study also had the advantage of health data from a period of secure employment before any rumor of future change had circulated. Furthermore, as the privatization of PSA came early in the process, the study had the additional advantage of an internal control group of civil servants as yet unaffected by change.

The target population for the Whitehall II study was all London-based office staff working in 20 civil service departments between 1985 and 1988. With a response rate of 73 percent, the final cohort consisted of 6,895 men and 3,413 women (30). Although mostly white-collar, participants covered a wide range of grades from office support staff to the highest-level administrators and policymakers. Baseline screening (phase 1) took place between late 1985 and early 1988. This involved a clinical examination and a self-administered questionnaire that contained sections on demographic characteristics, health, personality and lifestyle factors, and psychosocial work characteristics, such as job control, work demands, and social support at work. In 1989–90, (phase 2) the same questionnaire data were collected by mail; and between 1992 and 1993 a further round of clinical screening and questionnaire data collection was completed, (phase 3).

THE PSA STUDY

As it happened, the first three data-collection phases of the Whitehall II study coincided with the stages of the downsizing/closure/privatization process at PSA (Figure 5.2) Data from phase 1 of the Whitehall II study derive from a time of relatively secure employment for all participants. By the time of the phase 2 questionnaire, the structure and organization of PSA had started to change, but the future of the department was uncertain. Phase 2 for PSA participants thus fits the description of an anticipation phase. The sale of PSA Projects, the stand-alone business in which most of PSA's Whitehall II participants worked, took place during the phase 3 data collection. Ninety-one percent of PSA participants were screened before the sale, 84 percent between September and November 1992,

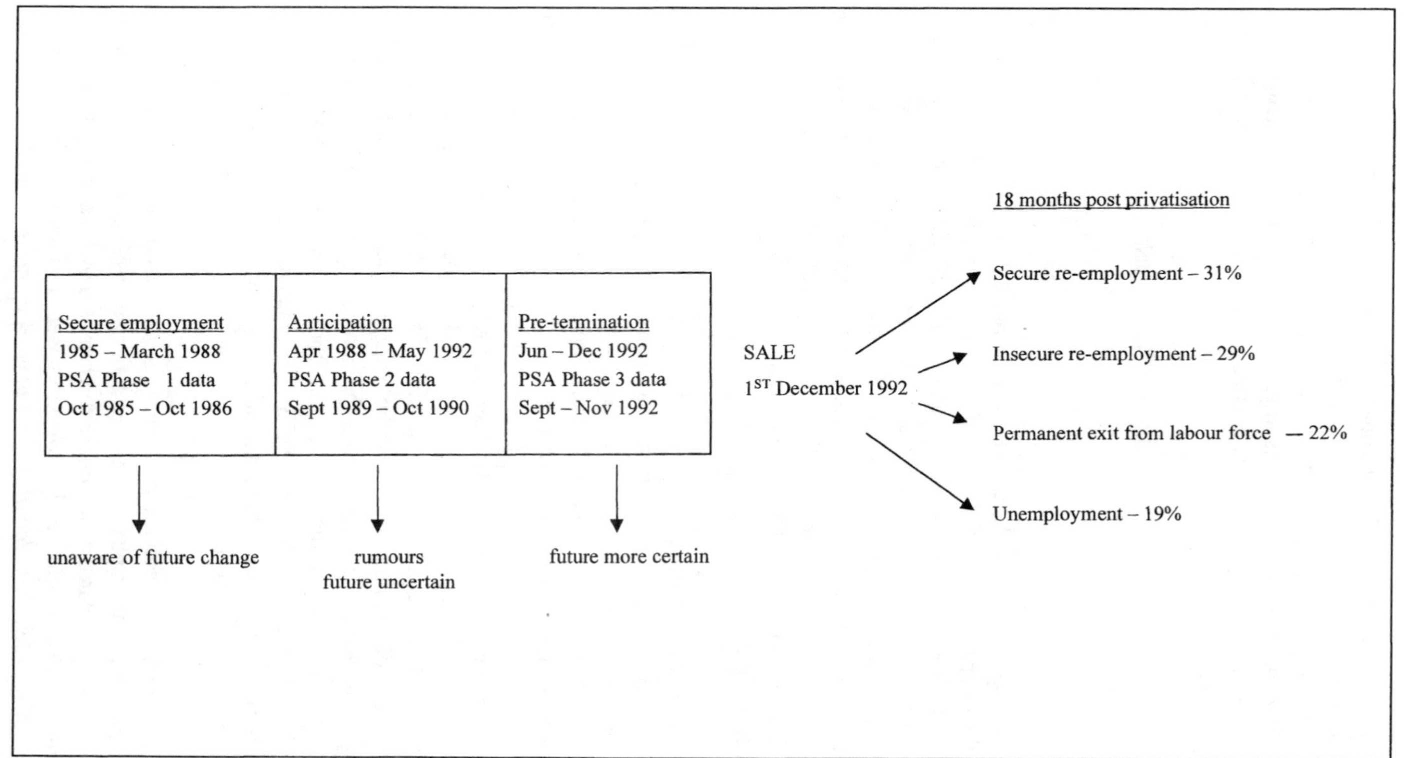

Figure 5.2. Stages of the PSA privatization process. "Phase" refers to the phase of data collection for PSA participants in the Whitehall II study. *Note:* "permanent exit from labour force" includes 26 participants who retired from the civil service at the usual age of 60.

immediately prior to the transfer of undertakings on December 1. This period, immediately before the sale, fits the description of a pre-termination phase. In addition to the regular phases of data collection, a further questionnaire was sent to all PSA participants 18 months after the privatization. The methods and findings of the PSA study, before and after privatization, are detailed in the next two sections.

BEFORE THE PRIVATIZATION

Methods

The target population for the PSA study was all participants in Whitehall II who recorded their department as PSA in the phase 1 questionnaire (Table 5.1). These participants formed the PSA study population for the duration of the study, from 1986 to 1994. During the anticipation and pre-termination phases, health and other outcomes for participants in the PSA study were compared with those for Whitehall II participants in the remaining 19 departments not facing the prospect of direct privatization at the time. The exposure for PSA participants at both the anticipation and pre-termination phases was job insecurity attributed to the forthcoming privatization.

Outcome Measures. Self-reported health outcomes examined before the privatization were taken from the questionnaires at all three phases of Whitehall II: self-rated health over the past 12 months (average, poor, or very poor vs. good or very good), presence of longstanding illness, presence of 17 different symptoms in the previous 14 days, number of health problems in the last year, angina pectoris and possible myocardial infarction assessed with the London School of Hygiene cardiovascular questionnaire, and absence from work for health reasons. Mental health assessed using the 30-item General Health Questionnaire (GHQ) (31) comprised "GHQ caseness," defined as a score of 5+, and depression as measured using a four-item depression subscale of the GHQ (32), derived by factor analysis. Physiological measures obtained during the clinical screening examinations at phases 1 and 3 included blood pressure, body mass index (BMI), serum cholesterol, and electrocardiogram (ECG). Participants were judged to suffer ischemia if their ECG was abnormal and/or if angina was diagnosed from responses to their questionnaire.

Explanatory Factors. Potential explanatory factors examined during the anticipation and pre-termination phases included four other psychosocial work characteristics, three health-related behaviors, divorce or separation, and negative affect.

Job control, skill discretion, and *job demands* were adapted from the job content instrument of Karasek (33). *Social support at work* comprised three components:

support from colleagues, support from supervisors, and information from supervisors. All the questions required responses on a four-point scale from "often" to "never/almost never." Each scale was divided into thirds; for analysis, change to a more adverse or more beneficial third at follow-up formed the outcome of interest. Those who experienced adverse change were compared with those who experienced no change or beneficial change, and vice versa. The three health-related behaviors were *alcohol consumption* over the recommended limits, *smoking,* and *exercise. Divorce and separation* was measured only among those married or cohabiting at baseline. *Negative affect,* a personality trait characterized by a disposition to accentuate the negative and to experience chronically high levels of distress (34), was assessed using the five negative affect items from Bradburn's Affect Balance Scale (35). Sociodemographic factors taken from the phase 1, 2, and 3 questionnaires included age, marital status, and civil service grade of employment.

Statistical Analysis. The overall aims of the analyses were to determine whether change in measures of health between baseline (phase 1) and follow-up (phase 2 or phase 3) was significantly different for women and men in PSA relative to women and men in the control sample, and to determine whether any significant changes in morbidity could be explained by changes in the potential explanatory factors measured.

Analysis of such data using simple differences is usually not recommended, since the magnitude of the change could depend on the level at baseline (36). Thus, analyses usually adjust for baseline (phase 1) values using analysis of covariance (ANOVA). This form of analysis has two advantages. First, it takes account of regression to the mean and is independent of the baseline value; second, using the follow-up values as the outcome, it allows for continuous and discrete variables to be analyzed and presented in a similar manner.

Following the analysis of health outcomes, factors with the potential to explain significant increases in morbidity were identified. These were explanatory factors in which change between baseline and follow-up, relative to the control group, reached conventional levels of statistical significance ($P < .05$). Such factors were included in the final model for each health outcome. Models were also adjusted separately for negative affect.

Findings

Of the 10,308 participants in phase 1 of Whitehall II, 666 were PSA employees on entry to the study. The remaining 9,642 participants from the other 19 departments comprised the control group. Response rates for the study are shown in Table 5.1.

Table 5.1

PSA study response rates

Phase of Whitehall II study and exposure measure for PSA	PSA participants	Control participans
Phase I: baseline (secure employment phase)	666 (153 F; 513 M)	9,642 (3,260 F; 6,382 M)
Phase 2: anticipation phase for PSA	526 (79%)	7,607 (79%)
Phase 3: pre-termination phase for PSA		
Questionnaire	567 (85%)	8,075 (84%)
Clinical screening	509 (76%)	7,595 (79%)

Note: Numbers of male and female participants at baseline (phase 1) are shown. Percentages given for phases 2 and 3 are percentage of the number of participants at baseline.

Secure Employment Phase. In general, during the secure employment phase there was greater morbidity among control women than women in PSA. This pattern of greater morbidity among the controls was repeated for men. For number of symptoms in the past 14 days, GHQ depression, and diastolic blood pressure, the health advantage of the PSA men was significant, partly reflecting the higher proportion of men from the lower grades in the control group. Furthermore, a greater proportion of PSA women and men than controls were nonsmokers, drank under the recommended weekly limit of alcohol, and took vigorous exercise. However, as adjustment was made for baseline values of the health and health-related behavior measures in all analyses at follow-up, differences between PSA and control participants were independent of these baseline differences.

Anticipation Phase. Although the prevalence of self-reported morbidity was generally lower among PSA women than among control women during the anticipation phase, the relative increase in morbidity between baseline and follow-up in PSA women was greater for GHQ caseness, symptom score, and number of health problems in the last year. For all these measures, relative increases were similar to or greater than those for men, but due to the smaller number of women the increases were not statistically significant (Table 5.2).

There was a greater increase between baseline and the anticipation phase for all the self-reported morbidity measures among men in PSA than among control men. This relative increase in morbidity was significant for poor self-rated health, symptom score, and number of health problems, and it was considerable for longstanding illness. Relative changes in minor psychiatric morbidity and depression were similar in PSA and control men.

Table 5.2

Effects of the anticipation phase on health outcomes

Health measure[b]	Odds ratio (95% confidence interval)[a]	
	Women	Men
Poor self-rated health	0.82 (0.5 to 1.3)	1.51 (1.2 to 2.0)
Longstanding illness	0.79 (0.5 to 1.4)	1.22 (0.9 to 1.6)
GHQ caseness	1.20 (–0.8 to 1.8)	1.11 (0.9 to 1.4)
Symptom score	0.47 (–0.0 to 1.0)	0.35 (0.1 to 0.6)
No. of health problems	0.10 (–0.2 to 0.4)	0.12 (0.0 to 0.2)

[a]Except for symptom score and health problems, which are differences (95% confidence intervals).
[b]All analyses of health measures are adjusted for age, employment grade, marital status, and baseline value of the outcome of interest.

Divorce or separation among PSA women was twice that among control women during the anticipation phase, but the difference was not significant. No trends were apparent in the relative changes in work characteristics, adverse or beneficial, between PSA and control women. PSA women experienced a significant relative loss of social support at work and a significant increase in job demands (Figure 5.3). Compared with control men, divorce or separation was more common among PSA men, but the difference was not significant. For men, relative changes in characteristics of the work environment tended to follow the pattern of increased adverse change and decreased beneficial change. In common with the women, PSA men suffered a significant relative loss of social support at work. They also experienced a significant relative drop in skill discretion and a considerable increase in job demands.

Drinking over the recommended limits had increased among PSA women by the anticipation phase, and there had been a significant increase in smoking relative to control women. A small increase in the proportion of PSA men drinking over the recommended limits was observed, but overall they retained their advantageous health-related behavior profile (Table 5.3).

As all the health outcomes examined during the anticipation phase were self-reported, theoretically, negative affect could have produced overestimates of odds ratios and differences, if PSA participants had tended to overreport negative events. Adjustment for negative affect, however, strengthened the associations, indicating that if men from PSA and men from control departments had been equal with respect to this trait at baseline, increases in measures of morbidity among the PSA men would have been greater (Figure 5.4). Adjustment for loss of

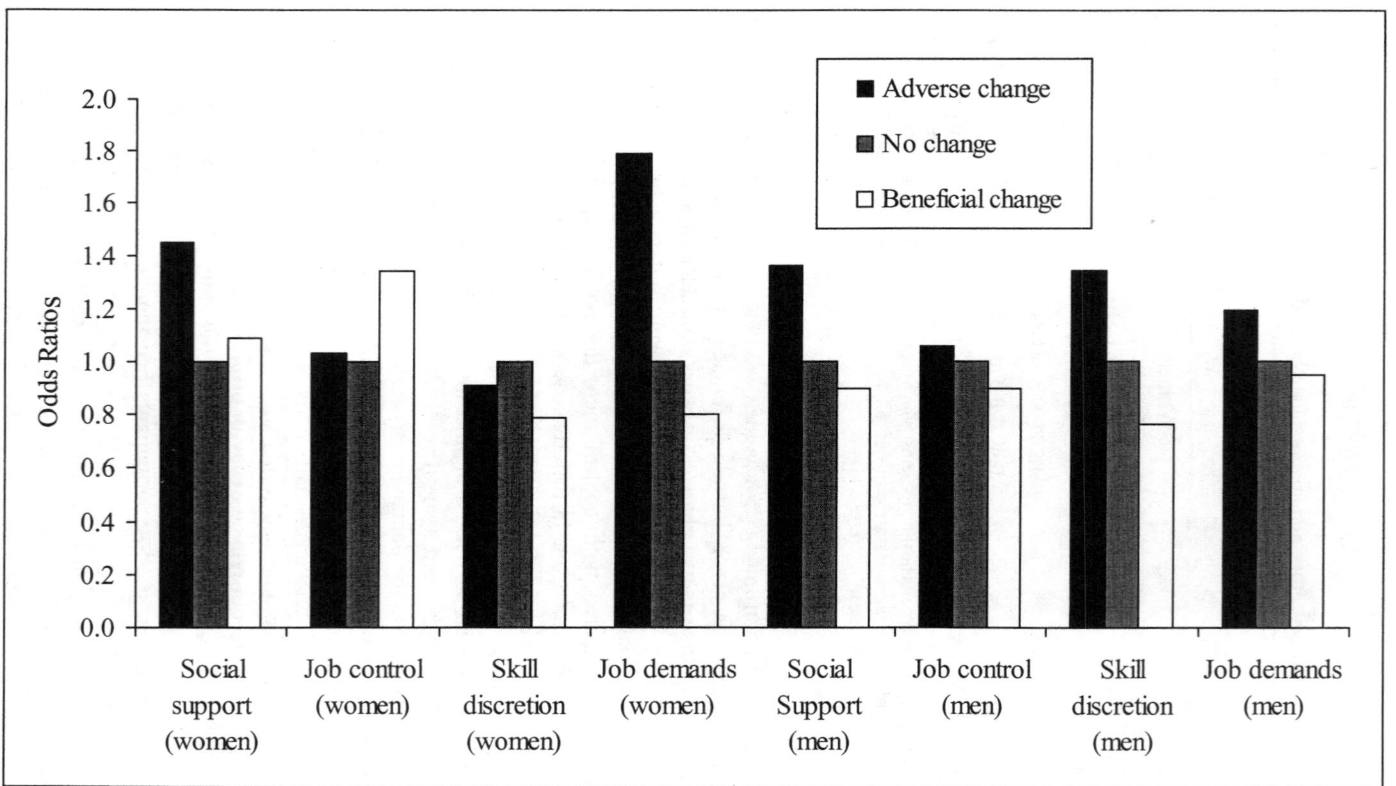

Figure 5.3. Effects of the anticipation phase on other characteristics of the work environment.

Table 5.3

Effects of the anticipation phase on health-related behaviors

Health-related behavior[a]	Odds ratio (95% confidence interval)	
	Women	Men
Units of alcohol per week 15 or more (women), 22 or more (men)	1.64 (0.7 to 3.7)	1.15 (0.8 to 1.6)
Current smoking	3.05 (1.3 to 7.2)	0.70 (0.4 to 1.3)
Vigorous exercise 1 hr or more per week	0.93 (0.7 to 1.2)	0.98 (0.8 to 1.2)

[a]All analyses of health-related behaviors are adjusted for age, employment grade, marital status, and baseline value of the outcome of interest.

social support explained 7 percent and 8 percent, respectively, of the relative increase in poor self-rated health and number of health problems. Otherwise, social support and skill discretion explained little of the relative increase in self-reported morbidity among PSA men during the anticipation phase. Adjustment for all the potential explanatory factors combined also had little explanatory power, showing that the effects of these factors were partly independent and partly overlapping. These relatively minor changes mean that the increase in morbidity associated with the anticipation phase in PSA participants cannot be attributed to negative affect or change in any of the potential explanatory factors measured.

Pre-termination Phase. A rather inconsistent picture showed some adverse changes in self-reported morbidity among PSA women relative to control women during the pre-termination phase. Among PSA men, there was a general increase in self-reported morbidity compared with controls and in both sexes the relative proportion sleeping nine hours or more per night on an average weekday increased significantly (Table 5.4).

By the pre-termination phase absence from work had decreased in all groups. However, decreases were smaller among controls (0.8 to 5.7 percent) than among PSA participants (3.9 to 14.5 percent). Relative decreases for PSA women were significant for both absence of one working week or more and two working weeks or more, and among PSA men for absence of one working week or more (Figure 5.5).

Adverse changes were seen in all physiological measures among PSA women compared with control women. The proportion of incident cases of ischemia during the pre-termination phase was greater among PSA women than among

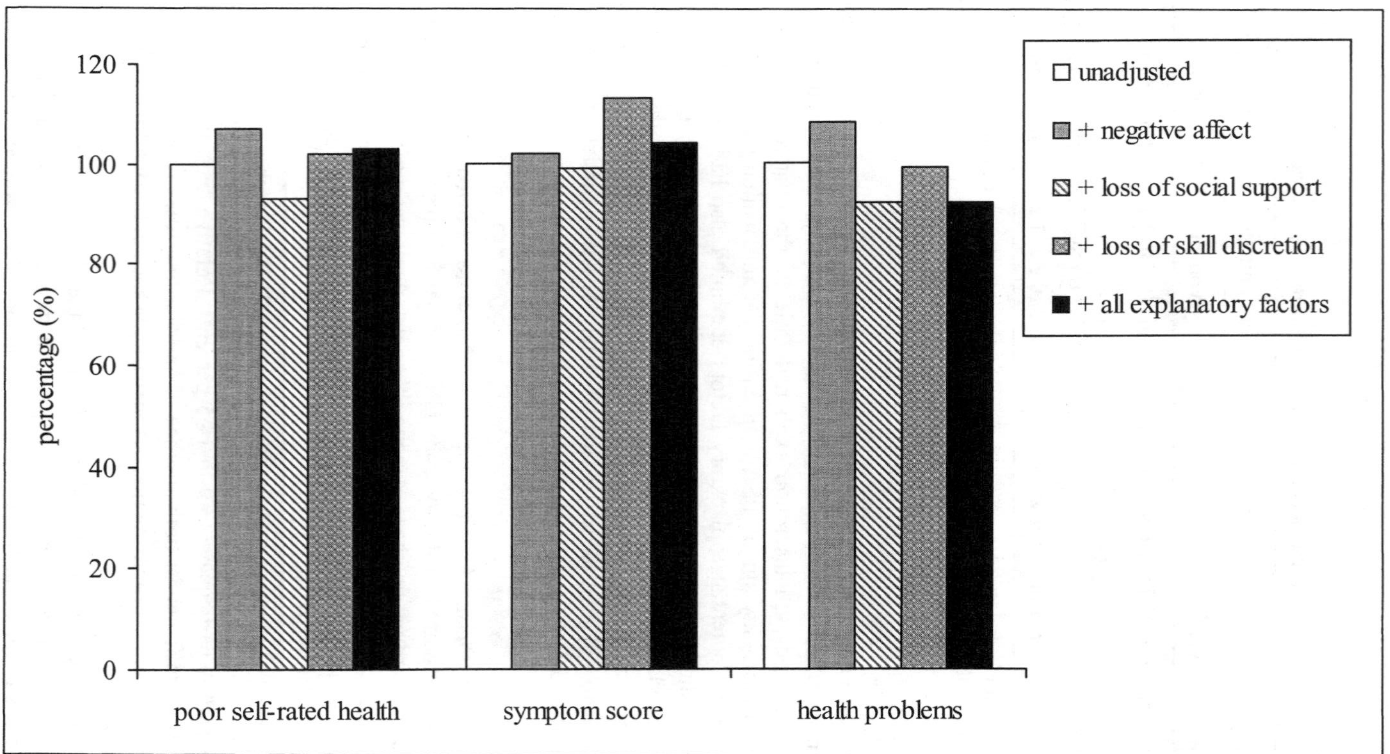

Figure 5.4. Effects of the anticipation phase on self-reported health measures, adjusted for potential explanatory factors, men only. *Note*: "Unadjusted" means adjusted for age, sex, grade, marital status, and baseline value of health outcome.

Table 5.4

Effects of the pre-termination phase on self-reported health

	Odds ratio (95% confidence interval)	
Health measure[a]	Women	Men
Poor self-rated health	0.86 (0.5 to 1.4)	1.18 (0.9 to 1.5)
Longstanding illness	0.80 (0.5 to 1.4)	1.13 (0.9 to 1.5)
Sleep 5 hrs or less per night	1.36 (0.6 to 3.0)	0.99 (0.6 to 1.8)
Sleep 9 hrs or more per night	2.22 (1.1 to 4.7)	1.82 (1.1 to 2.9)
GHQ caseness	1.06 (0.7 to 1.7)	1.16 (0.9 to 1.5)
GHQ depression	0.75 (0.5 to 1.2)	1.07 (0.8 to 1.4)

[a]Except for symptom score and health problems, which are differences (95% confidence intervals).
[b]All analyses of health measures are adjusted for age, employment grade, marital status, and baseline value of the outcome of interest.

controls, and relative increases in systolic and diastolic blood pressure and BMI were significant. Compared with control men, adverse changes were observed among PSA men for all physiological measures except blood pressure. Cholesterol concentration increased considerably among PSA men relative to control men (P = .07), and, as among the women, the relative increase in BMI was significant (Table 5.5).

By the pre-termination phase, divorce or separation among PSA women was nearly 2.5 times that among control women. A greater proportion of PSA women than control women lost social support at work and job control. However, a significantly greater proportion of PSA women gained job control; concurrent with this change was a significant increase in job demands, which more than doubled. Divorce or separation during the pre-termination phase differed little between PSA and control men. As among the PSA women, a greater proportion of men experienced a relative loss of social support at work. Slightly greater proportions of PSA men both lost and gained job control, and they experienced an overall significant loss of skill discretion relative to control men. Changes in job demands were very similar for both PSA and control men (Figure 5.6).

As during the anticipation phase, a small relative increase in drinking over the recommended limits was observed in both sexes, and there was a considerable though nonsignificant increase in smoking among the women. The relative proportion of men taking vigorous exercise increased significantly in the PSA group.

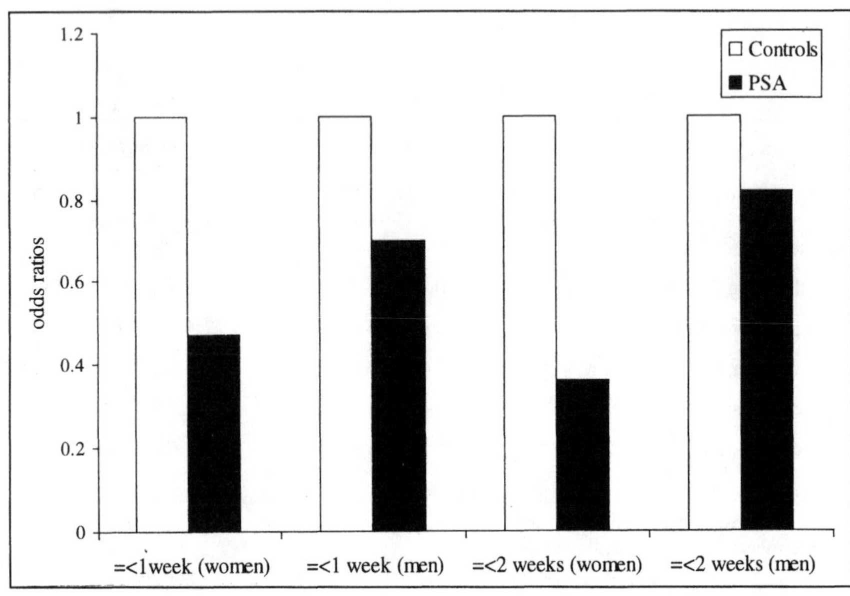

Figure 5.5. Effects of the pre-termination phase on annual sickness absence rates.

Negative affect explained little of the association with nine hours or more of sleep or sickness absence in either sex. Adjustment for job control and job demands strengthened the association with sleep among women (Figure 5.7), as did adjustment for skill discretion and vigorous exercise in men. Adjustment for increased job demands and job control explained the inverse association with sickness absence of one working week or more in PSA women by 12 percent and 18 percent, respectively. However, the effect on absence of two working weeks or more was less pronounced. Among men, adjustment for loss of skill discretion had little effect, but adjustment for vigorous exercise explained 8 percent of the difference between PSA men and controls for absence of one working week or more. Increased job demands among the PSA women explained 20 percent, 15 percent, and 15 percent of the relative increase in systolic blood pressure, diastolic blood pressure, and BMI, while increased job control explained 15 percent, 9 percent, and 20 percent, respectively. In PSA men, adjustment for either loss of skill discretion or increase in vigorous exercise had little effect on the relative increase in BMI. These findings indicate that, apart from the role of increased job demands and job control in PSA women, most of the increase in morbidity associated with the pre-termination phase among PSA participants remains unexplained.

Table 5.5

Effects of the pre-termination phase on physiological measures

	Difference (95% confidence interval)[a]	
Physiological measure[a]	Women	Men
Systolic blood pressure, mm Hg	3.49 (1.2 to 5.7)	–1.03 (–2.1 to 0.0)
Diastolic blood pressure, mm Hg	2.23 (1.7 to 2.8)	–0.10 (–0.9 to 0.7)
Cholesterol concentration, mmol/L	0.09 (–0.1 to 0.3)	0.07 (–0.0 to 0.2)
Body mass index, kg/m^2	0.65 (0.2 to 1.1)	0.30 (0.1 to 0.5)
Possible/probable ischemia on ECG or angina[c]	1.60 (0.8 to 3.3)	1.41 (0.9 to 2.2)

[a]Except for possible/probable ischemia, which is an odds ratio (95% confidence interval).

[b]Analyses of physiological measures are adjusted for age, employment grade, marital status, and baseline value of the outcome of interest.

[c]Possible/probable ischemia is adjusted for age, employment grade, and marital status only.

AFTER THE PRIVATIZATION

Methods

In addition to data from Whitehall II, the PSA study involved a further stage of data collection by self-completed questionnaire 18 months after the privatization. Due to cost constraints, this questionnaire was sent only to participants who were in PSA on entry to the Whitehall II study. Overall, the PSA questionnaire was very similar in content to the Whitehall questionnaires used at phases 1, 2, 3. An additional section gathered retrospective data about the effects of the privatization process, a question was added to determine the number of general practitioner (GP) consultations in the preceding 12 months, and the 12-item GHQ replaced the 30-item GHQ.

Employment status 18 months after the privatization was derived from questionnaire items. The question "How secure do you feel in your present job?" facilitated division of the employed into two groups: those who were "secure" or "very secure" and those who were "not very secure" or "very insecure." Exposure to job insecurity after the privatization was thus self-reported rather than attributed. Participants not in paid employment were divided according to their response to the question "would you like to find another job?" Those seeking work were classified as unemployed and those not seeking work as permanently out of paid employment. Thus the final categories were *secure reemployment, insecure reemployment, unemployment,* and *permanent exit from paid employment.*

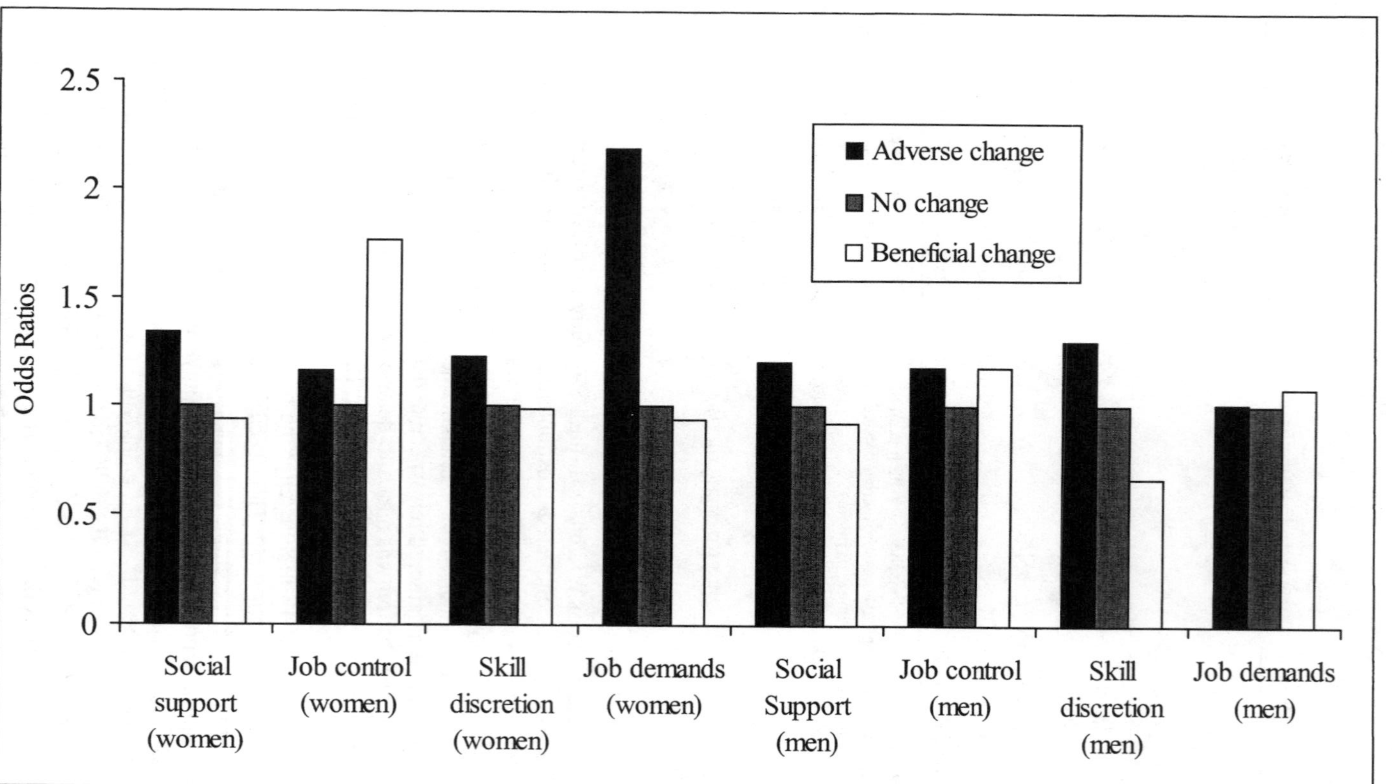

Figure 5.6. Effects of the pre-termination phase on other characteristics of the work environment.

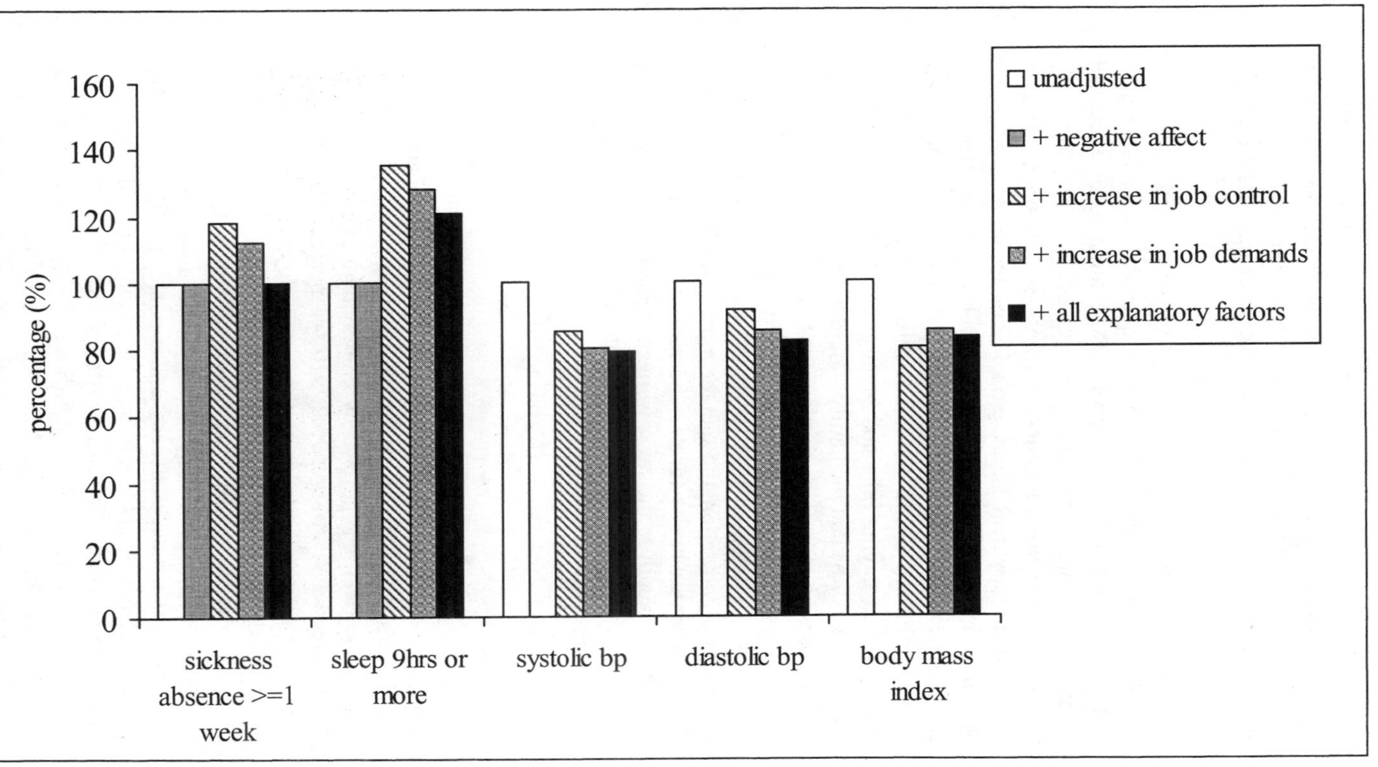

Figure 5.7. Effects of the pre-termination phase on sleep, sickness absence, and physiological measures, adjusted for potential explanatory factors, women only. *Note:* "Unadjusted" means adjusted for age, sex, grade, marital status, and baseline value of health outcome.

Outcome Measures. The self-reported health and health-related outcomes determined after the privatization were the same as those for the anticipation and pre-termination phases, except for the omission of sleep and sickness absence and the addition of number of GP consultations in the preceding 12 months.

Explanatory Factors. Potential explanatory factors examined after the privatization were taken from the baseline and PSA questionnaires. Financial strain, perception of low ability to influence one's health (external locus of control), two or more adverse life events in the last year (vs. zero or one), negative affect, alcohol consumption over the recommended limits, smoking, and exercise were investigated in all employment status groups. For those in employment, job control, job demands, skill discretion, and social support at work were also investigated. The measure of financial strain was derived from responses to two questions from Pearlin and Schoolers' list of chronic strains (37): the questions covered problems with paying bills and buying the kind of food and clothing the respondent felt she or he and the family should have.

The aim of analyses after the privatization was to determine whether change in morbidity between baseline and follow-up differed among participants in the four employment status categories. In the absence of a control group, one that had not experienced privatization, those in the most favorable employment status category (secure reemployment) formed the reference group. Sex differences for all measures were small, so the sexes were combined for analysis. In all other respects, the analysis of data after the privatization was the same as that at the anticipation and pre-termination phases.

Findings

Of the 666 participants who were in PSA on entry to the Whitehall II study, 541 (81 percent) responded to the PSA questionnaire. Findings for the 539 participants who provided usable data, categorized by employment status 18 months after the privatization, are shown in Figure 5.2: 219 (41 percent) of the participants were no longer working (permanent exit or unemployment), and of the 320 (60 percent) in employment, 155 (48 percent of all participants in employment) felt insecure or very insecure in their jobs. Less than 10 percent of the participants in the study population transferred to the private sector purchaser.

In general, there was greater morbidity and a poorer profile of psychosocial factors and health-related behaviors at baseline among participants in the less favorable employment status categories after-privatization. Tests of heterogeneity between the groups were not significant for psychosocial factors and health-related behaviors, but were significant for all health measures except long-standing illness. However, analyses of these health outcomes 18 months after the privatization, adjusted for the baseline values of all the health measures and all the potential explanatory variables, were very similar to the unadjusted outcomes.

After adjustment for baseline measures, morbidity was greater among participants insecurely reemployed or unemployed after the privatization than among those in secure reemployment. For minor psychiatric morbidity and consulting a GP four or more times in the past year, differences were statistically significant (Table 5.6). Among participants permanently out of paid employment, outcomes for poor self-rated health and number of symptoms compared favorably with the reference group. There was little difference in number of health problems, but the relative difference in longstanding illness was statistically significant. Levels of minor psychiatric morbidity were very similar in the two groups, but, although GP use was considerably higher, the relative difference was not statistically significant.

In general, for participants in insecure jobs compared with those in secure employment, changes in work characteristics followed a pattern of greater adverse and less beneficial change. The exception to this pattern was job demands, in which considerable beneficial change was observed. Insecure employment was associated with a significant relative loss of job control and skill discretion (Figure 5.8).

Table 5.6

Health outcomes for participants in insecure reemployment, permanently out of paid employment, and unemployed compared with those in secure reemployment 18 months after privatization

	Odds ratio (95% confidence interval)[a]		
Health measure[b]	Insecure reemployment	Permanent exit from employment	Unemployment
Poor self-rated health	1.48 (0.9 to 2.5)	0.88 (0.5 to 1.7)	1.20 (0.7 to 2.2)
Longstanding illness	1.31 (0.7 to 2.3)	2.25 (1.1 to 4.4)	1.62 (0.7 to 3.0)
Symptom score	0.27 (–0.3 to 0.8)	–0.30 (–1.0 to 0.4)	0.32 (–0.3 to 1.0)
No. of health problems	0.10 (–0.2 to 0.4)	–0.06 (–0.5 to 0.3)	0.16 (–0.2 to 0.5)
GHQ (12) score	1.56 (1.0 to 2.2)	0.07 (–0.7 to 0.8)	1.25 (0.6 to 2.0)
Health service use: 4 or more GP visits[c]	2.04 (1.1 to 3.8)	1.93 (0.9 to 4.0)	2.39 (1.2 to 4.7)

[a]Except for symptom score, health problems, and GHQ score, which are differences (95% confidence intervals).

[b]Analyses of health measures are adjusted for sex, age, grade, marital status, and baseline value of the outcome of interest.

[c]Analyses of GP visits are adjusted for sex, age, grade, and marital status only.

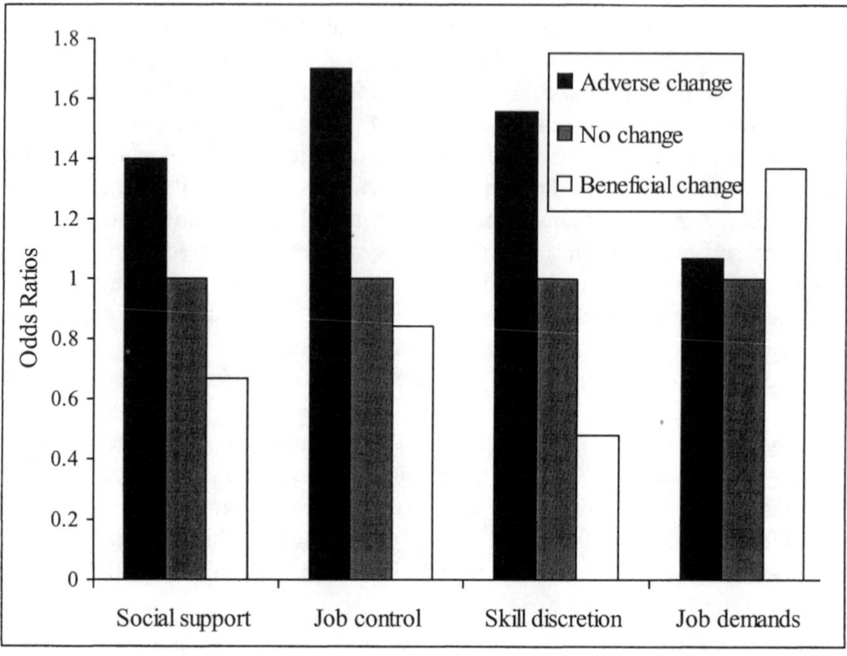

Figure 5.8. Effects of insecure employment 18 months after privatization on other characteristics of the work environment.

All the less favorable employment status categories were associated with a relative increase in financial strain, which was statistically significant in the unemployed. Locus of control over health did not differ significantly between the groups. Similarly, although there was a relative increase in two or more life events in the past year in all the less favorable employment categories, particularly the nonworking categories, differences were not significant. Generally, the health-related behavior profile associated with the less favorable employment status categories was better than that for the securely reemployed, and there was a significant relative increase in vigorous exercise among unemployed participants. A similar relative increase in vigorous exercise was seen among those permanently out of paid employment, but this group also saw a considerable relative increase in smoking (Table 5.7).

Adjustment for negative affect had a negligible effect on the relationship between permanent exit from paid employment and longstanding illness. The only potential explanatory factor that attenuated the relationship between insecure reemployment and GHQ score was loss of job control (6 percent). Financial strain attenuated the relationship between unemployment and GHQ score by 9 percent (Figure 5.9). Adjustment for GHQ score explained the

Table 5.7

Effects of employment status after privatization on health-related behaviors

	Odds ratio (95% confidence interval)		
Health related behavior[a]	Insecure reemployment	Permanent exit from employment	Unemployment
Units of alcohol per week 15 or more (women), 22 or more (men	0.84 (0.4 to 1.7)	0.62 (0.2 to 1.6)	0.98 (0.5 to 2.1)
Current smoking	0.82 (0.3 to 2.6)	1.87 (0.4 to 8.0)	0.90 (0.2 to 3.6)
Vigorous exercise 1 hr or more per week	0.96 (0.6 to 1.6)	1.71 (0.9 to 3.3)	1.92 (1.1 to 3.5)

[a]All analyses of health-related behaviors are adjusted for sex, age, employment grade, marital status, and baseline value of the outcome of interest.

association between insecure employment or unemployment and GP consultations in the past year by 26 percent and 27 percent, respectively. Financial strain explained 9 percent of the association between unemployment and GP consultations, but adjustment for increased exercise strengthened the association by 11 percent.

DISCUSSION

Health Outcomes

Health Effects of Job Insecurity before Privatization. Overall, the PSA study shows that job insecurity before privatization has a modest adverse effect on many self-reported health outcomes, with effects more pronounced during the anticipation phase, particularly among men. Job insecurity generated by the pre-termination phase is also associated with a significant relative increase in BMI in both sexes and a significant relative increase in blood pressure in women. An association between attributed job insecurity and increased self-reported morbidity has been confirmed by other longitudinal data from Whitehall II, in a study examining job insecurity attributed to major organizational change across the civil service (38). Both studies confirm results from an early, seminal study of workplace closure, the Michigan study (39). Studies also show morbidity reported to a GP to be significantly increased in the pre-closure phases (40–42).

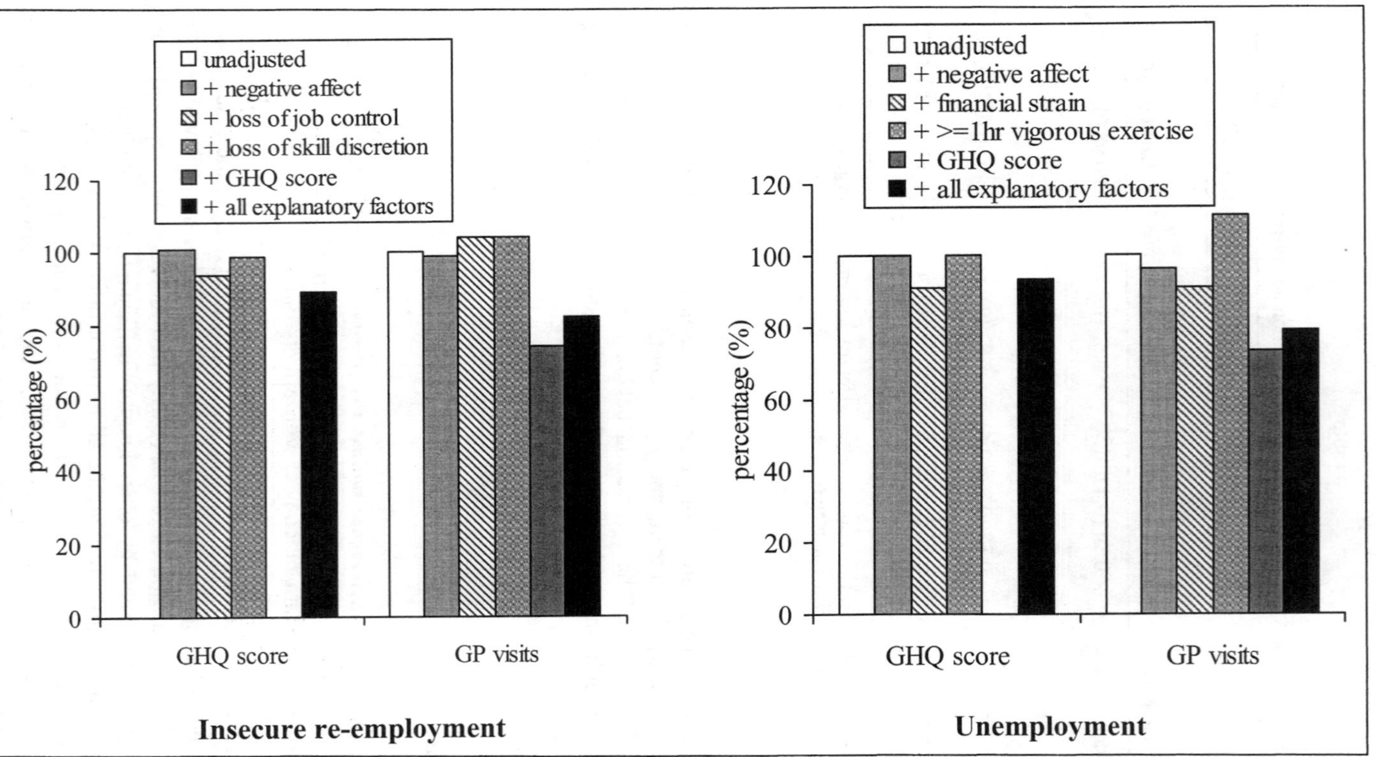

Figure 5.9. Effects of employment status 18 months after privatization on GHQ score and GP visits adjusted for potential explanatory factors.
Note: "Unadjusted" means adjusted for age, sex, grade, marital status, and baseline value of health outcome.

Few studies have looked at the effect of attributed job insecurity on physiological measures. Three other longitudinal studies have reported data on blood pressure. Two showed blood pressure to be elevated prior to redundancy (43–45), but a third, which compared change in blood pressure over time between participants and controls, found no effect (46). There has been even less interest in physiological measures other than blood pressure. In one study, a nonsignificant increase in cholesterol was observed in blue-collar women (47), and in the Michigan study no change was observed in BMI in the run-up to workplace closure (39). Job insecurity associated with the pre-privatization phases had no significant effects on minor psychiatric morbidity. This finding is in contrast to most studies of attributed job insecurity: consistent and significant associations have been demonstrated in all (45–49) but the Michigan study (50).

Health Effects of Employment Status after Privatization. Reemployment following either redundancy (51) or unemployment (52) has been shown to decrease self-reported morbidity. Likewise among PSA participants, those who found secure employment after the privatization enjoyed the best self-reported health, while those who were insecurely reemployed or unemployed had the worst outcomes for most measures.

Other data from the United Kingdom have shown that self-ratings of health for workers in insecure jobs were much closer to those for the unemployed than those for the securely employed, and the findings overall pointed to a gradient in health that paralleled the gradient in labor market advantage (53). Most cross-sectional population studies have documented more illness (54–56) and poorer self-rated health among the unemployed compared with the employed, after adjustment for social class and other sociodemographic factors (57–61), although others have failed to observe adverse effects (62, 63).

Most workplace closure studies and numerous population studies have shown unemployment to have adverse effects on a variety of mental health measures (47, 53, 64–74), with some evidence of adaptation over time (68, 75, 76). Similarly, among the PSA study participants, minor psychiatric morbidity was significantly higher among those unemployed after the privatization relative to those in secure employment.

Many workplace closure studies have compared post-closure mental health between the unemployed and the reemployed (39, 65, 74, 77, 78). Apart from one (74), such comparisons show the reemployed to have fewer mental health problems than the unemployed. However, differences obtained by such comparisons may merely reflect the selective reemployment of those with better mental health (79, 80). After the privatization in the PSA study, however, the reemployed were divided by security of employment. This division showed GHQ-12 score to be significantly elevated among the insecurely employed compared with those in secure employment. These findings are consistent with the observation that, for men, increased depression scores associated with unemployment are not reduced by reemployment in an insecure job (81). Unsatisfactory reemployment following closure among U.S. steel workers (82) and auto workers (77) significantly increased depression. A study of school leavers in Australia found the poorest levels of psychological health and well-being among those who were dissatisfied with their work; those who were satisfied had the highest levels. The unemployed of any duration, students, and workers who were neither satisfied or dissatisfied fell between these two extremes, indicating that what happens in the workplace has a greater health impact than finding a job or remaining in employment (83). Thus any job is not necessarily better than no job, and it has been proposed that cumulative labor market disadvantage may have more relevance for psychological well-being than does unemployment alone (81).

Among PSA study participants permanently out of paid employment, physical health measures were generally better than those for participants wanting work, except for longstanding illness, which was significantly higher than in any other group. Other studies have shown longstanding illness to be associated with permanent exit from paid employment, particularly at times of high unemployment (59). PSA study participants permanently out of paid employment had GHQ-12 scores almost identical to those of the securely employed. Similar observations have been made in other studies. One-year post-closure securely employed U.S. auto workers and those who had retired had similarly low levels of depression (77), as did older Swedish shipyard workers who accepted early retirement on full pay (46).

Health-Related Outcomes

Despite significant increases in a number of ill-health measures, the pre-termination phase of the PSA study was associated with a significant relative decrease in sickness absence from work. This finding was not unexpected, as work output is frequently seen as a buffer against job loss (22). Similar findings have been observed before closure in workplace closure studies (84, 85), and decreases in sickness absence have been associated with the threat of job loss (86, 87).

Sleep quality has been shown to be adversely affected during the pre-termination phase in three workplace closure studies (46–48). A significant relative increase in sleeping for nine hours or more per night on an average weekday was observed among PSA participants during the pre-termination phase. Sleeping five hours or less and nine hours or more per night has been associated with increased morbidity (88) and mortality (89, 90).

All the less favorable employment status categories in the PSA study were associated with increased GP consultations after the privatization. This association was significant for the insecurely reemployed and the unemployed, which were also the employment status categories associated with the greatest levels of morbidity. Other studies with data on this outcome have shown insecure reemployment (42, 49) and unemployment (54, 58, 91, 92) to be associated with increased GP consultations. In the PSA study, adjustment for GHQ score showed that over a quarter of this increase was explained by increased minor psychiatric morbidity.

Potential Explanations

Divorce and Separation, Financial Strain and Negative Affect. A considerable but nonsignificant relative increase in divorce and separation in women was associated with both pre-privatization phases in the PSA study. Divorce or separation represents the extreme end of marital difficulty, and elevated rates may indicate a much wider prevalence of marital discord. Job insecurity has been shown to have adverse effects on marital and family relations (93–95). Conflict with spouse increased in U.S. auto workers during a pre-termination phase (93), and adverse effects on marriages were reported among journalists threatened with the sale of their newspaper (48). It is possible that the marital discord associated with unemployment in workplace closure (96–98) and other studies (94, 99) starts during the period of job insecurity preceding redundancy.

All the less favorable employment status categories in the PSA study were associated with financial strain, and for unemployment the relative difference was significant. Insufficient money for food, clothes, and bills appeared partly to explain the relationship between unemployment and GHQ-12 score. Studies show that associations between unemployment and psychological symptoms weaken or disappear on adjustment for financial hardship (100) and proportional change in family income predicts GHQ scores (101). Household heat, food, clothing, and debt poverty have been shown to play a significant role in mediating the impact of unemployment on GHQ-12 score, although unemployment continued to have a substantial independent effect (102). Similarly, in the Netherlands, present or anticipated financial problems were found to be the mediating factors between unemployment and reported health problems (103).

Negative affect was not analyzed as an outcome and had very little explanatory power at any phase of the PSA study. The only study that appears to have examined negative affect in relation to job insecurity found that negative affect was the most important predictor of minor psychiatric morbidity among white-collar workers confronted with imminent job loss (34).

Psychosocial Work Characteristics. In the PSA study the anticipation phase was associated with a significant relative increase in job demands among women and a significant loss of social support and skill discretion among men. Again, during the pre-termination phase there was a significant relative increase in job demands among women, accompanied by a significant increase in job control; among men there was a significant relative lack of improvement in skill discretion. These findings for women concur with those from studies documenting work intensification after downsizing, in which efficiency savings are manifest as increased workloads and responsibilities among survivors (12). Little other work seems to have examined the effect of situations that generate job insecurity on other psychosocial work characteristics, with the exception of job satisfaction (104–107). However, recent work on the correlates of downsizing in Finland reveals that major (relative to minor) downsizing was significantly associated with increased job insecurity and physical demands and decreased skill discretion and participation in decision-making, but it was not associated with significant changes in social support at work (108).

In our data, loss of social support among men during the anticipation phase explained only a small fraction of the association with poor self-rated health and number of health problems. Other research that has examined social support at work in the context of job insecurity has focused almost exclusively on explanations of psychological ill-health (23, 109).

Before the privatization of PSA, many men who had previously worked as architects and surveyors were moved into project management as PSA was forced to outsource its work. For these participants, both the anticipation and pre-termination phases were associated with a significant loss of skill discretion. In a Finnish study of municipal employees, the only research to have looked at the effect of skill discretion on the relationship between job insecurity and health, a reduction in skill discretion attenuated the ratio of medically certified sickness absence related to major versus minor downsizing by 12 percent (108). However, among PSA participants, adjustment for skill discretion had virtually no explanatory power for any health outcome.

Among women in the PSA study, the pre-termination phase was characterized by increased control at work and job demands, as colleagues who left were not replaced or were replaced by employment agency staff. Adjustment for this combination of work characteristics attenuated the relationship between BMI, diastolic and systolic blood pressure, and chronic job insecurity by 21 percent, 18 percent, and 17 percent, respectively. Little work has examined the role of job demands and control at work in the association between attributed job insecurity and changes in physiological measures. Adjustment for the significant increase in job demands and job control in the PSA study partly explained the significant relative decreases in measures of sickness absence during the pre-termination phase. The combination of high demands and high control has been shown to be associated with better health (110).

Health-Related Behaviors. For alcohol consumption, the findings for PSA participants reflect those of other workplace closure studies that include pre-closure data on alcohol (46–48): no significant changes. It is possible that the increased smoking among women during the anticipation phase was a coping mechanism, as has been shown in previous research (111). In common with findings for the PSA men, a Finnish study found that economic recession was associated with a decrease in smoking, particularly among white-collar workers (112). No studies appear to have examined the effect of job insecurity on physical activity.

Adjustment for smoking and exercise had little effect on the association between job insecurity and health in the PSA study. The only other study that has considered health-related behaviors (alcohol consumption, smoking, and exercise) as possible explanations of the relationship between downsizing and health found no association between downsizing and alcohol consumption or exercise, and found that adjustment for an increase in smoking had little explanatory power (108). None of the workplace closure studies have reported data on exercise. Cross-sectional studies have found the unemployed to report levels of physical activity comparable to those for the employed (57, 113). However, a cross-sectional population study in Sweden found that men unemployed for one year or more had higher levels of physical activity than men who had experienced little unemployment (114), and a study of male construction workers in Finland found a relative increase in exercise among those unemployed long-term (more than 24 months) (115). Exercise data from our study seem to indicate that the nonemployed were spending some of their "free" time in physical activity. Most sports and leisure facilities in the United Kingdom have special rates for unemployed and retired people to encourage uptake in these groups. Adjustment for exercise in the PSA study showed GP consultations among the unemployed would have been 11 percent higher had this group not embraced this health-enhancing behavior.

IMPLICATIONS AND POSSIBLE INTERVENTIONS

Causation always remains a matter of belief or judgment based on all the available evidence. However, it is rare for the evidence on causation to be as unequivocal as that for cigarette smoking and lung cancer. Thus, there comes a point at which it becomes prudent to act on the premise that a causal relationship exists, rather than await further evidence (116).

Evidence of a relationship between unemployment and health reached critical mass some time ago. The findings presented here, together with previous work, will help move the evidence on labor market change and job insecurity in the same direction. Unfortunately, however, the impact of research on policy and practice is often tenuous and indirect, if it exists at all (117). For example, although the evidence against unemployment is overwhelming, in terms of effects not only on health but also on the economy and society, interventions have tended to be piecemeal and ameliorative.

Interventions to reduce the effects of labor market change could be aimed at the level of the individual, the organization, or the whole of society. At the individual level, enhancing ability to cope with job insecurity has been suggested. Social support, which has been shown to buffer the adverse effects of unemployment (52, 118) and work stress (119), is a possibility. However, this would have to come from outside work, as findings on the buffering role of social support at work in relation to job insecurity are mixed (23, 109, 120), and the findings described here show social support at work to be a casualty of the privatization process.

Few interventions aimed at unemployed individuals have reached the scientific literature, although the governments of most industrialized societies have numerous such projects running at any time. One intervention in the United States, designed to prevent psychological morbidity and promote reemployment, demonstrated higher levels of employment, higher earnings, fewer employer and job changes, and less depressive symptomatology at both short- and long-term (30 months) follow-up. Further, a cost-benefit analysis showed large net benefits of the intervention for the participants and for the federal and state government programs that supported the project (121).

However, the drawback with individual-level interventions is that they tend to view the deficiencies or inadequacies of unemployed persons as the cause of the problem, when it may be more appropriate to locate the deficiency or inadequacy in inequitable social relationships and the structural constraints that cause unemployment. An illustration of this can be found in monetarist policies that target inflation rather than unemployment, the former being more injurious to capital accumulation than the latter (122). Further, although many studies report that reemployment is an antidote to the harmful effects of unemployment, for a proportion of the reemployed the new job is hazardous, unsatisfactory, insecure, low-paid, or stressful (123). Interventions predicated on reemployment need to take such factors into account.

At the level of the organization, once a wave of redundancies has been deemed inevitable, managers should consider ways to help job losers leave and to help the insecure cope with uncertainty. Three types of coping strategy have been put forward. Initially, coping strategies should be preventive, aimed at precluding a job insecurity crisis, particularly where the intention is to keep a workforce basically intact. If job loss cannot be avoided, then ameliorative strategies are needed to minimize the hardships experienced by job losers and also to affect the reactions of survivors. In the aftermath of a period of uncertainty or job loss, restorative strategies should be aimed at repairing the damage done to the commitment and morale of the survivors (22, 124).

At the societal level, it has been suggested that self-reported job insecurity is significantly lower in countries with a better economic performance, higher unemployment benefits, a higher level of collective bargaining coverage, and more centralized collective bargaining (123). In the United Kingdom, the post–welfare state consensus around a minimalist state based on free market principles has led to an abandonment or drastic reduction in social welfare provisions and social security safety nets for those in and out of employment, and a tranche of legislation has decimated the power of trade unions to protect their members. Some authors suggest that this model should be abandoned in favor of policies that invest adequately in the pursuit of sustainable economic growth (6), reinstate index linking of benefits, and restore collective bargaining rights (125, 126).

Numerous other proposals, targeted mainly at academic audiences, advocate radical changes to the organization of societies and economies in the interest of health and well-being (127–129). Shortt (130) has suggested that long-term policy should address the complex issue of work, unemployment, and health in the 21st century. While this would demand little less than a basic restructuring of the relationship between work and the state, exactly such a consequence grew out of the last period of prolonged economic crisis, the Depression of the 1930s, resulting in the contemporary welfare state (130). In a report commissioned by the Dutch government, Karasek has proposed a new means of production (conducive production) and an alternative social economic model for a section of the workforce (131). However, a more comprehensive solution to the problems associated with today's labor market requires change in the means of production and economic relations on a scale unprecedented in recent history (132).

REFERENCES

1. OECD. A review of labor markets in the 1980s. In *The OECD Employment Outlook*, pp. 29–61. Paris, 1991.
2. Griffiths, J., and Ziglio, E. Health and work: Concluding remarks. In *Labor Market Changes and Job Insecurity: A Challenge for Social Welfare and Health Promotion,* edited by J. Ferrie et al., pp. 241–250. WHO Regional Publications, European Series No. 81. Copenhagen, 1999.
3. Beatson, M. Labor market flexibility. *Employment Depart. Res. Ser.* 48, 1995.
4. Mustard, J. F. Major technological change, socio-economic change and society's response. In *Labor Market Changes and Job Insecurity: A Challenge for Social Welfare and Health Promotion,* edited by J. Ferrie et al., pp. 151–167. WHO Regional Publications, European Series No. 81. WHO, Copenhagen, 1999.
5. *Work out—or Work in? Contributions to the Debate on the Future of Work.* York Publishing Services, York, U.K., 1995.
6. Hutton, W. *The State We're In.* Jonathan Cape, London, 1995.
7. Ambrose, M., and Overell, S. DOE told to deny rights. *Morning Star*, March 9, 1995, p. 1.
8. Convery, P., and Finn, D. Autumn 1993 budget: Employment measures. *Working Brief* 50: 1–3, 1994.
9. Newman, K. S., and Attewell, P. The downsizing epidemic in the United States: Toward a cultural analysis of economic dislocation. In *Labor Market Changes and Job Insecurity: A Challenge for Social Welfare and Health Promotion,* edited by J. Ferrie et al., pp. 101–126. WHO Regional Publications, European Series No. 81. WHO, Copenhagen, 1999.
10. Sampson, A. Stuck in the nervous nineties. *Observer,* June 4, 1995, p. 23.
11. MacErlean, N. Down and out Britain. *Observer,* March 17, 1996, p. 1.

12. Burchell, B., et al. *Job Insecurity and Work Intensification.* Joseph Rowntree Foundation, York, U.K., 1999.
13. Walker D. Financial rule eased to assist PSA sale. *Times* (London), December 6, 1989, p. 4.
14. Draper, P. Noble beginnings to government works. *Government Purchasing,* April 1995, pp. 12–13.
15. The PSA stands by for the draft. *Building,* February 26, 1988, p. 23.
16. H.M. Treasury Efficiency Unit. *Using Private Enterprise in Government.* Her Majesty's Stationery Office, London, 1986.
17. Bill, P. Government to sell off PSA construction arm. *Building,* December 2, 1988, p. 7.
18. Draper, P. The rise and demise of the PSA. *Government Purchasing,* May 1995, pp. 8–9.
19. Beale, N., and Nethercott, S. A critical review of the effect of factory closures on health (letter). *Br. J. Ind. Med.* 49: 70, 1992.
20. *Social Trends,* No. 27. The Stationery Office, London, 1997.
21. Jackson, C., et al. *Staff Attitudes in the Benefits Agency.* Institute of Manpower Studies, Brighton, U.K., 1992.
22. Hartley, J., et al. *Job Insecurity: Coping with Jobs at Risk.* Sage, London, 1991.
23. Dooley, D., Rook, K., and Catalano, R. Job and non-job stressors and their moderators. *J. Occup. Psychol.* 60: 115–132, 1987.
24. Catalano, R., Rook, K., and Dooley, D. Labor markets and help-seeking: A test of the employment security hypothesis. *J. Health Soc. Behav.* 27: 277–287, 1986.
25. Ferrie, J. E. Is job insecurity harmful to health? *J. R. Soc. Med.* 94: 71–76, 2001.
26. Reid, D. D., et al. Cardiorespiratory disease and diabetes among middle-aged male civil servants. *Lancet* 1: 469–473, 1974.
27. Marmot, M. G., Shipley, M. J., and Rose, G. Inequalities in death—Specific explanations of a general pattern? *Lancet* 1: 1003–1006, 1984.
28. Marmot, M. G., et al. Employment grade and coronary heart disease in British civil servants. *J. Epidemiol. Community Health* 32: 244–249, 1978.
29. Davey Smith, G., Shipley, M. J., and Rose, G. The magnitude and causes of socioeconomic differentials in mortality: Further evidence from the Whitehall study. *J. Epidemiol. Community Health* 44: 265–270, 1990.
30. Marmot, M. G., et al. Health inequalities among British civil servants: The Whitehall II study. *Lancet* 337: 1387–1393, 1991.
31. Goldberg, D. P. *The Detection of Psychiatric Illness by Questionnaire.* Oxford University Press, London, 1972.
32. Stansfeld, S., Head, J., and Marmot, M. G. Explaining social class differences in depression and well-being. *Soc. Psychiatry Psychiatr. Epidemiol.* 33: 1–9, 1998.
33. Karasek, R. Job demands, job decision latitude, and mental strain: Implications for job redesign. *Adm. Sci. Q.* 24: 285–311, 1979.
34. Roskies, E., Louis-Guerin, C., and Fournier, C. Coping with job insecurity: How does personality make a difference? *J. Organ. Behav.* 14: 617–630, 1993.
35. Bradburn, N. M. *The Structure of Psychological Wellbeing.* Aldine, Chicago, 1969.
36. Glynn, R. J., Rosner, B., and Silbert, J. E. Changes in cholesterol and triglyceride as predictors of ischemic heart disease in men. *Circulation* 66: 724–731, 1982.
37. Pearlin, L. I., and Schooler, C. The structure of coping. *J. Health Soc. Behav.* 19: 2–21, 1978.

38. Ferrie, J. E., et al. An uncertain future: The health effects of threats to employment security in white-collar men and women. *Am. J. Public Health* 88: 1030–1036, 1998.
39. Cobb, S., and Kasl, S. V. *Termination: The Consequences of Job Loss.* DHEW-NIOSH Publication No. 77-224. National Institute for Occupational Safety and Health, Cincinnati, 1977.
40. Jacobsen, K. Afskedigelse og sygelighed. *Ugeskr. Laeg*; 134: 352–354, 1972.
41. Jacobsen, K. Arbejdsloshed og afsked som sygdomsfremkaldende faktorer. *Ugeskr. Laeg.* 136: 1650–1651, 1974.
42. Beale, N., and Nethercott, S. Job-loss and family morbidity: A study of a factory closure. *J. R. Coll. Gen. Pract.* 35: 510–514, 1985.
43. Kasl, S. V., and Cobb, S. Blood pressure changes in men undergoing job loss: A preliminary report. *Psychosom. Med.* 32: 19–38, 1970.
44. Kasl, S. V. Changes in mental health status associated with job loss and retirement. In *Stress and Mental Disorder*, edited by J. E. Barrett, pp. 179–200. Raven Press, New York, 1979.
45. Schnall, P. L., et al. The impact of anticipation of job loss on psychological distress and worksite blood pressure. *Am. J. Ind. Med.* 21: 417–432, 1992.
46. Mattiasson, I., et al. Threat of unemployment and cardiovascular risk factors: Longitudinal study of quality of sleep and serum cholesterol concentrations in men threatened with redudancy. *BMJ* 301: 461–466, 1990.
47. Arnetz, B. B., et al. *Stress Reactions in Relation to Threat of Job Loss and Actual Unemployment: Physiological, Psychological and Economic Effects of Job Loss and Unemployment.* Stress Research Reports No. 206. Karolinska Institute, Stockholm, 1988.
48. Jenkins, R., et al. Minor psychiatric morbidity and the threat of redundancy in a professional group. *Psychol. Med.* 12: 799–807, 1982.
49. Rowlands, P., and Huws, R. Psychological effects of colliery closure. *Int. J. Soc. Psychiatry* 41: 21–25, 1995.
50. Kasl, S. Strategies of research on economic instability and health. *Psychol. Med.* 12: 637–649, 1982.
51. Kasl, S. V., Gore, S., and Cobb, S. The experience of losing a job: Reported changes in health, symptoms and illness behaviour. *Psychosom. Med.* 37: 106–122, 1975.
52. Kessler, R. C., Turner, J. B., and House, J. S. Effects of unemployment on health in a community survey: Main, modifying and mediating effects. *J. Soc. Iss.* 4: 69–85, 1988.
53. Gallie, D., and Vogler, C. Labor market deprivation, welfare and collectivism. In *Social Change and the Experience of Unemployment,* edited by D. Gallie, C. Marsh, and C. Vogler, pp. 299–336. Oxford University Press, New York, 1994.
54. Mathers, C. D., and Schofield, D. J. The health consequences of unemployment: The evidence. *Med. J. Aust.* 168: 178–182, 1998.
55. Claussen, B. A clinical follow up of unemployed. I: Lifestyle, diagnoses, treatment and reemployment. *Scand. J. Prim. Health Care* 11: 211–218, 1993.
56. Blaxter, M. Evidence on inequality in health from a national survey. *Lancet* 2: 30–33, 1987.
57. Grayson, J. P. Health, physical activity level and employment status in Canada. *Int. J. Health Serv.* 23: 743–761, 1993.

58. D'Arcy, C., and Siddique, C. M. Unemployment and health: An analysis of "Canada Health" data. *Int. J. Health Serv.* 15: 609–635, 1985.
59. Bartley, M., and Owen, C. Relation between socioeconomic status, employment, and health during economic change, 1973–93. *BMJ* 313: 445–449, 1996.
60. Arber, S., and Lahelma, E. Inequalities in women's and men's ill-health: Britain and Finland compared. *Soc. Sci. Med.* 8: 1055–1068, 1993.
61. Arber, S. Integrating nonemployment into research on health inequalities. *Int. J. Health Serv.* 26: 445–481, 1996.
62. Hibbard, J. H., and Pope, C. R. Health effects of discontinuities in female employment and marital status. *Soc. Sci. Med.* 36: 1099–1104, 1993.
63. Ramsden, S., and Smee, C. The health of unemployed men: DHSS cohort study. *Empire Gazette,* 1981, pp. 397–401.
64. Hamilton, V. L., et al. Hard times and vulnerable people: Initial effects of plant closing on autoworkers' mental health. *J. Health Soc. Behav.* 31:123–140, 1990.
65. Iversen, L., and Klausen, H. Alcohol consumption among laid-off workers before and after closure of a Danish ship-yard: A 2-year follow-up study. *Soc. Sci. Med.* 22: 107–109, 1986.
66. Studnicka, M., et al. Psychological health, self-reported physical health and health service use: Risk differential observed after one year of unemployment. *Soc. Psychiatry Psychiatr. Epidemiol.* 26: 86–91, 1991.
67. Viinamaki, H., et al. Unemployment, financial stress and mental well-being: A factory closure study. *Eur. J. Psychiat.* 7: 95–102, 1993.
68. Morrell, S., et al. A cohort study of unemployment as a cause of psychological disturbance in Australian youth. *Soc. Sci. Med.* 38: 1553–1564, 1994.
69. Smith, R. "What's the point. I'm no use to anybody": The psychological consequences of unemployment. *BMJ* 291: 1338–1341, 1985.
70. Viinamaki, H., et al. Unemployment and mental well-being: A factory closure study in Finland. *Acta Psychiatr. Scand.* 88: 429–433, 1993.
71. Feather, N. T. *The Psychological Impact of Unemployment.* Springer Verlag, New York, 1990.
72. Fryer, D. Labor-market disadvantage, deprivation and mental health benefit agency? *Psychologist* 8: 265–272, 1995.
73. Arnetz, B. B., et al. Neuroendocrine and immunologic effects of unemployment and job insecurity. *Psychother. Psychosom.* 55: 76–80, 1991.
74. Dew, M. A., Bromet, E. J., and Penkower, L. Mental health effects of job loss in women. *Psychol. Med.* 22: 751–764, 1992.
75. Warr, P., and Jackson, P. Adapting to the unemployed role: A longitudinal investigation. *Soc. Sci. Med.* 25: 1219–1224, 1987.
76. Iversen, L., and Sabroe, S. Plant closures, unemployment, and health: Danish experiences from the declining ship-building industry. In *Unemployment, Social Vulnerability, and Health in Europe*, edited by D. Schwefel, P.-G. Svensson, and H. Zollner, pp. 31–47. Springer-Verlag, Berlin, 1987.
77. Hamilton, V., et al. Unemployment, distress, and coping: A panel study of autoworkers. *J. Pers. Soc Psychol.* 65: 234–247, 1993.
78. Iversen, L., and Sabroe, S. Psychological well-being among unemployed and employed people after a company closedown: A longitudinal study. *J. Soc. Iss.* 44: 141–152, 1988.

79. Lahelma, E. Unemployment and mental well-being: Elaboration of the relationship. *Int. J. Health Serv.* 22: 261–275, 1992.
80. Claussen, B., Bjorndal, A., and Hjort, P. H. Health and re-employment in a two year follow up of long term unemployed. *J. Epidemiol. Community Health* 47: 14–18, 1993.
81. Burchell, B. The effects of labor market position, job insecurity, and unemployment on psychological health. In *Social Change and the Experience of Unemployment*, edited by D. Gallie, C. Marsh, and C. Vogler, pp. 188–212. Oxford University Press, New York, 1994.
82. Leana, C. R., and Feldman, D. C. Finding new jobs after a plant closing: Antecedents and outcomes of the occurrence and quality of reemployment. *Hum. Relations* 48: 1381–1401, 1995.
83. Greatz, B. Health consequences of unemployment: Longitudinal evidence for young men and women. *Soc. Sci. Med.* 36: 715–724, 1993.
84. Beale, N., and Nethercott, S. Certificated sickness absence in industrial employees threatened with redundancy. *BMJ* 296: 1508–1510, 1988.
85. Owens, C. Sick leave among railwaymen threatened by redundancy: A pilot study. *Occup. Psychol.* 40: 43–52, 1966.
86. Virtanen, V. "An epidemic of good health" at the workplace. *Sociol. Health Illness* 16: 394–401, 1994.
87. Knutsson, A., and Goine, H. Occupation and unemployment rates as predictors of long-term sickness absence in two Swedish counties. *Soc. Sci. Med.* 47: 25–31, 1998.
88. Belloc, B., and Breslow, L. Relationship of physical health status and health practices. *Prev. Med.* 1: 409–421, 1972.
89. Breslow, L., and Enstrom, J. Persistence of health habits and their relationship to mortality. *Prev. Med.* 9: 469–483, 1980.
90. Belloc, N. Relationship of health practices and mortality. *Prev. Med.* 2: 67–81, 1973.
91. Yuen, P., and Balarajan, R. Unemployment and patterns of consultation with the general practitioner. *BMJ* 298: 1212–1214, 1989.
92. Carr-Hill, R. A., Rice, N., and Roland, M. Socioeconomic determinants of rates of consultation in general practices based on 4th national morbidity survey of general practices. *BMJ* 312: 1008–1012, 1996.
93. Broman, C. L., Hamilton, V. L., and Hoffman, W. S. Unemployment and its effects on families: Evidence from a plant closing study. *Am. J. Community Psychol.* 18: 643–659, 1990.
94. Lampard, R. An examination of the relationship between marital dissolution and unemployment. In *Social Change and the Experience of Unemployment*, edited by D. Gallie, C. Marsh, and C. Vogler, pp. 264–298. Oxford University Press, New York, 1994.
95. Larson, J. H., Wilson, S. M., and Beley, R. The impact of job insecurity on marital and family relationships. *Fam. Relations* 43: 138–143, 1994.
96. Hinde, K. Labor market experiences following plant closure: The case of Sunderland's shipyard workers. *Regional Stud.* 28: 713–724, 1994.
97. Buss, T. F., Redburn, F. S., and Waldron, J. *Mass Unemployment: Plant Closings and Community Mental Health.* Sage, Beverly Hills, 1983.
98. Grayson, J. P. The closure of a factory and its impact on health. *Int. J. Health Serv.* 15: 69–93, 1985.

99. Fagin, L., and Little, M. *The Forsaken Families.* Penguin, Harmondsworth, U.K., 1984.
100. Rodgers, B. Socio-economic status, employment and neurosis. *Soc. Psychiatry Psychiatr. Epidemiol.* 26: 104–114, 1991.
101. Jackson, P. R., and Warr, P. Unemployment and psychological ill-health: The moderating role of duration and age. *Psychol. Med.* 14: 605–614, 1984.
102. Whelan, C. The role of income, life-style deprivation and financial strain in mediating the impact of unemployment on psychological distress: Evidence from the Republic of Ireland. *J. Occup. Org. Psychol.* 65: 331–344, 1992.
103. Leeflang, R. L. I., Klein-Hesselink, D. J., and Spruit, I. P. Health effects of unemployment—II: Men and women. *Soc. Sci. Med.* 34: 351–363, 1992.
104. Armstrong-Stassen, M. The impact of organizational downsizing on the job satisfaction of nurses. *Can. J. Nurs. Adm.* 9: 8–32, 1996.
105. Roskies, E., and Louis-Guerin, C. Job insecurity in managers: Antecedents and consequences. *J. Organ. Behav.* 11: 345–359, 1990.
106. Bussing, A. Can control at work and social support moderate psychological consequences of job insecurity? Results from a quasi-experimental study in the steel industry. *Eur. J. Work Organ. Psychol.* 8: 219–242, 1999.
107. Heaney, C., Israel, B., and House, J. Chronic job insecurity among automobile workers: Effects on job satisfaction and health. *Soc. Sci. Med.* 38: 1431–1437, 1994.
108. Kivimaki, M., et al. Factors underlying the effect of organizational downsizing on the health of employees: A longitudinal cohort study of changes in work, social relationships and health behaviours. *BMJ* 320: 971–975, 2000.
109. Dekker, S. W. A., and Schaufeli, W. B. The effects of job insecurity on psychological health and withdrawal: A longitudinal study. *Aust. Psychol.* 30: 57–63, 1995.
110. Karasek, R. Job socialization and job strain: The implications of two related psychosocial mechanisms for job design. In *Working Life*, edited by B. Gardell and G. Johansson. Wiley, Chichester, U.K., 1981.
111. Graham, H. Women's smoking and family health. *Soc. Sci. Med.* 25: 47–56, 1987.
112. Hyyppa, M. T., Kronholm, E., and Alanen, E. Quality of sleep during economic recession in Finland: A longitudinal cohort study. *Soc. Sci. Med.* 45: 731–738, 1997.
113. Rodriguez, E. Health consequences of unemployment in Barcelona. *Eur. J. Public Health* 4: 245–251, 1994.
114. Janlert, U. *Work Deprivation and Health: Consequences of Job Loss and Unemployment.* Karolinska Institute, Lulea, Sweden, 1991.
115. Leino-Arjas, P., et al. Predictors and consequences of unemployment among construction workers: prospective cohort study. *BMJ* 319: 600–605, 1999.
116. Bradford Hill, A. The environment and disease: Association or causation? *Proc. R. Soc. Med.* 58: 295–300, 1965.
117. Walt, G. How far does research influence policy? *Eur. J. Public Health* 4: 233–235, 1994.
118. Turner, J. B., Kessler, R. C., and House, J. S. Factors facilitating adjustment to unemployment: Implications for intervention. *Am. J. Community Psychol.* 19: 521–542, 1991.
119. House, J. S. *Work Stress and Social Support.* Addison-Wesley, Reading, Mass., 1981.
120. Lim, V. K. G. Job insecurity and its outcomes: Moderating effects of work-based and nonwork-based social support. *Hum. Relations* 49: 171–194, 1996.

121. Vinokur, A. D., et al. Long-term follow-up and benefit-cost analysis of the jobs program: A preventive intervention for the unemployed. *J. Appl. Psychol.* 76: 213–219, 1991.
122. Ezzy, D. Unemployment and mental health: A critical review. *Soc. Sci. Med.* 37: 41–52, 1993.
123. OECD. Is job insecurity on the increase in OECD countries? In *The OECD Employment Outlook*, pp. 129–160. Paris, 1997.
124. Hartley, J. Models of job insecurity, and coping strategies by organizations. In *Labour Market Changes and Job Insecurity: A Challenge for Social Welfare and Health Promotion,* edited by J. Ferrie et al., pp. 127–149. WHO Regional Publications, European Series No. 81. WHO, Copenhagen, 1999.
125. Quick, A., and Wilkinson, R. G. *Income and Health.* Socialist Health Association, London, 1991.
126. Shaw, M., et al. *The Widening Gap: Health Inequalities and Policy in Britain.* Policy Press, Bristol, 1999.
127. Whitehead, M. *Inequalities and Public Policy: Part I—The International Perspective.* Equity in Health Research and Development Unit, Liverpool, UK, 1995.
128. Scott-Samuel, A., Whitehead, M., and Connelly, J. *Inequalities and Public Policy. Part II – The UK perspective.* Equity in Health Research and Development Unit, Liverpool, UK, 1995.
129. *Action on Social Inequalities and Health.* Proceedings of a European Conference. BMJ Publishing, London, 1994.
130. Shortt, S. E. D. Is unemployment pathogenic? A review of current concepts with lessons for policy planners. *Int. J. Health Serv.* 26: 569–589, 1996.
131. Karasek, R. Dutch labor participation and job quality policy for the late 1990s: Defining new alternatives and new visions. In *Labor Market Changes and Job Insecurity: A Challenge for Social Welfare and Health Promotion,* edited by J. Ferrie et al, pp. 168–239. WHO Regional Publications, European Series No. 81. WHO, Copenhagen, 1999.
132. Braverman, H. *Labor and Monopoly Capital: The Degradation of Work in the Twentieth Century.* Monthly Review Press, New York, 1974.

Section II

Work Demands

Chapter 6

WORKLOAD AND WORKPLACE STRESS

Wendy A. Macdonald

Don't tell me about the millions of jobs you've created. I've got four of them and I'm not all that impressed.

U.S. worker to President Bill Clinton

Over recent years, in many countries, there have been major workplace changes aimed at improving organizational performance and competitive advantage. Such changes include the introduction of new technologies, organizational restructuring and "downsizing," multi-skilling of employees, and associated changes in workplace practices and workplace or enterprise agreements between managements and employee groups. Whether or not organizational performance has improved, considerable evidence suggests that many of these changes have been associated with an intensification of work and in some countries (such as Australia and the United States) with increased hours of work, such that a large proportion of employees have experienced an increase in their workload and/or increased stress (1–10).

In most jurisdictions that have occupational health and safety legislation, employers are held responsible for providing safe and healthy "systems of work," regardless of particular enterprise or workplace agreements. Accordingly, the successful implementation of changes in work and organizations requires that staffing levels and individual workloads must be consistent both with productivity requirements *and* with health and safety requirements. In order to achieve this, managers must to be able to identify the workplace and job factors that commonly influence workload, and to understand and be able to monitor relationships between workload levels and employees' well-being and performance. Ergonomists currently have a wide range of methods for identifying and analyzing both physical and psychological task demands, related workload, and the goodness of "fit" between task demands and people's capacities to cope with them (see 11–13). However, current knowledge of broader workplace and job factors that may influence overall workload levels is less than adequate.

In particular, the relationship between workload and stress levels is not well understood. It cannot be described purely in terms of number of hours worked: even when total working hours are highly correlated with the quantity of work performed, an increase in hours is not necessarily associated with an increase in stress levels. For example, a recent European Union survey found that the national groups reporting the highest levels of stress were among those with the shortest working hours, probably due at least in part to their employment in short-term positions with low influence and low job security, performing repetitive work (10).

Among the most commonly cited factors contributing to workplace stress levels are job demand, job pressure, workload, work intensification, work pressure, and the like (e.g., 5, 8, 10, 14–16). There is a great deal of "fuzziness," however, about the particular workplace issues and experiences to which such labels refer. In everyday terms we know what someone means when she says she has a high workload: we assume that her job entails a lot of work, demanding considerable time and effort. That is, she has to perform a large quantity of work and, whether because of the sheer quantity or because of the quantity in combination with its difficulty or complexity, she has to invest a substantial amount of time and effort in performing it. We cannot assume, however, that high workloads are necessarily stressful, nor that people with high workloads are dissatisfied with their jobs (e.g., 17, 18). People in such jobs *might* be dissatisfied for various possible reasons, including high levels of stress and/or excessive workloads. In addition—or alternatively—they might experience feelings of considerable satisfaction, engagement, enthusiasm, or even exhilaration (17, 19–21). Further, we need to remember that it is not only excessively *high* workload levels that are stressful; excessively *low* workload levels can also be experienced as stressful, whether due to boredom or to the effort required to maintain the required performance standard for a highly monotonous task (e.g., 22–24).

What, then, determines relationships between job demands, performance, perceived workload, and occupational stress? How can workload levels be controlled to avoid excessively low or high levels, as part of a proactive approach to stress management? For example, how should we assess the impact on people's workloads of the introduction of new technology or work systems? On what basis should we determine required staffing levels when organizations are restructured? How should we evaluate alternative models of new, multifunction photocopiers to select the one that will have the most positive impact on a particular group of users' workloads? What limits, if any, should be placed on an individual's workload in terms of the total hours worked per shift, or over longer periods of weeks or months? Should such limits take account of the nature and level of work demands, as well as the total time spent working? If so, how might this be achieved? How should workload relate to rest-break requirements? This chapter presents a conceptual framework for tackling such questions.

AN ERGONOMICS VIEW OF WORKLOAD, ITS DETERMINANTS AND DIMENSIONS

A useful starting point for investigating the above questions is available within the domain of cognitive ergonomics, or human factors psychology, where workload has been the topic of a large amount of research over the past few decades (e.g., 24–29). This research arose from earlier studies that focused on the capacities and limitations of the human information-processing system (e.g., 30–34). Within this literature the terms "workload" and "mental workload" have come to be used interchangeably.

Gopher and Donchin (35) defined mental workload as ". . . the difference between the capacities of the information-processing system that are required for task performance to satisfy expectations and the capacity available at any given time." Similarly, Jex (36) defined mental workload as ". . . the operator's evaluation of the attention load *margin* (between their motivated capacity and the current task demands) while achieving adequate task performance. . . ." Jex's "motivated capacity" is similar to Kalsbeek's earlier notion (37) of a "willing to spend" capacity, acknowledging that an individual's *absolute* capacity in some physical sense is approached only under conditions of maximum possible motivation. According to this view, it is the size of the margin or gap between level of task demands and individuals' *motivated* capacity—influenced by the degree of effort they are willing to expend in that situation—that determines their workload level. Motivation is also important in the context of Kahneman's model (34), in which available attentional resources can to some extent increase in response to perceived demands, provided that the person is motivated to cope with the demands. It is evident, then, that factors affecting an individual's motivation to perform a task must be considered, along with the demands intrinsic to the task, when assessing the acceptability of workload levels in relation to people's coping capacity.

The multidimensional nature of workload is emphasized in the definition provided by Kantowitz, one of the most active researchers in this domain: "Workload is a subjective experience caused by external and internal factors such as motivation, ability, expectations, training, timing, stress, fatigue, and circumstances in addition to the number, type and difficulty of tasks performed, effort expended, and success in meeting requirements" (38, p. 97). Kantowitz's highly inclusive view of workload is reflected in the International Standards Organization (ISO) Standards 10 075 (39) and 10 075-2 (40) concerning "ergonomics principles related to mental workload," about which Nachreiner wrote: "Although mental workload is usually associated with tasks requiring information processing, it is made explicit in this standard that any human activity, even those that are primarily regarded as physical activities, includes mental activities and thus mental workload. The standard is thus relevant to all kinds of work design, not only to those kinds of work task that would be regarded as 'mental' in a restricted sense" (41).

As is evident from the above examples, some views of workload (e.g., 35, 36) remain largely embedded within the original, information-processing research framework, while others, such as those of Kantowitz (38) and the ISO papers (39, 40), portray workload as a more inclusive, multidimensional construct, incorporating external factors, internal factors, and the resultant costs and gains (Figure 6.1).

Figure 6.1 presents an "ergonomics" view of workload, according to which a more difficult task requires the expenditure of greater effort in its performance. The notion of "spare capacity" is important here. As demands increase, people may be able to maintain their performance at an acceptable level, but the decreasing gap between demands and their "coping capacity" is associated with an increase in perceived workload. When demands increase to "overload" level—exceeding the person's coping capacity—deterioration in *optimal* performance quality is inevitable. However, for many tasks, an optimal performance level—or even a minimum acceptable level—is not clearly specified. Also, there is often scope for people to adopt performance strategies that achieve less than optimal

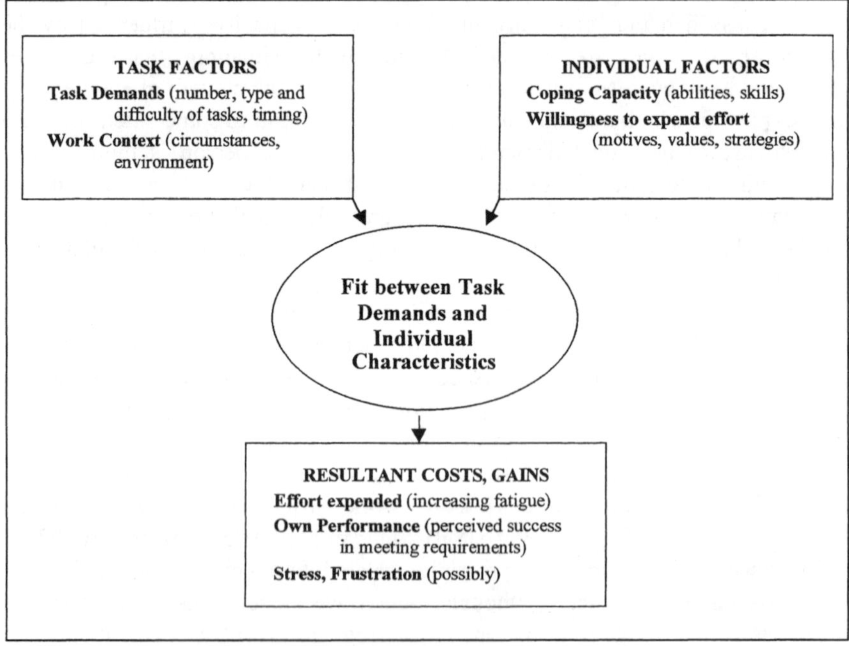

Figure 6.1 An ergonomics, multidimensional representation of workload. Adapted from Kantowitz (38).

performance but demand less attention, thus freeing some attentional resources to be "spent" in coping with other demands. Accordingly, there is often no clearly delineated point at which a person becomes overloaded and unable to cope with the demands of work. For these reasons, human performance typically "degrades gracefully" under overload conditions.

This ergonomics or human factors psychology view of workload is the conceptual basis for one of the most widely used workload measurement methods: the NASA Task Load Index (TLX; 42), according to which workload level is a function of "operator" ratings of the following six dimensions: three aspects of task demand (physical demand, mental demand, and temporal demand); two types of "cost" (amount of effort expended, and frustration or stress experienced, during task performance); and one "gain" (level of perceived success in achieving the task objectives and satisfaction with own performance level). Being subjective in nature, operator ratings of task demands necessarily reflect to some degree the interaction of external and internal factors shown in Figure 6.1. It is noteworthy that the TLX measures physical demands of task performance along with mental and temporal demands. Another widely used method is SWAT, the Subjective Workload Assessment Technique (43), which incorporates only three dimensions. In SWAT, task demands are represented by a single dimension, time load, along with two types of personal cost, mental effort load and stress load.

In the ergonomics domain, then, there is broad consensus that "workload" is not simply the *amount* of work that has to be done, although this factor is included in Kantowitz's definition and would be expected to influence levels of the TLX temporal demand and the SWAT time load factors. Rather, workload is determined by the demands *experienced* by the person performing the work, and this experience is a function of both the objectively measurable demands of work performance and the person's own perceived capacity to cope with those demands. Accordingly, the workload experienced by someone performing a specific task (e.g., taking an exam, or running a kilometer in a set time) will be much lower for people with a high capacity to perform that task than for people with a low capacity—assuming that all are equally motivated to succeed. "Workload" results from interactions between individual factors and work demands. Within this framework, "task demands" are the aspects that require the expenditure of some physical and/or mental effort and attention.

The broader ergonomics definitions of "workload" also encompass at least some of the *costs* incurred as people attempt to meet task demands, including effort expended and consequent fatigue. Thus, Hart and Staveland, who developed the NASA-TLX, viewed workload as "a hypothetical construct that represents the cost incurred by a human operator to achieve a particular level of performance," (42, p. 140). And Matthews and colleagues noted that "Workload . . . refers to people's experiences of cognitive task performance as effortful and fatiguing" (44, p. 87). Consistent with this, "effort" is one of the dimensions assessed by both the TLX and SWAT.

Another possible cost incorporated within the workload construct is the experience of negative emotions such as stress. The Kantowitz definition of workload quoted above incorporates stress; the TLX "frustration" dimension is defined operationally in terms that include stress, and stress is one of the three workload dimensions measured by SWAT. Such negative emotions are thought to arise when workload levels are too high or too low. When demands are so high that the required effort levels to cope with them are close to someone's maximum capacity, then workload is likely to be experienced as excessive.[1] Someone who is expending a high level of effort in an attempt to cope with demands, but perceives his performance as probably inadequate and feel that this matters, is likely to feel anxious or frustrated or depressed: that is, he is likely to experience stress (8, 45–49).

Negative emotions associated with very *low* workload levels are of a somewhat different nature, since they typically arise when task performance demands little thought and holds little interest, leading to boredom. Such circumstances are naturally de-arousing, and there is a natural tendency to decrease effort expenditure or to cease performance altogether; in these circumstances, a requirement to maintain good performance, in terms of either a high quantitative output or a low error rate (such as in a monitoring task) or both, can be experienced as unpleasantly stressful (22–24, 50).

Implicit in most of the ergonomics literature on workload is the assumption that negative emotions related to "stress" are effectively interchangeable. For example, operational definitions of the TLX dimension termed "frustration" are insecure, discouraged, irritated, stressed, or annoyed, versus secure, gratified, content, relaxed, or complacent. Clearly, the meanings of these words are not the same; in fact, an earlier version of the TLX had separate dimensions for frustration and stress, which in this later version were effectively combined. Such differences can sometimes have practical significance. For example, I conducted semi-structured individual interviews with a group of train controllers on their task demands and related workload issues, prior to conducting more formal task analyzes and workload assessments (51). I found that the controllers interpreted stress as anxiety related to performing their safety-critical work under conditions of very high task demands: for example, situations in which someone might not take a meal break during a work shift of many hours, or when someone left work after a very busy shift but within the next hour telephoned the person on the following shift with worries about tasks he or she might not have completed. In contrast to this, they interpreted frustration in terms of work situations where their work was more demanding, or unpleasant, due to a problem that could have been avoided—for example, if management had replaced faulty equipment. Clearly, it is useful in

[1] This is true as long as task performance is perceived as feasible; it obviously does not hold for someone who sees the task as requiring capacities that are clearly beyond those he possesses, such that there is no point in his seriously attempting to perform it.

some circumstances for such distinctions to be preserved, so that the particular kind of "negative affect" has greater diagnostic value.

It is noteworthy that, according to the ergonomics view, the only unequivocally *positive* dimension of workload is degree of perceived success in achieving performance objectives, with no reference to positive affect per se. Some degree of satisfaction could be expected to accompany perceived success, but unlike the negative emotions (frustration, stress) that may accompany the perceived risk of failure, this is not incorporated into workload definitions and is not measured as part of workload.

WORKLOAD AND JOB DEMANDS

Ergonomics measurement of workload typically has a fairly narrow focus, with any contextual effects either defined as part of the task or ignored. While some definitions of workload include reference to the circumstances or context in which task performance occurs—for example, Kantowitz (38, as quoted above) refers to "circumstances," and Meshkati (52, p. 307) includes "environmental factors" and the individual's "motivational state and personal utility system,"—the ergonomics research domain has not produced any workload assessment methods that systematically measure such contextual factors. Huey and Wickens (24) saw the most fundamental source of workload as demand factors inherent in task performance, but acknowledged that "the behaviour and workload experiences" of a particular operator are also influenced by particular goals and performance criteria, and by additional factors such as fatigue, stress, training, crew coordination, and environmental stressors (e.g., heat, cold, vibration, noise, and danger). Importantly, they note, "Although the influence of these factors is obvious in operational situations, little research has been performed to establish their relationship with operator workload, and they are ignored in most workload theories" (24, p. 57).

Huey and Wickens's book (24) presents one of the most detailed discussions of the workload concept as it applies to real world environments. The authors review evidence on relationships between performance and workload levels (in the ergonomics sense) for teams of operators performing mainly monitoring and control tasks, typically in safety-critical systems, including nuclear power plants, hospital emergency rooms, army maneuvers, and various types of vehicle control. In these, as in most workplaces, there is a wide range of demands that are broader than specific tasks (e.g., the need to maintain cordial interpersonal relationships), contextual factors (e.g., one or two team members away sick), and psychosocial environment factors (e.g., supervisor supportiveness), in addition to the physical environment and other factors noted above, that are likely to influence performance strategies, affective states, and hence workload levels.

Clearly, the workload of a whole job (job workload), as opposed to that experienced in relation to performance of a specific task, is very unlikely to be simply the sum of task-related workloads. Similarly, job workload is likely to have a broader range of determinants, including contextual factors, than those affecting each of the workloads of the component work tasks taken in isolation and out of context. The whole set of demands associated with job performance, including but not confined to task demands, is here termed "job demands."

Other task and job demands noted by Huey and Wickens that have relevance in a wide range of workplaces include task schedules, variability of task demands, factors influencing speed-versus-accuracy trade-offs, and total task duration. Operators' selection of performance strategies is a key mechanism by which the effects of such variables affect relationships between demands, effort, and performance, and hence workload. For example, ". . . people may be able and willing to exert considerable effort or to accept inactivity and boredom for brief intervals, but not for very long. Particularly in familiar and predictable situations, experienced operators will pace themselves, working at a rate and effort level that they can sustain for the expected duration of the task" (24, p. 67). This effect of task duration was observed during an investigation of mail sorting rates, where one of the factors found to significantly affect sorting rates was the known, total volume of mail for that day (53).[2] That is, people worked at a slower average rate when they knew that mail volume and hence their total task duration would be higher.

Such findings are important when considering shift durations and rest breaks, and have been acknowledged in some policies related to the adoption of "extended" shifts. For example, the Australian Council of Trade Unions (ACTU) Code of Conduct on Twelve Hour Shift Work stated that extended shifts should be introduced only where they would not impose "excessive" physical or mental workload (54), and a paper produced by the Australian Council of Commerce and Industry agreed that careful assessment of physical and mental workload is required prior to the introduction of extended shifts (55). Despite recognition of these issues, the past decade has seen the proliferation of extended shift systems in many countries (56–59).

A major obstacle to the implementation of policies to prevent excessive workload levels is the absence of measurement tools suitable for ordinary workplace use. There appears to have been remarkably little research on generic dimensions and determinants of job-related workload. Specific formulas of various sorts have been developed to determine appropriate workloads (sets of work tasks and related constraints) for a wide variety of particular occupations, including nurses, airline crews, and even academics (e.g. 60–62). However, given the domain-specific terms of these tasks, they have no value beyond the particular target group, and

[2] This factor was in addition to variables reflecting cognitive and psychomotor difficulties of the sorting task, in accord with both the Hick-Hyman law and Fitts' law (see 98).

appropriateness of resultant workload levels (in the ergonomics sense) appears not to have been evaluated.

The great majority of ergonomics research on workload has been concerned with the development or evaluation of equipment and related systems of work, usually with the aim of minimizing demands on operator capacity or, more broadly, aiming to maximize performance quality and system efficiency. For example, my colleagues and I have used the NASA-TLX workload scales (sometimes in modified form) in a series of small-scale projects for a variety of tasks and jobs, including those of assembly line workers (63), laboratory technicians (64), rehabilitation counselors (17, 65), and train controllers (51). In all these projects, information from the six TLX scales was used separately; as described earlier, the standard scales measure three types of task demand (physical, mental, and temporal demands), two types of cost (effort and frustration/stress), and one gain (perceived performance success and related satisfaction).

Two of these projects were primarily concerned with task demands in accord with conventional ergonomics practice. O'Bryan and coworkers (63) found significant differences between two industrial assembly line tasks in terms of three of its six dimensions: physical difficulty, time pressure, and effort. These differences were validated in terms of a range of standard work-analysis techniques, including heart rate and an engineering Predetermined Motion Time System. I developed a modified set of TLX scales, based on initial interviews with train controllers, to analyze the dimensions of controller workload for automated versus nonautomated control systems (51). The performance scale was omitted, since it was found to be unlikely that ratings would vary below a "reasonably good" level, and previous studies had found very little variation (63, 64)—not surprising, given that people were performing the normal work for which they were employed. The modified TLX scales were:

- *Perceptual demands:* task information able to be noticed easily when needed; able to be seen or heard easily
- *Mental demands:* thinking and planning; decision-making; switching attention between different aspects of the work while maintaining task priorities; remembering to do things; recalling information when needed
- *Importance of avoiding errors:* awareness of consequences of errors[3]
- *Physical demands:* physical discomfort or tiredness related to posture; reaching and twisting; effects of seating and work-station layout; adequacy of opportunities to walk around
- *Time pressure:* work rate demands; time available to deal with things
- *Effort required:* concentration level; how much attention needed
- *Frustration experienced:* stress, annoyance, irritation

[3] This scale was particularly relevant given the nature of the expected impact of automation; some earlier researchers have found this to be a significant determinant of workload level (e.g., 99, 100).

Effects of varying automation levels and varying overall demand level were investigated in terms of the rated relative importance of the different scales. Results were of considerable practical value; for example, with the nonautomated task condition, avoiding errors was rated as less important with near-capacity workload than when things were quieter, suggesting an enforced change in speed-versus-accuracy performance strategy. Overall workload levels were assessed using unidimensional magnitude estimation ratings (e.g., 66).

Our other two projects looked more broadly at the nature of job demands and workload. So and Mert-Iljin (64) used semi-structured interviews to explore workload dimensions for university technical staff of varying seniority level (junior assistant through to manager). Expected differences between junior and more senior staff in the relative significance of different workload dimensions were reflected by the TLX. However, interview results indicated a need for measures of additional workload dimensions, particularly those concerning relationships with other people, and levels of task identity or role clarity. Upsdell (65) and Macdonald and Upsdell (17) reported use of the TLX in conjunction with measures of occupational stress, burnout, and job satisfaction to identify predictors of stress-related illness and to explore correlations between these measures. High levels of TLX mental demand were associated with *low* levels of stress and *high* levels of job satisfaction. Such relationships are a salutary reminder that, as noted earlier, demanding jobs need not necessarily be stressful. (This issue is discussed further by Payne and Morrison [18].) Overall, this group of studies has demonstrated that the TLX—modified or otherwise—is an inadequate method for assessing either job demands or overall job workload: it ignores several important types of job demand (discussed further below), and it does not adequately assess positive affect. However, it can provide useful diagnostic information on different types of task demands, particularly if adapted to suit particular task characteristics.

In a recently reported study, Jung and Jung (67) developed a method for overall workload assessment that involved workers judging the relative workload intensity of various task demands and workplace environment factors, as required by the analytical hierarchy process (AHP) (68). Following the AHP procedure, the authors developed mathematical algorithms to rank the workload of a range of specific work tasks. Results were validated in that they were significantly related to a physiological index of metabolic demands and to the NASA-TLX overall workload score. However, the AHP method is a very time-consuming one and appears to offer no advantage over the TLX.

WORKLOAD AND STRESS

The widely accepted transactional view of occupational stress has much in common with the ergonomics workload construct, according to which stress is "a perceptual phenomenon arising from a comparison between the demand on the person and his ability to cope . . . an imbalance in this mechanism, when coping is important, gives rise to the experience of stress, and to stress response" (22, p. 25).

For both workload and stress, the balance, or fit, between demands made on someone and that person's ability to cope with the demands plays a key role, as shown by comparing Figure 6.1 with the above definition of stress. In the case of stress, the demand side of the equation encompasses a somewhat wider range of factors than in the case of workload, although many of the job-related stressors are also determinants of job workload. On the other hand, the experience of workload has been operationally defined to incorporate affective states such as stress or frustration, as discussed earlier (although I argue below that incorporating affective states within "workload" is undesirable).

The key role of various types of task and job demands in relation to occupational stress is recognized by the ISO's papers on mental workload (39, 40), although its treatment of the topic largely conflates the concepts of mental workload and stress/strain. Gaillard wrote, "Macroconcepts, such as mental load [workload] and stress, are often confounded because they refer to similar phenomena and are used interchangeably in daily life" (69, p. 623). He argues that despite their evident similarities and overlaps, they should not be regarded as synonymous: "A proper distinction among these concepts is not only important for theory building but also for the reconstruction of the work environment." Figure 6.2 presents a conceptual framework that is intended to clarify this distinction and to provide a clear basis for developing more satisfactory methods of assessing job workload.

This framework retains as its focus the ergonomics concept of workload depicted in Figure 6.1, although in Figure 6.2 the individual's fit is not just with task demands, which are still centrally important, but *also* with broader job demands, with the workplace environment, and with additional influences from within and outside the work organization. Workload is depicted in Figure 6.1 as the total of all elements in the diagram, consistent with definitions such as that of Kantowitz and with operational definitions such as the structure of the NASA-TLX measurement technique; that is, workload incorporates within it performance costs and gains, including stress. In Figure 6.2, however, the workload experience is shown as a hypothetical construct resulting from the fit between individual and job demand factors, but *not* incorporating either positive or negative affect. In terms of the six NASA-TLX dimensions, the three demand dimensions and the effort dimension are retained, but the frustration/stress and performance success/satisfaction dimensions of workload are considered here as possible concomitant or resultant states, rather than inherently part of the workload experience. Intuitively, this departure from previous, more inclusive conceptions seems defensible, and it certainly reduces the gap between our everyday understanding of workload and the more specific meaning defined here.

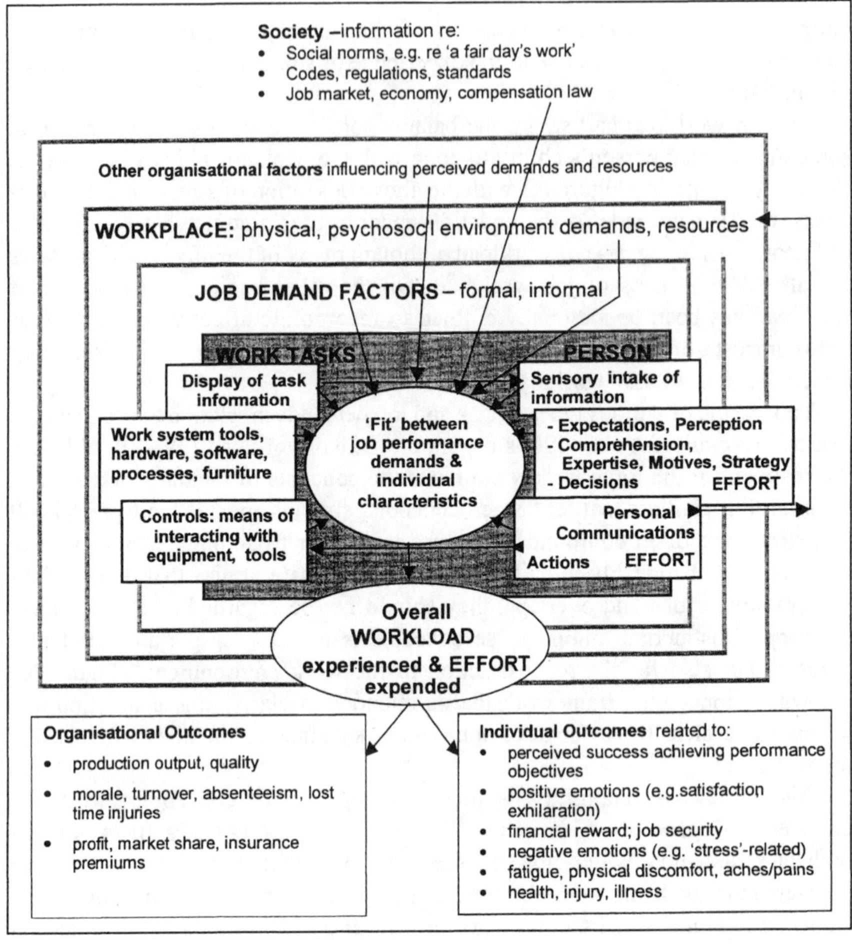

Figure 6.2 A conceptual framework for identifying determinants of job workload.

There are additional, more specific reasons for the narrower conception of workload presented in Figure 6.2. It provides a clearer conceptual framework for research to elucidate the complex and poorly documented relationships between workload and associated constructs, including stress; related to this, it provides a more useful framework for analyzing and developing solutions to the practical workplace questions about workload raised at the beginning of this chapter. It also removes the need to measure affective states as part of workload measurement (as in the TLX and SWAT methods), which is desirable given the existing methods that will do this more effectively. For ergonomists interested in workload measurement in the context of job performance issues (rather than related to more specific task or equipment issues), this framework emphasizes the possible importance of broader, system issues. Finally, for those whose primary interest is in workplace stress, it highlights the potential significance of specific task demands in addition to broader workload issues.

WORKLOAD DETERMINANTS AND OCCUPATIONAL STRESSORS

Task Demands

The Figure 6.2 framework highlights the central importance to our experience of job-related workload of the tasks we are required to perform. Task demands are a product of the amount and difficulty of work that has to be performed per unit time in relation to individual coping characteristics, including both their information-processing and physical capacities. They are moderated by the effects of work-station and equipment design, design of work processes in terms of the imposed time pressures and other constraints, immediate consequences of errors or inaccuracies, and so on.

This type of demand is typical of those considered in ergonomics task analyzes, for example in a recent study of work-rate standards for assembly line tasks in the manufacturing industry (see Chapter 7). Specific task factors can be categorized as follows; their common defining characteristic is that they require increased effort expenditure (above rest) of some kind, and hence are contributors to workload:

- *Sensory/perceptual factors*: form of stimulus-information coding; compatibility between stimulus-information coding/format and person's mental model(s); number of sources of stimulus information; stimulus uncertainty (number of possible types of stimuli and their relative probabilities); rate of occurrence of stimuli; predictability of time/place of stimulus occurrence
- *Decision/memory factors:* required decision rate; decision complexity (based on clarity of relevant issues, clarity of their interrelationships); demands on memory (short term and long term); decision information (uncertainty resolved per decision); attention-sharing between different sources of information, different activities; concentrated attention; care to avoid errors or to get things exactly right, especially when errors or poor quality output can have major consequences; repetitiveness, short cycle times: monotononous, de-arousing
- *Affective factors*: hiding own feelings, presenting required feelings, such as dealing with situations that would normally be extremely distressing, or with people who are hurt, upset, or angry
- *Interpersonal factors*: communicating with others during course of work performance in ways required to maintain appropriate social relationships (some overlap likely with affective factors)

- *Psychomotor factors*: response uncertainty (number of possible types of responses and their relative probabilities); predictability of time of required response; response precision (target "tolerance" in relation to distance moved); compatibility between required response and relevant mental model; required response rate; repetitiveness—short cycle time, small number of different action components—risk of "overuse" injuries (overlap with decision/memory factors, and physical factors)
- *Physical factors*: significant force, such as lifting, pushing, pulling; significant local force, such as gripping, squeezing, trigger; physical effort causing faster breathing; postures that are awkward and so require increased effort, such as twisting, bending; static postures including standing still, sitting, and holding arms in set positions such as at a keyboard

Job Demand Factors

Moving from task demands to broader job demands, we enter the domain of occupational stress, since most stress measurement scales that incorporate stressors include "job demand" as one of the potential stressors. However, with the focus on stress rather than stressors there has been comparatively little analysis or research on the particular aspects of work that are most appropriately categorized as job demands. Varied terminology is used, such as "workload" (referring to the amount and difficulty of work; 16); "work pressure" (70); "job pressure" (15); "cognitive demands," "quantitative job demands" (71); "psychological demands and mental workload," "physical demands" (14).

A wide range of recent research substantiates the importance of job demands (both cognitive and physical) as a predictor of employee stress and related health problems, including musculoskeletal disorders (e.g., 8–10, 15, 72–76). In the case of the latter, most research interest has focused on the role of specific physical demand factors, but a large body of evidence now indicates that psychological demands, and stress itself, can also be important risk factors (e.g., 14, 77–81). The nature of causal mechanisms underlying such associations is poorly understood, but there is an evident need to recognize the possible roles of both physical and psychological work demands in relation both to physical overuse injuries and to stress.

A second important set of job factors that can act as workplace stressors relate to "control"; many of the studies cited in the above paragraph have shown level of control to predict stress levels and related health problems. Control is less directly related to workload than is demand. However, according to one account of the mechanism that relates increased control to reduced stress, a higher level of control enables people to take actions to reduce actual or potential stressors (82). Hockey and colleagues (83) presented a control model of stress regulation that explained this mechanism specifically in terms of people being able to gain greater control over their workload level by providing access to alternative performance strategies—for example, decreasing demand to avoid stressfully high workloads, or increasing demand to avoid stressful boredom—and by providing access to additional coping resources of various kinds, again to avoid stressfully high workloads. This view of the relationship between control and workload is consistent with more recent research showing that when the effects of different types of control are analyzed separately, higher levels of instrumental control (relating to influence over task factors such as amount and rate of work, which would directly influence workload) are related to lower levels of "work pressure," whereas higher levels of decision control (relating to influence over organizational processes, procedures, and policies, which might be associated with greater responsibilities without any counteracting decrease in demand) are related to higher work pressure (69).

The third major category of stress-related job factors are those affecting "support." The original demand/control model of Karasek and coworkers was modified by addition of a third dimension, "social support" (84), based on the hypothesis (confirmed in some but not all studies) that "jobs which are high in demands, low in control, and also low in social support at work carry the highest risk of illness" (14). More recently, the importance of support mechanisms in relation to stress was demonstrated by a factor analysis of responses to the Job Stress Survey (15), from which two factors emerged: job pressure and organizational support. Within the Figure 6.2 framework showing job demands as workload determinants, support is a job factor that can reduce workload either by reducing task demands or by increasing resources to cope with existing demands, whether through instrumental or affective support (e.g., 14, 75, 85). Consistent with this, Van Der Doef and Maes (86) concluded from their major review of research evidence, "Only aspects of job control that correspond to the specific demands of a given job moderate the impact of high demands on well-being." Such findings emphasize the importance of analyzing the specific demands of particular jobs, in order to manage workload, stress, and well-being more effectively.

Instrumental support might reduce task demands by, for example, improving the availability and/or quality of various types of supportive resources, such as equipment, adequate staffing level, helpful supervisors, and management policies that facilitate work performance. Affective or interpersonal support would tend to increase morale, which might increase individuals' maximum "willing to spend" effort level, thus increasing their coping capacity and reducing their perceived workload level. It might also be associated with workload reduction due to the provision of informal, instrumental support, particularly during brief peaks in demand levels. Provision of performance feedback can function both as affective or interpersonal support and as instrumental support, in that it conveys information that can be used to "fine-tune" performance strategies with consequent improved performance and reduced effort expenditure and hence workload; this has been shown in a laboratory vigilance task for which workload was measured by the TLX (87).

It is possible that the personal "reward" value of some types of support might reduce imbalance in the effort/reward equation, which would be expected to reduce stress levels (88), and, depending on the nature of the work and available strategies, this might produce flow-on effects leading to reduced workload. More generally, the satisfaction experienced in relation to performance of jobs with high "motivating potential" (89) might also have some reward value in this sense, although such jobs can also be more demanding, to the extent that their motivating potential is derived from high levels of task variety and autonomy. There is a need for empirical data on these relationships.

Job role clarity, ambiguity, and conflict are recognized stressors that have the potential to affect workload through their effects on energy expenditure level, and on selection of performance strategies, to an extent dependent on their interaction with other factors such as job insecurity. For example, someone who is unclear about how much work she is expected to complete, and to what standard, and who is anxious about the possibility of losing her job, may expend more effort in producing a larger amount and/or higher quality of work than otherwise.

Other job factors with significant implications for workload include working hours and shift-system design. In addition to the demands of work performance at particular points in time, job demands are determined by the total time worked—the duration of "exposure" to task and job demands—and the opportunities for recovery from accumulated fatigue. Fatigue tends to increase workload in accordance with the associated reduction in coping capacity, although changes in performance strategy may offset such effects, at least partially.

Workplace Environment and Additional Organizational Influences

A wide variety of work environmental/organization factors might affect workload, directly or indirectly. Employee perceptions of organizational values and expectations regarding acceptable work practices and the quantity and quality of work performance are likely to affect performance strategies and effort expenditure, and thus to affect workload.

Some environmental influences are not clearly delineated from job factors. A supervisor, for example, might instrumentally support an employee's task performance by arranging for the timely provision of new equipment (job factor level), while also contributing to low job satisfaction through poor interpersonal skills that generate interpersonal conflicts (organizational level). Similarly, noisy machinery might make it more difficult for its operators to communicate with others in the vicinity and to make complex decisions; for them, this could be categorized as a direct job demand. For other people, more distant from the source of noise, it might be categorized as an aspect of their general environment affecting their general "arousal level" and perhaps their mood. Both effects would have the potential, to a greater or lesser degree, to affect workload and stress.

Influences from Outside the Work Organization

The influence of social norms and values concerning "a fair day's work" is likely to affect many aspects of work performance and workload. More formally, legislation regarding specific "risky" or highly demanding work practices (e.g., heavy lifting, work in high temperatures) can be expected to affect the workloads of people performing such work. More general factors such as perceived job security, and the low availability of alternative employment, may influence people's workload. The suggested mechanism here is that people feeling insecure in their job will perceive the potential cost to them of inadequate work performance as higher than otherwise; this might motivate them to invest more effort in their work performance (thus increasing workload), as well as increasing their anxiety level. Finally, individual employee variables, such as levels of both nonwork demands and supportive resources external to the workplace, are recognized as factors likely to affect people's capacity to cope with workplace demands and hence affect their workload within this ergonomics framework.

PRACTICAL UTILITY OF THE WORKLOAD CONSTRUCT IN WORKPLACE APPLICATIONS

At the beginning of this chapter, I raised a series of questions on how workload should be managed as part of a proactive approach to stress management: for example, how should we assess the impact on people's workloads of the introduction of new equipment or work systems? On what basis should we determine required staffing levels when organizations are restructured? How should workload levels be related to working hours, rest breaks, and shift systems? I argue here that these questions can most effectively be addressed by (*a*) directly assessing both *workload* levels and levels of *task, job, and environmental demand and support factors,* and (*b*) determining relationships between workload, demand and support factors, and *a range of employee outcomes*, including positive affect as well as stress-related negative affect, fatigue, and related somatic states. These points are discussed below.

The ergonomics workload construct is well established and can be clearly defined and assessed separately from work task demands. This construct has proven its usefulness in the processes of developing and evaluating a wide range of equipment, systems, and related work tasks, typically with the aim of optimizing task demands on operators and thus maximizing performance quality and system efficiency. Workload evaluations are now routinely conducted during system design and development in many safety-critical or "high technology" operations, where, somewhat paradoxically, increasing levels of automation do not necessarily result in reduced workload (e.g., see 51, 90–92). In environments such as aircraft flight decks or nuclear power station control rooms, analysis of workload is accepted as necessary both to optimize equipment and system design and to determine required numbers of crew or staff. In workplaces that have no particular risk of catastrophic failure, evaluations of employee workloads in this sense are rare.

I argue here that the wider, more explicit application of the ergonomics workload construct has considerable potential value to researchers and practitioners in the domains of industrial engineering, workplace health and safety, and human resource management more generally. In particular, I suggest that occupational stress and associated problems would be more effectively managed within such a framework. In particular, it would focus greater attention on the role of specific task demands as workload determinants, thus providing a better basis for the development of appropriate "supports." To set standard work rates that are both equitable and efficient, identification and assessment of specific task demands is likely to be essential (see Chapter 7). Task demand analysis is also important for purposes such as establishing appropriate staffing levels, optimizing system interface design, and determining various aspects of job design such as shift rosters and rest-break regimens (e.g., 51, 55, 93, 94).

I suggest that, even when stress prevention or management is the primary objective, a workload framework is a more useful basis for dealing with stress than the occupational stress frameworks that provide the conceptual basis for assessment of job demands in most workplace studies. A workload framework is also more useful in dealing with a range of other, more performance-oriented workplace issues such as staffing levels and work rates. Stress is only one of several negative outcomes that may occur if workload levels are not managed appropriately. As shown in Figure 6.2, at the individual level fatigue is another outcome; increased fatigue is a direct outcome of effort expenditure, which in turn is directly related to workload level. Fatigue has the potential to impair performance in many ways, including a higher rate of mistakes, omissions, and more subtle temporal disturbances to performance; a narrower focus of attention, with decreased capacity for complex or creative decision-making; the adoption of more effort-conserving strategies, which are likely to be less proactive and to entail higher levels of risk-taking (leading to inefficient work scheduling, inappropriate crisis management, and decreased innovation); and increased levels of negative emotions (see 29, 44). Such fatigue-mediated effects on performance may manifest themselves in increased organizational costs related to accidents and associated costs including lost-time injuries and insurance premiums, higher absenteeism, reduced product or service quality, and lower productivity.

Consistent with the above account, fatigue and stress are depicted in Figure 6.2 as possible individual outcomes of workload, with concurrent effects on organizational functioning; a range of potentially *positive* outcomes is also shown. Individuals' workload may be affected by their perception of their success in achieving performance objectives (e.g., 42), and in the NASA-TLX workload measurement tool this factor is combined with performance-related satisfaction to form a single TLX scale. However, I argue here that the role of positive affective states, such as someone's satisfaction with his own performance, is sufficiently important to warrant its separate assessment in most workplace applications. I argue further that affective states should not be operationally defined as part of the workload construct, since this can obscure important underlying relationships. For example, Upsdell found in a study of rehabilitation counselors that while the TLX overall workload score (average of TLX scales) was not related to measures of stress (including vocational strain from the Occupational Stress Inventory [95] and measures of "burnout": emotional exhaustion, depersonalization, personal accomplishment [96]), the TLX frustration subscale was strongly correlated with vocational strain, emotional exhaustion, and personal accomplishment. In addition, the TLX mental demand scale was *negatively* correlated with these other "stress" measures and with general satisfaction from the Job Diagnostic Survey (89).

It is likely that relationships between workload and affective states, both positive and negative, are mediated by the context in which work is performed. This has been suggested by studies of jobs such as nursing and policing, which typically expose people to relatively high levels of physical and emotional demands. For example, McIntosh (20) found in a study of nurses that "exhilaration" was an important factor related to their work performance, and that jobs rated high in exhilaration provided significant protection against burnout. Discussing reasons for such findings, McIntosh invoked the concept of "edgework," from Lyng (97), "who suggested that edge-work—carried out on the border between order and chaos and reflecting both psychological and contextual factors—provides workers in dangerous occupations a sensation of being in control" (20, p. 314). Accepting this interpretation, one might suggest that workload itself would be modified by such positive feelings, mediated by the perception of enhanced control and hence a perceived increase in coping capacity. There is a need for research to explore demands that are inherent in such work in relation to both contextual and individual factors and, importantly, in relation to performance quality.

Someone who is generally satisfied with his job may find a high workload more acceptable than someone who is not, and may be willing to invest higher levels of effort, perhaps resulting in improved performance. Workload acceptability is also likely to be influenced by the context. I have suggested elsewhere that employees' frustration with some types of increased demands was moderated by their perception that management could have eliminated the demand—that it was avoidable (51). On the other hand, emergency service workers do not resent working at near-maximal levels for some of the time, since this is an inherent, unavoidable part of the job. To take another example, having to work harder or faster to meet deadlines is typically defined as part of "work pressure" and thus associated with increased stress. However, in the context of repetitive and seemingly monotonous assembly line work, the increased demand associated with deadlines was associated with lower stress (see Chapter 7).

Even if people are generally satisfied with their jobs and accept high demands as unavoidable, near-maximal effort is unlikely to be sustainable for extended periods without the development of high levels of fatigue and significant performance decrements. The requirement to maintain performance despite significant fatigue would be expected to induce high stress levels, but there is a paucity of research evidence of relationships between clearly defined and measured task demands, workload levels, fatigue, and stress. In order to better understand such undoubtedly complex relationships, I have argued here that a focus *only* on stress is unhelpful—that both positive and negative affective states related to work performance also need to be considered. Employees' positive and negative affective states influence stress very directly, but can also influence workload *level,* employee perceptions of workload *acceptability,* and the quantity and quality of work performance.

Further, to facilitate effective management of occupational stress and to achieve or maintain performance standards, it is important to retain clear distinctions between objective task/job demand factors and the workload that people experience. Current frameworks for addressing occupational stress give virtually no attention to workload, although the framework proposed here has some conceptual overlap with Siegrist's effort-reward imbalance model of stress causation (88), in that "extrinsic work pressures" (incorporating task and job demands) are conceptualized as what drives "effort" (a central component of workload), with stress occurring when there is a lack of reciprocity between effort and potential rewards. This argument has something in common with that of Eriksen and Ursin (76), who emphasized the importance of "coping" with demands rather than "control" over them. The extent to which individuals cope, or feel that they are coping, with their work demands, is a key determinant of their perceived workload. However, Eriksen and Ursin defined and measured coping in terms of coping capacities and styles, rather than success in coping per se.

As depicted in Figure 6.2, the present workload approach focuses on the task and job factors with which employees have to cope, and I argue that measures of these factors, along with resultant workload levels, would be better predictors of employee well-being (encompassing both positive and negative affective states) than the more commonly measured job demands or work pressures. The present model highlights the potentially important role of specific task demands, rather than more general job demands. The significance of both task demands and workload levels in relation to stress, arousal, and fatigue is described in Chapter 7.

REFERENCES

1. Wright, C., and Lund, J. Best practice Taylorism: "Yankee speed up" in Australian grocery distribution. *J. Ind. Relations* 38: 196–212, 1996.

2. Lund, J., and Wright, C. Computer Monitoring and Scientific Management in Grocery Warehousing: A Comparative Case Study of Management Strategy and Union Response in the Unites States and Australia. Paper presented at the Globalisation of Production and Regulation of Labour Conference, University of Warwick, U.K., September 11–13, 1996.
3. O'Donnell, M. Work intensification, female NESB workers, public hospital and contracting out. In *Work Intensification: The Darker Side of Workplace Reform.* Workplace Studies Centre, Victoria University, Melbourne, 1997.
4. Cooper, C. L. Introduction. In *Theories of Organizational Stress,* edited by C. L. Cooper, pp. 1–5. Oxford University Press, Oxford, 1998.
5. ACTU Occupational Health and Safety Unit. *A Report on the ACTU 1997 National OHS Survey on "Stress at Work."* Australian Council of Trade Unions, Melbourne, April 1998.
6. Charyszyn, S., and Tucker, P. New light on working hours. *Ergonomist,* May 2001.
7. U.S. Department of Labor. *Are Managers and Professionals Really Working More?* Issues in Labor Statistics, Summary 00-12. Bureau of Labor Statistics, Washington, D.C., May 2000.
8. Cox, T., Griffiths, A., and Rial-Gonzalez, E. *Research on Work-Related Stress.* European Agency for Safety and Health at Work, 2000. http://agency.osha.eu.int/publications/reports/stress/.
9. Cooper, C. L., Dewe, P. J., and O'Driscoll, M. P. *Organizational Stress: A Review and Critique of Theory, Research, and Applications.* Sage, London, 2001.
10. Paoli, P., and Merllie, D. *Third European Survey on Working Conditions 2000.* European Foundation for the Improvement of Living and Working Conditions, Dublin, 2001.
11. Kirwan, B., and Ainsworth, L. K. (eds.). *A Guide to Task Analysis.* Taylor and Francis, London, 1992.
12. Wilson, J. R., and Corlett, E. N. (eds.). *Evaluation of Human Work,* Ed. 2. Taylor and Francis, London, 1995.
13. Salvendy, G. (ed.). *Handbook of Human Factors and Ergonomics.* Wiley, New York, 1997.
14. Karasek, R., et al. The Job Content Questionnaire (JCQ): An instrument for internationally comparative assessments of psychosocial job characteristics. *J. Occup. Health Psychol.* 3: 322–356, 1998.
15. Vagg, P. R., and Spielberger, C. D. Occupational stress: Measuring job pressure and organizational support in the workplace. *J. Occup. Health Psychol.* 3: 294–305, 1998.
16. Williams, S., and Cooper, C. L. Measuring occupational stress: Development of the pressure management indicator. *J. Occup. Health Psychol.* 3: 306–321, 1998.
17. Macdonald, W., and Upsdell, T. Measuring job-related mental workload—Or should that be stress? In *Proceedings of the 1996 National Occupational Stress Conference: Health and Well-Being in a Changing Work Environment.* Australian Academic Press, Brisbane, 1996.
18. Payne, R. L, and Morrison, D. The importance of knowing the affective meaning of job demands revisited. *Work Stress* 13: 280–288, 1999.
19. Warr, P. B. Decision latitude, job demands, and employee well-being. *Work Stress* 4: 285–294, 1990.

20. McIntosh, N. J. Exhilarating work: An antidote for dangerous work? In *Organizational Risk Factors for Job Stress,* edited by S. L. Sayter and L. R. Murphy, pp. 303–316. American Psychological Association, Washington, D.C., 1995.
21. Leiter, M. The Impact on Staff Members of a Hospital Merger in Dublin. Paper presented to APA-NIOSH Conference on Work, Stress, and Health '99: Organization of Work in a Global Economy, Baltimore, March 1999.
22. Cox, T. *Stress.* Macmillan, Basingstoke, U.K., 1978.
23. Hancock, P. A., and Warm, J. S. A dynamic model of stress and sustained attention. *Hum. Factors* 31: 519–537, 1989.
24. Huey, B. M., and Wickens, C. D. (eds.). Workload Transition: Implications for Individual and Team Performance. National Academy Press, Washington, D.C., 1993.
25. Moray, N. (ed.). *Mental Workload: Its Theory and Measurement.* Plenum, New York, 1979.
26. Moray, N. Mental workload since 1979. *Int. Rev. Ergonomics* 2: 123–150, 1988.
27. Hancock, P. A., and Meshkati, N. (eds.). *Human Mental Workload.* North Holland, Amsterdam, 1988.
28. Xie, B., and Salvendy, G. Review and reappraisal of modelling and predicting mental workload in single- and multi-task environments. *Work Stress* 14: 74–99, 2000.
29. Hancock, P. A., and Desmond, P. A. *Stress, Workload and Fatigue.* Lawrence Erlbaum, Mahwah, N.J., 2001.
30. Mowbray, G. H. Simultaneous vision and audition: The comprehension of prose passages with varying levels of difficulty. *J. Exp. Psychol.* 46: 365–372, 1953.
31. Broadbent, D. E. *Perception and Communication.* Pergamon Press, London, 1958.
32. Fitts, P. M., and Posner, M. I. *Human Performance.* Brooks Cole, Belmont, Calif., 1967.
33. Welford, A. T. Single-channel operation in the brain. *Acta Psychol.* 27: 5–22, 1967.
34. Kahneman, D. *Attention and Effort.* Prentice-Hall, Englewood Cliffs, N.J., 1973.
35. Gopher, D., and Donchin, E. Workload—An examination of the concept. In *Handbook of Perception and Human Performance,* edited by K. R. Boff, L. Kaufman, and J. P. Thomas, Vol. II, pp. 41.1–41.49. Wiley, New York, 1986.
36. Jex, H. R. Measuring mental workload: Problems, progress and promises. In *Human Mental Workload,* edited by P. A. Hancock and N. Meshkati, pp. 5–39. North Holland, Amsterdam, 1988.
37. Kalsbeek, J. W. H. Measurement of mental work load and of acceptable load. *Int. J. Production Res.* 7(1): 33–45, 1968.
38. Kantowitz, B. H. Mental workload. In *Human Factors Psychology,* edited by P. A. Hancock, pp. 81–121. North Holland, Amsterdam, 1987.
39. International Standards Organization. *Ergonomic Principles Related to Mental Workload—General Terms and Definitions.* ISO 10 075. Geneva, 1991.
40. International Standards Organization. *Ergonomic Principles Related to Mental Workload—Part 2: Design Principles.* ISO 10 075-2. Geneva, 1994.
41. Nachreiner, F. Standards for ergonomics principles relating to the design of work systems and to mental workload. *Appl. Ergonomics* 26: 259–263, 1995.
42. Hart, S. G., and Staveland, L. E. Development of the NASA-TLX. In *Human Mental Workload,* edited by P. A. Hancock and N. Meshkati, pp. 139–183. North Holland, Amsterdam, 1988.

43. Wierwille, W. W., Rahimi, M., and Casali, J. G. Evaluation of 16 measures of mental workload using a simulated flight task emphasizing mediational activity. *Hum. Factors* 27: 489–502, 1985.
44. Matthews, G., et al. *Human Performance: Cognition, Stress, and Individual Differences.* Psychology Press, Hove, U.K., 2000.
45. Salvendy, G., and Smith, M. J. (eds.). *Machine Pacing and Occupational Stress.* Taylor and Francis, London, 1981.
46. Carayon, P. A longitudinal test of Karasek's job strain model among office workers. *Work Stress* 7: 299–314, 1993.
47. Burke, R. J. Organizational-level interventions to reduce occupational stressors. *Work Stress* 7: 77–87, 1993.
48. Marsella, A. J. The measurement of emotional reactions to work: Conceptual, methodological, and research issues. *Work Stress* 8: 153–176, 1994.
49. Siegrist, J., and Peter, R. Job stressors and coping characteristics in work-related disease: Issues of validity. *Work Stress* 8: 130–140, 1994.
50. Welford, A. T. *Skilled Performance: Perceptual and Motor Skills.* Scott, Foresman, Glenview, Ill., 1976.
51. Macdonald, W. A. Train controllers, interface design and mental workload. In *People in Control,* edited by J. M. Noyes and M. L. Bransby, pp. 239–258. IEE Press, Stevenage, U.K., 2001.
52. Meshkati, N. Toward development of a cohesive model of workload. In *Human Mental Workload,* edited by P. A. Hancock and N. Meshkati, pp. 305–314. North Holland, Amsterdam, 1988.
53. Macdonald, W. A. *Factors Influencing V-Sort "Throwing Off" Rates: Report to Australia Post.* Centre for Ergonomics and Human Factors, Faculty of Health Sciences, La Trobe University, Melbourne, October 1999.
54. ACTU. ACTU Code of Conduct on Twelve Hour Shift Work. *Health Safety Bull.* 58, December 1988.
55. Macdonald, W., and Bendak, S. Effects of workload and 8- versus 12-h workday duration on test battery performance. *Int. J. Ind. Ergonomics* 26: 399–416, 2000.
56. Kogi, K. Job content and working time: The scope for joint change. *Ergonomics* 34: 757–773, 1991.
57. Pollock, C., Cross, R., and Taylor, P. Influences of 12- versus 8-hour shiftwork on injury patterns. In *Proceedings of the 12th Triennial Congress of the International Ergonomics Association,* Vol. 5, pp. 19–21, Toronto, 1994.
58. Rosa, R. R. Extended workshifts and excessive fatigue. *J. Sleep Res.* 4(Suppl. 2): 51–56, 1995.
59. Wallace, M., and Greenwood, K. Twelve-hour shifts (editorial). *Work Stress* 9: 105–108, 1995.
60. Freund, L. E. Measuring the difficulty of nursing assignments. In *Human Factors in Health Care,* edited by R. M. Pickett and T. J. Triggs, pp. 211–235. Lexington Books, Lexington, Mass., 1975.
61. Russell, A. B. *Faculty Workload: State and System Perspectives.* Education Commission of the States, State Higher Education Executive Officers, Denver, Colo., November 1992.

62. Canada, Health Services Directorate, Health Services and Promotion Branch. *Operating Room Workload Measurement System and Staffing Methodology.* Health and Welfare Canada, Ottawa, 1985.
63. O'Bryan, S. J., Macdonald, W. A., and Evans, O. M. A comparison of some workload analysis techniques. In *Proceedings of the 27th Annual Conference of the Ergonomics Society of Australia,* pp. 139–147. Ergonomics Society of Australia, Canberra, 1991. www.ergonomics.org.au.
64. So, C., and Mert-Iljin, V. Measuring Mental Workload in an Occupational Setting. Research project conducted in partial fulfillment of the requirements of the Graduate Diploma in Ergonomics, La Trobe University, Melbourne, 1990.
65. Upsdell, T. *Occupational Burnout, Stress, Mental Workload, and Job Satisfaction among Rehabilitation Counsellors.* Research project conducted in partial fulfillment of the requirements of the Graduate Diploma in Ergonomics, La Trobe University, Melbourne, 1994.
66. Alteras-Webb, S., and Dekker, D. K. Measuring perceived task difficulty using magnitude estimation: A demonstration and replication. In *Proceedings of the Human Factors and Ergonomics Society 38th Annual Meeting,* pp. 335–339. Human Factors and Ergonomics Society, Santa Monica, Calif., 1994.
67. Jung, H. S., and Jung, H.-S. Establishment of overall workload assessment technique for various tasks and workplaces. *Int. J. Ind. Ergonomics* 28: 341–353, 2001.
68. Saaty, T. *The Analytic Hierarchy Process.* McGraw-Hill, New York, 1980.
69. Gaillard, A. W. K. Stress, workload, and fatigue as three biobehavioral states: A general overview. In *Stress, Workload, and Fatigue,* edited by P. A. Hancock and P. A. Desmond, pp. 623–639. Lawrence Erlbaum, Mahwah, N.J., 2001.
70. Carayon, P., and Zijlstra, F. Relationship between job control, work pressure and strain: Studies in the USA and in the Netherlands. *Work Stress* 13: 32–48, 1999.
71. Hurrell, J. J., and McLaney, M. A. Control, job demands, and job satisfaction. In *Job Control and Worker Health,* edited by S. L. Sauter, J. J. Hurrell, and C. L. Cooper, pp. 97–103. Wiley, Chichester, U.K., 1988.
72. Ganster, D. C., Hurrell, J. J., and Thomas, L. T. Development of a scale to assess occupational cognitive demands. In *Social, Ergonomic, and Stress Aspects of Work with Computers,* edited by G. Salvendy, S. L. Sauter, and J. J. Hurrell. Elsevier, Amsterdam, 1987.
73. Karasek, R., and Theorell, T. *Healthy Work: Stress, Productivity, and the Reconstruction of Working Life.* Basic Books, New York, 1990.
74. Kasl, S. V. Measuring job stressors and strains: Where we have been, where we are, and where we need to go. *J. Occup. Health Psychol.* 3: 390–409, 1998.
75. Theorell, T. Job characteristics in a theoretical and practical health context. In *Theories of Organizational Stress,* edited by C. L. Cooper, pp. 205–219. Oxford University Press, Oxford, 1998.
76. Eriksen, H. R., and Ursin, H. Subjective health complaints: Is coping more important than control? *Work Stress* 13: 238–252, 1999.
77. Andries, F., Kompier, M. A. J., and Smulders, P. G. W. Do you think that your health or safety are at risk because of your work? A large European study on psychological and physical work demands. *Work Stress* 10: 104–118, 1996.
78. Bernard, B. P. (ed.). *Musculoskeletal Disorders (MSDs) and Workplace Factors.* National Institute of Occupational Safety and Health, Cincinnati, 1997.

79. Devereux, J. J., and Buckle, P. W. Adverse work stress—A review of the potential influence on work related musculoskeletal disorders. In *Proceedings of the IEA 2000/HFES 2000 Congress,* Vol. 5, pp. 457–460. Human Factors and Ergonomics Society, Santa Monica, Calif., 2000.
80. Devereux, J. J., and Buckle, P. The risk of neck, shoulder and upper limb musculoskeletal disorders due to interactions between physical and psychosocial work risk factors. In *Proceedings of the IEA 2000/HFES 2000 Congress,* Vol. 5, p. 597. Human Factors and Ergonomics Society, Santa Monica, Calif., 2000.
81. Evans, O., and Patterson, K. Predictors of neck and shoulder pain in non-secretarial computer users. *Int. J. Ind. Ergonomics* 26: 357–365, 2000.
82. Frese, M. Theoretical models of control and health. In *Job Control and Worker Health,* edited by S. L. Sauter, C. L. Cooper, and J. J. Hurrell, pp. 107–128. Wiley, Chichester, U.K., 1989.
83. Hockey, G. R., et al. Assessing the impact of computer workload on operator stress: The role of system controllability. *Ergonomics* 32: 1401–1418, 1989.
84. Johnson, J. V., and Hall, E. M. Job strain, workplace social support, and cardiovascular disease: A cross-sectional study of a random sample of the Swedish working population. *Am. J. Public Health* 78: 1336–1342, 1988.
85. Greller, M. M., Pasons, C. K., and Mitchell, D. R. D. Additive effects and beyond: Occupational stressors and social buffers in a police organization. In *Stress and Well-being at Work: Assessments and Interventions for Occupational Mental Health,* edited by J. C. Quick, L. R. Murphy, and J. J. Hurrell, pp. 33–47. American Psychological Association, Washington, D.C., 1992.
86. Van Der Doef, M., and Maes, S. The job demand-control-support model and psychological well-being: A review of 20 years of empirical research. *Work Stress* 13: 87–114, 1999.
87. Becker, A. B., Warm, J. S., and Dember, W. N. Effects of feedback on perceived workload in vigilance performance. In *Proceedings of the Human Factors Society 35th Annual Meeting,* pp. 1491–1494. Santa Monica, Calif., 1991.
88. Siegrist, J. A. Adverse health effects of high-effort/low-reward conditions. *J. Occup. Health Psychol.* 1: 27–41, 1996.
89. Hackman, J. R., and Oldham, G. R. *Work Redesign.* Addison-Wesley, Reading, Mass., 1980.
90. Karwowski, W., et al. Human factors in manufacturing. In *Handbook of Human Factors and Ergonomics,* edited by G. Salvendy, pp. 1865–1925. Wiley, New York, 1997.
91. Moray, N. Human factors in process control. In *Handbook of Human Factors and Ergonomics,* edited by G. Salvendy, pp. 1944–1971. Wiley, New York, 1997.
92. Woods, D. D., Sarter, N., and Billings, C. Automation surprises. In *Handbook of Human Factors and Ergonomics,* edited by G. Salvendy, pp. 1926–1943. Wiley, New York, 1997.
93. Kantowitz, B. H., and Simsek, O. Secondary-task measures of driver workload. In *Stress, Workload, and Fatigue,* edited by P. A. Hancock and P. A. Desmond, pp. 395–408. Lawrence Erlbaum, Mahwah, N.J., 2001.
94. Mouloua, M., Hitt, J. M., and Deaton, J. Automation and workload in aviation systems. In *Stress, Workload, and Fatigue,* edited by P. A. Hancock and P. A. Desmond, pp. 334–350. Lawrence Erlbaum, Mahwah, N.J., 2001.

95. Osipow, S. H., and Spokane, A. R. *Occupational Stress Inventory (OSI).* Psychological Assessment Resources, Odessa, Fla., 1987.
96. Maslach, C., and Jackson, S. *Maslach Burnout Inventory Manual,* Ed. 2. Consulting Psychologists Press, Palo Alto, Calif., 1986.
97. Lyng, S. Edgework: A social psychological analysis of voluntary risk taking. *Am. J. Sociol.* 95: 851–886, 1990.
98. Proctor, R. W., and Van Zandt, T. *Human Factors in Simple and Complex Systems.* Allyn and Bacon, Boston, 1994.
99. Herbert, A. *Factors in the Perception of Work Difficulty.* Report from the Institute of Applied Psychology, No. 53. University of Stockholm, Stockholm, 1974.
100. Moray, N., and King, B. *Error as a Cause and Effect of Workload: Mental Workload as a Closed Loop System.* Department of Industrial Engineering, Working Paper No. 84-11, Toronto, 1984.

Chapter 7

WORK DEMANDS AND STRESS IN REPETITIVE BLUE-COLLAR WORK

Wendy A. Macdonald

Work demands often play a significant role in the generation of occupational stress (1–6). Demand levels are determined by the physical, cognitive, and emotional difficulty of specific work tasks, as well as by the total amount of work that must be performed within a given time period, and by broader job characteristics, as discussed in Chapter 6. My emphasis here is on the effects on employee stress levels of work demands related to work rates and performance pacing, as well as effects of specific task demands and perceived workload levels.

In this chapter I present information from a research project that documented and evaluated the formal and informal methods used to determine standard work rates or production targets within a sample of Australian work organizations. It focused particularly on employees performing repetitive work tasks, mostly in manufacturing industry. The project documented employees' evaluations of their required work rates and their levels of affective well-being (stress, arousal), and related these to various characteristics of the work: the factors "pacing" task performance; the nature and level of task difficulty; the level of employees' perceived control or participation in decision-making; and the quality of job design factors related to job satisfaction.

The project originated because of evidence that the formal methods sometimes used to set work rates for repetitive work tasks, including predetermined motion time systems (PMTS) such as Modapts (7),[1] may make insufficient allowance for task difficulty, resulting in required work rates being too high. There was also some prior evidence that work rates or targets are better accepted by workers who have participated in the process of setting their levels or who

[1] See the later section "Processes Used in Determining Work Rate" for a brief account of PMTS. Modapts is a simple form of PMTS, developed originally in Australia with the intention of its being usable by employees themselves; it is now applied in many countries.

have a greater sense of control over their workpace. Some of this background evidence is summarized below.

WORK DEMANDS AND STRESS

As work demands increase and the gap between demand levels and individual capacity to cope with the demands decreases, people need to expend increasingly more effort to maintain performance at an acceptable level, with an associated increase in their perceived workload (see Chapter 6). Work task demands include the various aspects of task difficulty—physical, mental, and emotional—as well as temporal constraints on performance and the sheer amount of work that has to be done within a specified time. These factors are interrelated: performing a larger amount of work in a given time requires a faster work rate, and the effort needed to achieve this is likely to be greater if the work is more difficult. Time pressure might also be influenced by the nature and extent of work "pacing," such as by a moving assembly line, and by having to meet orders or other deadlines. When work demands are either too high or too low in relation to people's performance capacities, workload levels will probably be experienced as excessively high or low, and stress is a likely outcome (see Chapter 6), although clear research evidence detailing these particular relationships is largely lacking.

Stress itself is associated with a higher incidence of various musculoskeletal disorders (8–10), despite the most commonly identified risk factors for such injuries being purely physical task demands such as high levels of repetitive movements; static, bending, or twisting postures; and the exertion of significant physical forces. There is also evidence of increased injury risk when work performance entails very precise movements at a fast rate (e.g., 11, 12). The use of PMTS in setting work rates takes account, to some extent, of the required level of precision, but there is some evidence that PMTSs are not always applied in a way that achieves this objective (13).

EMPLOYEE CONTROL, PARTICIPATION, AND STRESS

People's level of control over their own work performance is another potentially important factor likely to influence their stress levels (e.g., 1, 14–17; see Chapter 6). Stress is more likely when "individuals are constrained in the way they carry out their work and cope with its demands: they have little control over their work or how they cope with it" (18, p. 790).

The particular interest of the project presented here was in work *rate* and in how much control employees had over their own work, particularly the extent to which they could choose to vary their work rate over time (self-pacing), as opposed to having a pace imposed by external factors. Machine pacing such as by a moving assembly line imposes a high level of external control over the pace of work, minimizing opportunities for employees to decide when to speed up and when to slow down. Performance may also be paced by the operation of production systems in which subsequent stages, performed by different people, cannot commence until work on an earlier stage has been completed, thus imposing a series of performance deadlines; the product of each phase of the system must be made available in time to meet the need of the next phase. A specified daily production target imposes much less constraint than a moving assembly line, but imposes more than a weekly production target.

A high level of external pacing is generally associated with increased stress (see 19). For example, a comparison of machine-paced and self-paced jobs in a sawmill showed that machine pacing was associated with higher levels of catecholamines, a physiological indicator of increased stress (20). All forms of external pacing impose a specific rate of work, but it is important to note that this *rate* might be high or low: that is, a high level of external *pacing* does not necessarily impose a high work *rate.* Other influences on average work rate might be piece-work payment systems and, more subtly, social pressures that define "a fair day's work."

There is evidence that participation in setting the work rate may to some extent counteract the negative effects of "machine" or external pacing. In an experimental study by Johansson (21), two groups performed the same laboratory task at the same work rate. For one group the rate was self-selected, changeable every five minutes, while for the other group the rate was imposed on them (pairing subjects across groups). Those who selected their own work rate reported much lower levels of both effort and stress, despite both groups performing the same task at the same rate. There is also laboratory evidence that when people participate in setting their own performance goals or standards, particularly when they receive performance feedback, they are more highly motivated and their performance improves (see 22).

However, evidence on such effects among employees in industry is more limited. Using workers in a fish-processing plant who trimmed and sorted fish fillets, Shikdar and Das (22) investigated the effects on productivity of three production standards, all anchored to a standard (100 percent) rate calculated using a PMTS: "set 100 percent," "set 140 percent," and "self-selected hard" (specified as something higher than 100 percent that would be challenging—the average value selected was 120 percent). Conditions also varied according to whether or not participants received performance feedback and monetary incentives. Productivity during the one-week period of the experiment was better with a 120 percent self-selected standard than with the 140 percent imposed standard; apparently, people were able to work more effectively under the first condition. This might have been because they felt it was a more acceptable rate, so invested greater effort (see Chapter 6). It might also have been because, when confronted by the need to achieve an excessively difficult rate (140 percent), participants were more stressed and their performance capacity suffered as a consequence. Possible long-term effects of higher work rates on stress or health were not investigated in that study.

In some workplaces, participation entails giving employees full responsibility for applying a PMTS to set their own line speed. In addition to the motivational benefits of people having control over their own work, this ensures that "rebalancing" of the production line due to changed work processes and task times can be done immediately rather than forgotten or greatly delayed. If the person responsible for line rebalancing is someone who is less directly involved, such as a production engineer with a wide range of other responsibilities, then there is likely to be some delay before adjustments are made (23).

The broader benefits of employees participating in the general management of their own work and workplace have been well documented, particularly in terms of scores on the "control" dimension of the Karasek model (e.g., 4). There is also evidence of a more qualitative nature (e.g., 24–26). Optimizing levels of employee control and participation can be expected to result in improved job satisfaction and morale, yielding a range of organizational benefits (e.g., 27–29).

Typically, machine-paced work gives little job satisfaction. Such work is often simple and repetitious with short cycle times, which many people experience as highly monotonous and unsatisfying. This kind of work can be stressful (see 30). Shikdar and Das (22) noted, "Motivating workers, . . . especially in repetitive production tasks, remains a major concern. These tasks are viewed as monotonous, boring and unmotivating, resulting in reduced worker productivity." Employees in manufacturing environments commonly experience some social isolation due to high noise levels, which would be expected to reduce their coping capacity and resistance to stress. Such isolation means they are less likely to receive social support from colleagues, which also effectively reduces their capacity to cope and has been associated with increased stress (e.g., 1, 18, 31).

Overall then, there is greater risk of high stress and low job satisfaction when work tasks are highly repetitive and performance is externally paced. For this study, we hypothesized that such risks will increase if the rate at which work is paced is excessive in relation to the difficulty or demands of the work.

PROCESSES USED IN DETERMINING WORK RATE

The process of determining work rates needs to take adequate account of task difficulty and the other factors that affect overall workload, so that employees do not feel they have to work at an excessively high rate with resultant negative effects on stress, health, and productivity (e.g., 32, 33). The methods used to determine line speeds or production targets, and hence work rates, should also enable participation by the employees performing the work. Apart from its value in enhancing general job satisfaction, participation in determining the work rate may result in the rate itself being perceived as more acceptable and less stressful, even when the work is externally paced.

Work rate requirements may be determined by production managers or supervisors using informal guesstimate and trial. Alternatively, more formal methods may be used, such as Time Study, in which the times taken to perform the specific tasks in question are directly measured, or PMTS, in which the time required for task performance is calculated using standard times and formulas. PMTSs are based on an industrial engineering concept of "work measurement," entailing task analysis and identification of the standard time for each necessary step of the task, plus additional standard allowances for "personal" time and fatigue.

However, some evidence suggests that PMTS calculations take insufficient account of the physical and/or mental difficulty of work that is significantly more demanding than average (34–38). Also, one small-scale study found considerable variation between individual PMTS practitioners in the extent to which they allowed for varying task difficulty, with a general tendency to underestimate task demands (13).

The aim of this project was to evaluate the methods used to set work rates within a sample of Australian work organizations. I present some of the project team's findings, including analyses of work task and job characteristics in relation to employees' evaluations of required work rates and their levels of stress and arousal. Further details are reported elsewhere (39).

PROJECT OVERVIEW

We collected data during the late 1990s from 20 companies at 22 sites (two of the larger companies were represented by two worksites). The project had two main stages. In stage 1, information about tasks was collected by both direct observation and questionnaire; selected tasks were described and employee characteristics and perceptions documented. Stage 2 focused in more depth on a subset of these tasks, with more detailed analyzes of work demands, job design, stress, and job satisfaction, using a variety of formal methods outlined below.

All participating companies had one or more types of repetitive, short-cycle work tasks that were paced by the production process or by a production target, with several employees per task who spent a substantial part of their work time on that task and who were potentially available for interview. Support from relevant unions was obtained at this stage. Data were collected for about 82 work tasks. Questionnaires were administered, by personal interviews, to 37 production managers or supervisors, 12 staff with responsibility for occupational health and safety, and 186 employees familiar with the specific tasks nominated for investigation. Employees included 78 women and 108 men, with an average age of 39 years; between them, they reported speaking 43 languages and their birthplaces were distributed over 50 countries.

In stage 2, we collected more extensive data on a subset of 36 work tasks within ten of the companies. Two concurrent video recordings of each task being performed were made from fixed cameras at different angles, supplemented in most cases by a hand-held video camera/recorder. Based on these recordings, standard ergonomics techniques (or methods based on these) were used to determine postural demand, force demand, cardiovascular demand, and actual work rate. Interviews with employees performing these tasks provided more detailed information on their levels of workload, quality of job design, fatigue, and affective well-being.

CHARACTERISTICS OF THE WORK TASKS INVESTIGATED

Work Pacing and Work Rate Determinants

It became evident at a fairly early stage during the project that many companies had no formal methods or procedures for establishing standard work rates or production targets, and relatively few used any kind of formal method. In view of this, we implemented an additional selection criterion during the latter part of the project, requiring that the company used some type of formal method, such as some form of PMTS or Time Study. This requirement was introduced because the project was intended to include some evaluation of the effects of such methods.

A simple, ordinal rating of the extent to which each task was externally paced could not be established. Instead, tasks were categorized according to which of a range of factors paced their performance. Many of these factors were inherent in the production system itself, and in varying combinations and to varying degrees they determined work rates. Factors found to be significant determinants of work rate for each task were as follows: machine operating or production process time, 62.3 percent of tasks (including 13.5 percent of all tasks, which had a moving line, and 16 percent classified as "end of line"); production targets, 70 percent of tasks; production orders and related deadlines, 46 percent of tasks. For many tasks, more than one of these determinants applied.

Some kind of incentive or bonus payment system was reported for 15 percent of tasks. The apparent purpose of most such systems was to reward non-absenteeism or general performance quality; one system was specifically related to product reject rate. Others were in the form of general profit sharing, with no particular aspect of performance being the focus. Overall, it seemed that these bonus systems would have little impact on work rates.

Formal methods of calculating appropriate levels for production targets or line speeds were reported for 48 percent of the tasks surveyed. The percentage for standard times (PMTS) is an overestimate of the incidence in the total population, since it proved difficult to find companies using formal methods and a deliberate effort was made to recruit them. Of the subset of tasks for which a formal method had been used, Time Study (any form of timing, usually fairly informal, of task performance) was reported for 72 percent, or 34.5 percent of the total task sample. Some form of standard times, based either on industry standards or on a PMTS such as Modapts—was reported for 28 percent, or 13.5 percent of tasks in the whole sample.

A wide range of other factors were reported as sometimes affecting the actual rate at which people worked at any given time, and variations in this rate. These factors included looking for rejects or being careful to ensure product quality; variation in staffing level; process holdups; amount of work backlog; the need, or wish, to finish work by a particular time; people in another section waiting for the product; other people's attitudes or expectations; personal goals; and whether the person worked alone or with others. Almost all managers reported that line speed was never increased as a means of coping with an increased amount of work or an urgent deadline; however, for 18 percent of tasks, they reported that in these circumstances, targets were sometimes increased.

The project team used Modapts to analyze and calculate an appropriate standard work rate for each Stage 2 task. Most of the actual task performance times were found to cluster quite close to Modapts standard times; 20 percent of tasks were performed faster than the standard time without addition of the usual 15 percent "fatigue allowance"; when this allowance was included within the standard Modapts time, approximately 45 percent of tasks were performed faster than the standard. However, the distribution of actual performance times had a long "tail," with some very slow times. Reviewing the videotapes of these slow performances, we saw that many were in situations where total cycle time was governed primarily by machine process times—that is, employees sometimes performed more slowly than the standard because otherwise they would have a longer waiting time before the start of the next machine cycle. For such tasks, the application of a PMTS to set or evaluate actual work rates was clearly invalid, since performance of these tasks was limited by the production process rather than by human performance characteristics.

Task Demands and Workload

One of the selection criteria for participating companies was repetitiveness of the work. Fifty-two percent of the tasks had a cycle time of less than a minute; 30 percent, one to five minutes; and 18 percent, longer than five minutes. Tasks were categorized in terms of the following physical and mental demands:

- *Physical demand factors*: heavy loads (lift/push/pull); local loads (manual pinch, squeeze grips); static postures; metabolic demands
- *Mental demand factors*: perceptual load; motor control (precision); working memory load; concentration (mental effort)

Each of these eight task demand factors was allocated a subscore, based on the joint decision of at least two members of the research team: 0, no significant demand; 0.5, significant to some degree or for some of the time; or 1.0, definitely a significant demand. Thus, three scores were calculated for each task: physical demand factors (maximum score = 4); mental demand factors (maximum score = 4); and total demand factors (sum of physical + mental; maximum score = 8). These scores reflect partly the *variety* of task demand factors and partly the *level* of demand. Figure 7.1 shows the distributions of physical demand and mental demand scores for all tasks.

Employees rated all tasks on a 10-point scale of "overall task difficulty." For the whole set of tasks, mean rating of overall difficulty was 5.35 (S.D. = 2.37). The stage 2 subset of tasks was not significantly different, with a mean of 5.20 (S.D. = 2.39). Employee ratings on this scale were significantly correlated with total task demand scores, based on a separate analysis of the tasks by the research team. In fact, the mean correlation (Spearman's rho) was .405 ($P = .002$), which provides some validation of the employee ratings, remembering that task demand scores reflected the variety as well as the intensity of task demands, so a very high correlation with employee ratings of "overall difficulty" would not be expected.

Employees also rated stage 2 tasks on each of seven scales (0 to 100) representing different workload components or dimensions, based on the NASA-TLX scales and other workload literature (40–42; see Chapter 6). The scales used were as follows: physical demand, mental demand, time pressure, effort, frustration (all standard TLX scales), plus two additional scales: "working automatically or thinking things out" and "working carefully to avoid errors." The first of these

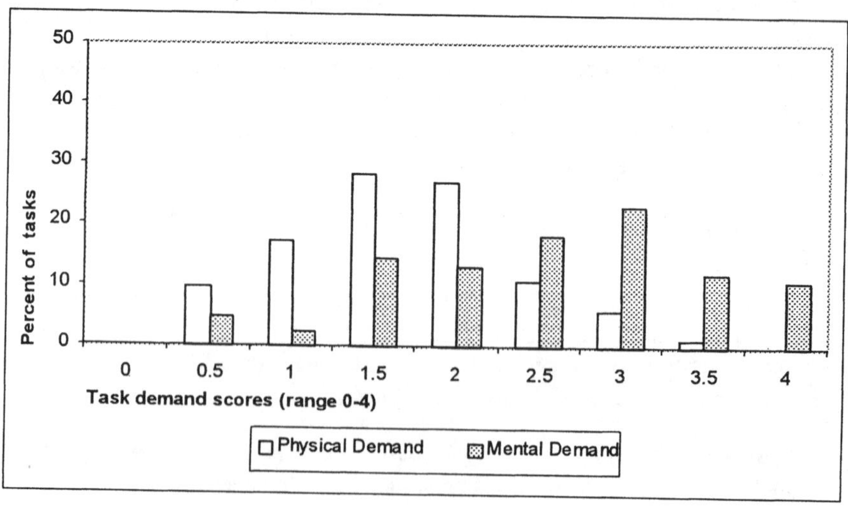

Figure 7.1 Distribution of physical and mental task demand scores for stage 1 tasks.

new scales was included because of its appropriateness for the largely repetitive process work under investigation in this project; it is also similar to one of the scales considered during the process of developing the TLX (40). The "working carefully to avoid error" scale was formulated to assess subjects' concerns about their own performance in a way that was less personally threatening than the standard TLX "own performance" scale. Previous investigations have found the latter scale to lack sensitivity in ordinary workplace use, presumably due to the unwillingness of many people to rate their own job performance as less than adequate, despite assurances of confidentiality (34, 43, 44).

The highest mean rating (74 on the 100-point scale) was on this last scale, in which the specific question was, "How affected are you by knowing it is very important to get things right?" The importance of this factor was related to employees' perceptions of the need to maintain high quality standards rather than simply to maintain a high output or work rate. It was evident that in many tasks this factor was experienced as a major demand. Second in importance as sources of workload were, equally, mental demand and effort, both with means of 70, followed by physical demand with a mean of 65, and time pressure with 63. The *relatively* low value for time pressure indicates that for many tasks this was not a major determinant of workload, suggesting that for most tasks work rates were not excessive.

The second lowest rating was for the question, "Are you able to work automatically, or do you have to consciously think things out?" The relatively low mean rating of 49 indicated a high degree of working "on auto," as is typical of highly repetitive work. The lowest mean rating, of 42, was on the frustration dimension: "How frustrated, discouraged, irritated, annoyed, etc. do you feel?"; this indicates that frustration was a relatively less important element in the workload experienced by this sample of employees.

For each of the stage 2 tasks, we evaluated three specific aspects of physical demands:

- A composite *forces stress* score (range, 0 to 3) was calculated, based on the Snook and Ciriello (45) or University of Michigan (46) method. Only 40 percent of tasks scored above zero, and very few required forces that presented any significant injury risk.
- *Cardiac cost,* working heart rate minus resting heart rate, was measured. Heart rate elevation was generally below the maximum acceptable level of 30 to 35 beats per minute (47); only 7.5 percent of tasks had heart rate elevations of more than 40 beats per minute.
- Postural demands were evaluated using OWAS and/or RULA (48), and from the resultant data we created a new composite measure *postural stress,* scored from 0 to 3 (see 39 for details of these three scores). In contrast to results for forces stress and cardiac cost, there was an elevated injury risk due to the required postures for a high proportion of these tasks.

Job Diagnostic Survey Scores

We evaluated job design in terms of the motivating potential score (MPS) from the Job Diagnostic Survey (JDS) (49, 50). A direct measure of job satisfaction (the JDS "general satisfaction" scale) was also used. There is evidence that JDS scores are predictive of workers' health (see 51, 52), and some small studies have found scores for a range of Australian jobs to correspond quite closely with the U.S. normative data for these families of jobs (43, 53, 54).

The normative MPS mean for "processing" jobs, which are directly comparable to those in this project, is 105 (S.D. = 70), whereas for our data set it was 85 (S.D. = 44). On the face of it, the much lower value of 85 for the present sample suggests that the jobs sampled were relatively poor in terms of factors such as task variety, task significance, autonomy, and feedback. However, it is possible that the focus of our study on specific tasks, rather than on whole jobs, might have biased responses more narrowly than if employees had been questioned about all elements of their job, resulting in lower MPS scores than otherwise. Also, one would expect the significant degree of organizational restructuring and downsizing that has occurred throughout the 1990s to have changed some job characteristics to an extent that decreases the validity of older normative data, such as those for the JDS used here.

Affective Well-Being of Employees

Affective well-being was assessed in terms of the two dimensions of the Stress Arousal Checklist (SACL): stress and arousal. These are well established as valid constructs to represent people's mood or emotional state (e.g., 18, 55, 56). Recently, a series of studies by Van Katwyk and coworkers (57) identified and confirmed these two dimensions as representative of people's affective states at work, describing them as pleasure–displeasure, and degree of arousal. Similarly, the SACL stress dimension is said to be related to feelings of pleasantness–unpleasantness or hedonic tone (e.g., comfortable, cheerful, distressed, worried), and the arousal dimension is related to the physiological and behavioral states of attentiveness, sleepiness, and energy level (e.g., stimulated, energetic, sluggish). In the present study, the SACL arousal score was 7.41 (S.D. = 3.06) and the stress score was 6.54 (S.D. = 3.98), which are within 1 S.D. of normative means (18).

Factors associated with variations in stress and arousal are described below. Stress was expected to increase both with very monotonous work (highly repetitive, externally paced) and when task demands were excessively high. Arousal was expected to be positively correlated with high levels of work rate and task demands, and negatively correlated with high levels of monotony. Within the constraints of this study, we could not measure or control for likely variations in stress and arousal related to individual differences among employees.

FACTORS INFLUENCING VARIATIONS IN AFFECTIVE WELL BEING

Variation in Stress

Using multiple regression analysis, we developed a predictive equation in which variables representing the various task factors were entered, initially in order of the strength of their bivariate correlations with stress. Where there was both a researcher-generated measure and an employee rating for the same construct, and where these were significantly correlated, as was usually the case, initial preference was given to variables from the researchers' analyses. Work task factors were also given a higher preference than employee ratings. However, whenever a relevant employee rating proved more effective in accounting for variance, this measure was substituted. The model finally developed ($F = 7.57$; $P < .000$; adjusted $R^2 = .32$) is shown in Table 7.1.

Overall Task-Related Workload. The best measure of task demands as a predictor of stress was the mean of the following scales: physical demands; mental demands, time pressure; effort, frustration and "working carefully." This measure provides a comprehensive index of task-related workload. Stress was higher with higher levels of workload.

Motivating Potential Score. The next best predictor was MPS, representing a set of job characteristics that facilitate both coping capacity and job satisfaction based on reasonable autonomy and feedback, some variety, and the opportunity for some sense of "ownership" and pride in the work performed. Stress was lower with higher MPS scores.

Task Cycle Time. This variable represented categories of cycle-time duration, ranging from 0-30 seconds to more than 10 minutes. Higher values represented

Table 7.1

Predictors of stress

Predictor	Beta	Sig.
Overall task-related workload (rating scales)	.42	.000
Motivating potential score (from JDS)	–.28	.019
Task cycle time code	–.21	.106
Rate set by process, machine, or line speed	.14	.299

longer cycle times. Before the entry of the "rate set by process, machine, or line speed" factor, the beta value for task cycle time was –.28 (P = .013). However, cycle time was highly correlated with this factor, and on its entry, beta dropped to –.21. As shown in Figure 7.2, employees with stress scores in the lowest three categories (0 to 6) were performing tasks spread across all cycle-time categories, but among those with higher stress scores (the three categories from 7 to 12), proportionately more were performing short-cycle-time tasks. There were only three scores in the highest two categories, and these were distributed across the cycle-time groups.

Work Rate Determined by Work Process or Machine Times or Line Speed. This self-explanatory variable did not make a large additional contribution to the model, due to its correlation with task cycle time. However, it was one of the stronger bivariate correlates of stress. Its effects are depicted in Figure 7.3. Higher proportions of people with low stress scores were performing tasks in which the work rate was *not* influenced by the production process, while those with higher

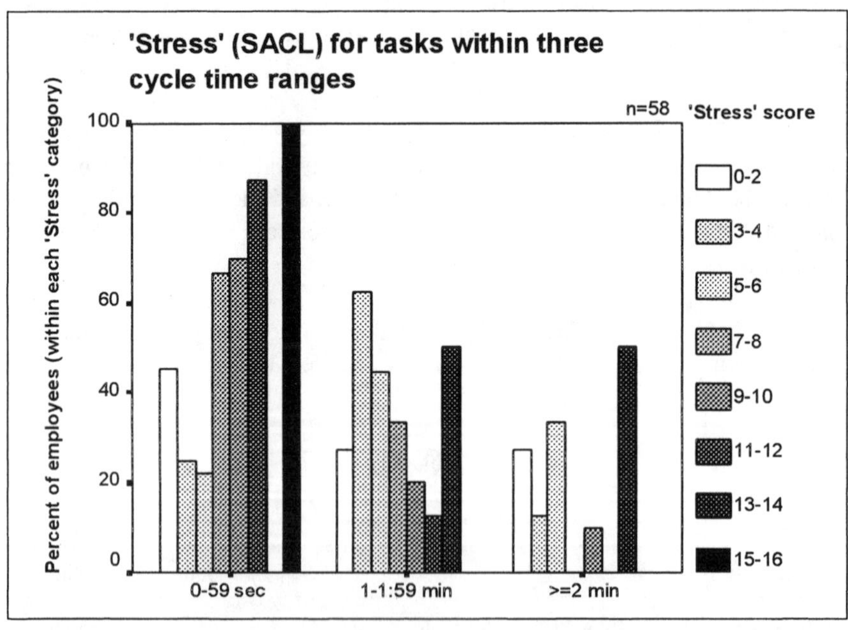

Figure 7.2 Relationship between stress and cycle time: distribution of stress scores shown separately for cycle times categorized as short, medium, and long. Total numbers within each stress category: 0–2, 11; 3–4, 8; 5–6, 9; 7–8, 9; 9–10, 10; 11–12, 8; 13–14, 2; 15–16, 1.

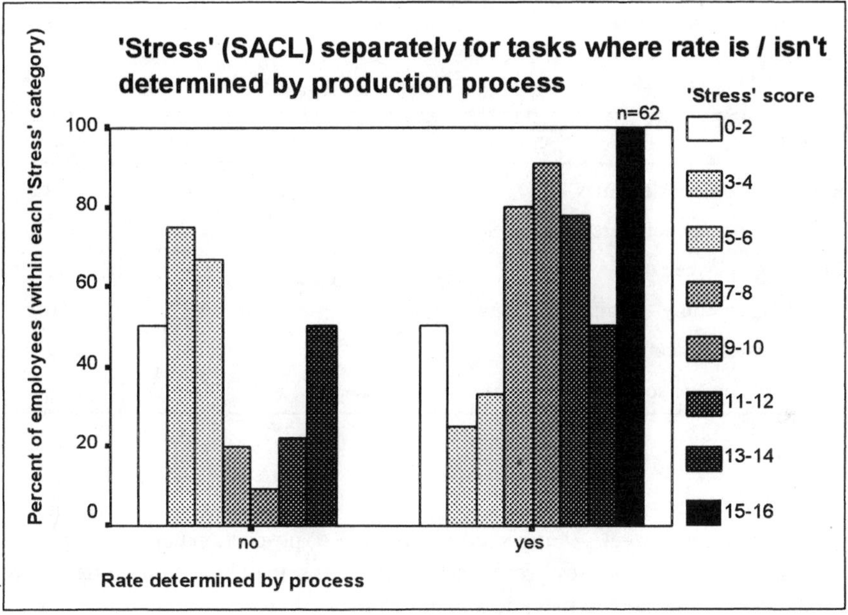

Figure 7.3 Relationship between stress (from stress arousal checklist) and whether or not work performance was "paced" by the production process or line speed. Numbers in each stress category: 0–2, 12; 3–4, 8; 5–6, 9; 7–8, 10; 9–10, 11; 11–12, 9; 13–14, 1; 15–16, 1.

stress scores were much more likely to be performing "machine-paced" tasks, consistent with some earlier, experimental work (e.g., 19).

Other variables, not included in the predictive model but each having significant bivariate correlations with higher stress, were the following: higher force demand score, higher fatigue rating, lower general satisfaction score, larger worksite (where work tasks tended to be more demanding), and higher ratings on the individual TLX scales of mental demand, time pressure and frustration.

Variation in Arousal

Using the same regression strategy as that outlined above for stress, we developed the predictive model for arousal (F = 6.402; P < .000; adjusted R^2 = .36) (Table 7.2).

Rate Set by Orders, Deadlines. This was the best predictor within the final model. It represents the time pressures associated with urgent deadlines, and it is strongly

Table 7.2

Predictors of arousal

Predictor	Beta	Sig.
Rate set by orders, deadlines	.32	.009
Motivating potential score (from JDS)	.23	.048
Effort—employee rating	.24	.101
"Working carefully"—employee rating	.19	.156
Postural stress score	.13	.279
Total task demand score	.07	.624

related to arousal level. As depicted in Figure 7.4, proportionately more people with higher arousal scores were performing tasks in which work rates were influenced by the need to meet deadlines or orders.

Motivating Potential Score. Arousal was higher with higher MPS scores. This variable represents the positive influence of good employee motivation on work performance—being related both to decreased stress (as shown above) and, here, to increased arousal.

Effort Rating. Higher effort was related to higher arousal. Ratings on this standard TLX scale were one of the strongest predictors of arousal. In the final model its value was reduced due to its correlation with "working carefully."

"Working Carefully" Rating. High ratings on "working carefully" were associated with high arousal. This scale required employees to rate, "How affected are you by knowing that when doing this task it is *very important* to get things just right, or to avoid errors?" It had one of the highest bivariate correlations with arousal, just slightly lower than Effort.

Total Task Demand Score. Arousal was higher with higher total task demand Scores. This variable had the strongest bivariate correlation with arousal, and it was retained in the model in view of both this strong correlation and its central role within the project's conceptual framework. It comprises the sum of researchers' scores for eight different aspects of physical and mental task demands and provides a comprehensive, objective index of task demands.

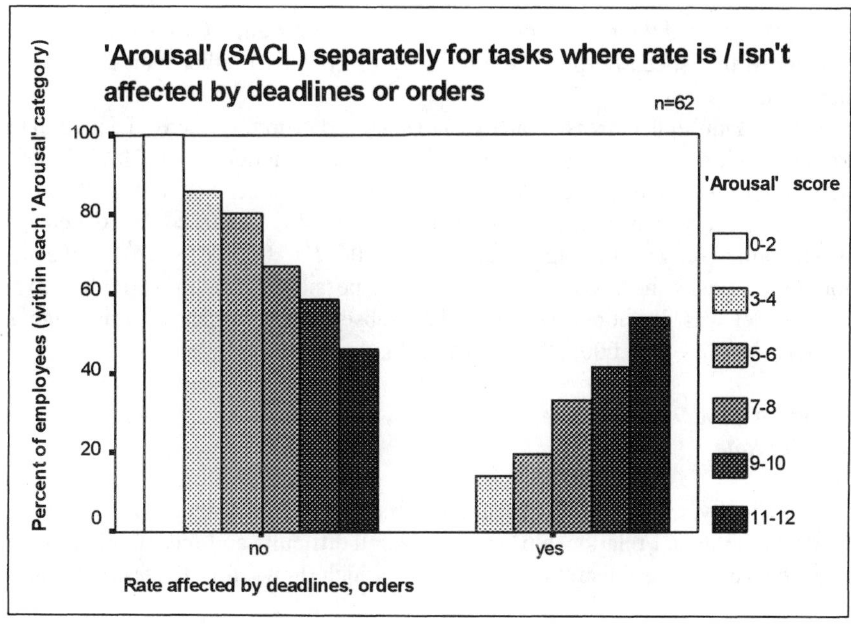

Figure 7.4 Relationship between arousal (from stress arousal checklist) and whether or not work rate was affected by deadlines or orders. Numbers in each arousal category: 0–2, 5; 3–4, 7; 5–6, 10; 7–8, 15; 9–10, 12; 11–12, 13.

Postural Stress Score. Arousal was higher with higher postural stress scores. This variable had the second highest bivariate correlation with arousal. It was retained in the model despite its low contribution to the final version, because it represents a formal measure of the aspect of physical task demands that was found to be most in need of remedy to reduce risk of musculoskeletal injury.

Other variables, not included in the predictive model but each having significant bivariate correlations with higher arousal, were the following: higher mental task demand score, longer task cycle time, higher general satisfaction score, higher ratings on TLX scales of mental and physical demand, and lower rating on the "working automatically" scale.

FACTORS INFLUENCING VARIATIONS IN ACCEPTABILITY OF WORK RATE

Employees evaluated the acceptability of line speeds or targets using a five-point scale ("much too slow/low" to "much too fast/high"). The majority of employees

(65 percent) rated their target or line speed as "about right." Of the others, most responded that speeds/targets were too high (30 percent) rather than too low (5 percent).

We used multiple regression analysis of stage 1 data to formulate an equation to predict work rate acceptability ratings. The resultant model ($F = 6.51$; $P < .000$; adjusted $R^2 = .11$) is presented in Table 7.3. The model accounted for only 11 percent of variance in stage 1 data, although this increased to 16 percent when applied only to the stage 2 subset ($F = 4.06$; $P = .012$, $R^2 = .16$). However, for stage 2 tasks there was a wider range of possible predictor variables, so a new model was developed with this data subset. Table 7.4 shows this stage 2 model ($F = 9.28$; $P < .000$; adjusted $R^2 = .35$).

Effects of Task Difficulty on Acceptability of Work Rate

Task difficulty, represented by several factors, was an important predictor in both models. The stage 1 relationship between overall difficulty and acceptability of the required work rate is illustrated in Figure 7.5, which shows, for each task difficulty

Table 7.3

Stage 1 predictors of work rate acceptability

Predictor	Beta	Sig.
Satisfaction with overall "say"	–.27	.001
Overall difficulty rating	.15	.067
Speed vs. quality rating	–.11	.198

Table 7.4

Stage 2 predictors of work rate acceptability

Predictor	Beta	Sig.
Overall difficulty rating	.26	.052
(Not) working "on auto" rating	.18	.153
Fatigue rating	.45	.001
Mental task demand score	.15	.235

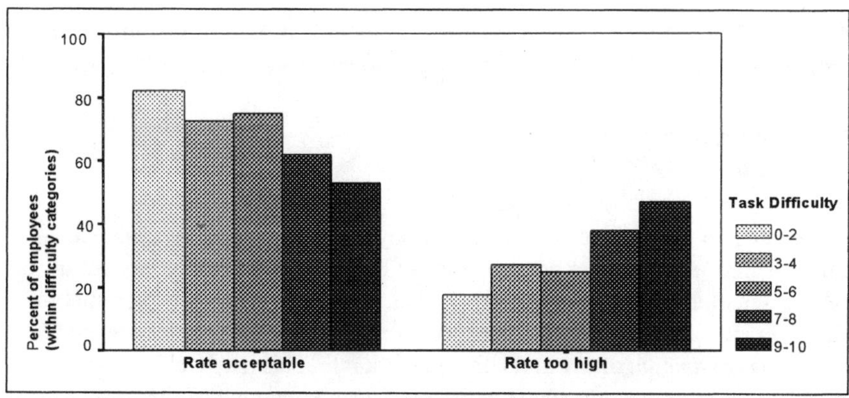

Figure 7.5 Relationship between employees' ratings of task difficulty and their perceptions of work rate acceptability. Numbers in each task difficulty category: 0–2, 17; 3–4, 22; 5–6, 56; 7–8, 29; 9–10, 17.

level, the proportions of people who recorded their target or line speed (and hence their work rate) as acceptable versus those who recorded it as too high.

In the above regression models, overall difficulty was the factor most directly representing task difficulty or demands; however, it was not the only one. The presence of the "speed versus quality" factor (employee ratings of their relative importance) in the stage 1 model suggests that the target or line speed was more likely to be rated as excessive when there was greater perceived pressure for speed than for product quality. This may indicate that for some tasks the time required to ensure high product quality was inadequately recognized. Ensuring high product quality may require precise movements and careful inspection—activities that tend to be associated more with perceptual/cognitive than with physical demands. Consistent with this, two of the highest correlates of work rate acceptability were working "on auto" and the researcher-generated mental task demand score, showing that work rates were more often perceived as excessive for tasks that were more mentally demanding and that required "thinking it out" rather than working "automatically." These results suggest an inadequate recognition of the time required to deal with perceptually and/or cognitively more demanding tasks. The fourth factor in the stage 2 model was fatigue, which, unsurprisingly, was higher when rates were perceived as too high.

To some extent, the above results might be due simply to a high work rate increasing the perceived difficulty of the task; indeed, temporal demand or time pressure is one of the six standard TLX workload dimensions. However, researchers' scores of task demands did not include work rate as a determining factor, and as noted above, we found a significant correlation between mental task demand score and work rate acceptability. Thus, results support the hypothesis that insufficient allowance had been made for task difficulty in setting targets or line speeds for some of the more mentally demanding tasks.

Effects of Employee Participation on Acceptability of the Work Rate

Being able to participate by "having a say" in things can be regarded as a component of autonomy or control, and we hypothesized that the amount of say people felt they had would influence their rating of work rate acceptability. However, no significant relationships were found between work rate acceptability and ratings of *amount* of say in relation to work rate. This may well have been due to lack of variation in ratings: the majority of people reported having no say at all about targets or line speeds. Ratings of *satisfaction* with overall amount of say were also recorded—referring to "say" in general terms rather than specifically in terms of work rate. This factor represents perceived *influence* at the general, organizational level, rather than any kind of direct, instrumental control (see 17). In the regression model using stage 1 data (reported above), satisfaction with overall say was the strongest predictor of work rate acceptability. As shown in Figure 7.6, employees who were dissatisfied with their amount of say were more likely to perceive their required work rate as too high. This result is consistent with previously documented evidence showing that work rates are more acceptable when people have participated in determining their level. However, in the present case, the effect arose from dissatisfaction with amount of say "in general" rather than with amount of say in setting work rates.

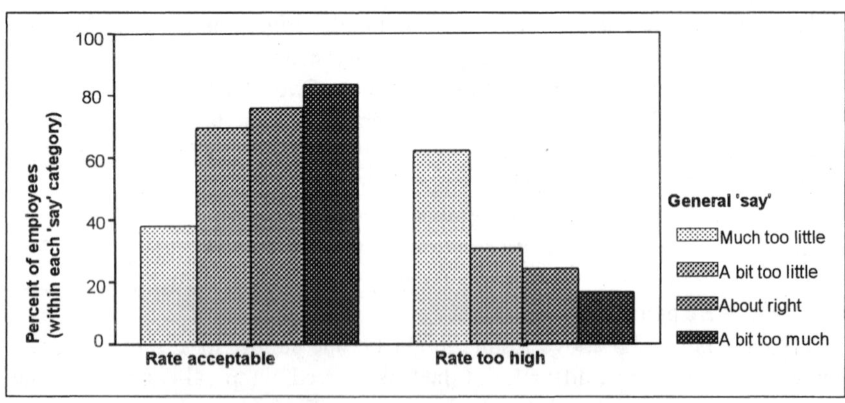

Figure 7.6 Relationship between employees' satisfaction with their general amount of "say" and their rating of work rate acceptability. Numbers in each "say" category: much too little, 16; a bit too little, 33; about right, 84; a bit too much, 6.

Contrary to expectation, satisfaction with overall say was not significantly related to acceptability of the work rate for the stage 2 subset of tasks. The companies recruited to participate in stage 2 included a higher proportion where work rates were set by PMTS or similar standard time systems (because, due to the relative rarity of PMTS, this became one of the inclusion criteria towards the end of the project). Stage 2 tasks also differed from the rest in that their work rates were more likely to have been influenced by orders or deadlines, and employees reported having more say in how the task was done. However, it is not obvious how these differences might have interacted with the relationship between satisfaction with overall say and acceptability of the work rate.

DISCUSSION

Use of formal methods such as a PMTS or Time Study in setting work rates had less effect on employee well-being than did the following characteristics of the production process: presence of production targets (a factor for 70 percent of tasks), deadlines and orders (for 46 percent of tasks), and performance pacing by the production process, machine operating time, or line speed (for 62 percent of tasks). Acceptability of work rate was little affected by these factors, but the stress score tended to be higher when performance speed was influenced by the timing of the production process, machine operating time, or line speed—that is, when level of external pacing was high. This result was expected, since external pacing decreases employee control. On the other hand, arousal levels were higher where work rate was significantly influenced by orders or deadlines.

The effectiveness of PMTS in setting appropriate work rates was difficult to evaluate. We attempted to evaluate one such method, Modapts, in terms of the discrepancy between actual work rates observed from video-recorded performance and Modapts-calculated rates. No strong relationships between stress or arousal and discrepancies between Modapts standard times and performance times were observed, and it was evident that in many cases work rates were limited by production process times rather than by the rate at which people could perform the work.

Did required work rates make adequate allowance for task difficulty? The evidence on this question was clear: employees performing the more difficult or demanding tasks were more likely to experience the required work rate as too high. This was particularly so for tasks where the demands were mental rather than physical, requiring workers to "think it out" rather than work more or less automatically. People doing the most demanding tasks also had higher stress scores. These results suggest that higher levels of task demand, particularly mental demands, had been inadequately recognized by those responsible for determining production targets or line speeds. In fact, the strongest predictor of stress scores was high levels of task difficulty or workload measures. Stress levels were substantially higher among people performing tasks with higher average TLX scores, with higher force demand scores, and, consistent with this, with higher fatigue ratings. These findings indicate the stressful effects of very high task demands.

However, highly repetitive, monotonous work, which is not difficult in the normal sense of the word, was also expected to be stressful. The finding that employees performing tasks with the shortest cycle times had higher stress scores is in accord with this expectation. It is also consistent with a much earlier finding of Johansson (58) that people performing very repetitive work in sawmills, with cycle times of 1 minute or less, suffered more frequently from depression, gastrointestinal disorders, and disturbed sleep patterns than those with work cycle times of 3 to 30 minutes.

As noted above, stress scores tended to be higher when the work rate was primarily determined by the production process time or line speed. However, the hypothesis that stress would be lower with higher levels of employee participation or "say" was not confirmed. It may be that with these tasks—where amount of say was usually so low that, even at its highest, it did not confer much sense of control—variation was unimportant relative to the much stronger influence on control of the level of external pacing of performance.

As hypothesized, arousal scores were predicted by a different set of variables from those predicting stress scores. The strongest single predictor of higher arousal was the presence of orders or similar deadlines as a significant influence on work rates, whereas the production system factor that had the greatest influence on stress was a higher level of external pacing. While very high levels of arousal may be associated with increased stress and perhaps with deteriorating performance, moderate levels are commonly associated with optimal task performance (e.g., see 59, 60), and good performance would be expected to produce higher job satisfaction. In fact, the second strongest predictor of higher arousal was a satisfying job design (higher MPS), supported by a higher general satisfaction score (JDS). This association of good job design with higher arousal contrasts with results for stress, which had a significant *negative* relationship with good job design.

Several task demand factors were predictors of arousal, but they were a different combination from those predicting stress. With arousal, the factors were effort rating, "working carefully" rating, postural stress score, and total task demand score. The first two are the workload rating scales, which most directly reflect the effort expended in performing the task. The last two were calculated by the researchers from objective analyses of task demands. Other variables that were significantly correlated with higher arousal included longer task cycle time, higher general satisfaction, and lower rating on the TLX scale "working automatically."

These results suggest that, at least with this sample of tasks, those tasks that had to be performed to meet deadlines were often experienced as positive, representing an enjoyable challenge rather than an unpleasant stressor. However, such tasks also tended to have longer cycle times and higher MPS scores, making it difficult to identify the primary determinants of the lower levels of stress and higher job satisfaction that were associated with them.

Overall, a wide range of task and work characteristics interact to influence different dimensions of employee well-being, and it was beyond the scope of the present project to elucidate the complexities of these interactions. However, we can draw some clear conclusions concerning workplace management strategies.

IMPLICATIONS FOR WORKPLACE MANAGEMENT

How might current workplace management practices be changed to improve both the well-being of employees and organizational productivity? In many companies, it appeared that the application of quite straightforward engineering methods study (see 61) could significantly improve production efficiency. In addition, the following possible changes should be considered:

- In determining required work rates, ensure that adequate allowance is made for all aspects of task demands, particularly mental demands.
- (Re)design work to minimize the need for people to work slowly or wait while production process or machine cycle times are completed.
- Minimize the periods that employees spend performing repetitive, short-cycle-time, monotonous work that presents little challenge.
- Reduce process hold-ups, machine problems, and poor-quality materials; apart from its obvious direct benefits, this will reduce both task demands and stress.
- Find ways to increase employees' sense of being able to have a say in issues affecting them, and more generally.
- Find ways to improve job design to increase its potential for providing job satisfaction (increase feedback, autonomy, task variety, task significance, task identity).
- In all of the above, involve employees in the processes of developing, as well as implementing, changes.

Acknowledgments — Thanks are due to the many people who have contributed to the project reported here, most importantly my co-researchers Gerri Nolan and Owen Evans. Other members of the project team were Liz Pratt, Michael Hui, David Caple, Deborah Vallance of the Amalgamated Metal Workers Union, Ann Taylor of the Metal Trades Industries Association, and Sandra Cowell of the Australian Industries Group. I especially thank all participating companies and their employees who generously gave their time.

REFERENCES

1. Karasek, R., and Theorell, T. *Healthy Work: Stress, Productivity and the Reconstruction of Working Life.* Basic Books, New York, 1990.
2. Houtman, I. L. D., and Kompier, M. A. J. Risk factors and occupational risk groups for work stress in the Netherlands. In *Organizational Risk Factors for Job Stress*, pp. 209–225. American Psychological Association, Washington, D.C., 1995.
3. Edwards, J. R., Caplan, R. D., and Van Harrison, R. Person-environment fit theory. In *Theories of Organizational Stress*, edited by C. L. Cooper. Oxford University Press, Oxford, 1998.
4. Karasek, R., et al. The Job Content Questionnaire (JCQ): An instrument for internationally comparative assessments of psychosocial job characteristics. *J. Occup. Health Psychol.* 3: 322–356, 1998.
5. Cox, T., Griffiths, A., and Rial-Gonzalez, E. *Research on Work-Related Stress.* European Agency for Safety and Health at Work, 2000. http://agency.osha.eu.int/publications/reports/stress/.
6. Ellis, N. *Work and Health Management in Australia and New Zealand.* Oxford University Press, Melbourne, 2001.
7. Heyde, C. *The Sensible Taskmaster.* Heyde Dynamics, Sydney, 1976.
8. Sauter, S. L., and Swanson, N. G. An ecological model of musculoskeletal disorders in office work. In *Beyond Biomechanics: Psychosocial Aspects of Musculoskeletal Disorders in Office Work*, edited by S. D. Moon and S. L. Sauter, pp. 3–21. Taylor and Francis, London, 1996.
9. Devereux, J. J., and Buckle, P. W. Adverse work stress—A review of the potential influence on work related musculoskeletal disorders. In *Proceedings of the IEA 2000/HFES 2000 Congress,* Vol. 5, pp. 457–460. Human Factors and Ergonomics Society, Santa Monica, Calif., 2000.
10. Evans, O., and Patterson, K. Predictors of neck and shoulder pain in non-secretarial computer users. *Int. J. Ind. Ergonomics* 26: 357–365, 2000.
11. Orr, S., and Wells, R. The effect of work speed and task precision on perceived fatigue and muscle activation in the arms and shoulders. In *Proceedings of the 12th Triennial Congress of the International Ergonomics Association,* Vol. 5, pp. 318–320, Toronto, 1994.
12. Bernard, B. P. (ed.). *Musculoskeletal Disorders (MSDs) and Workplace Factors.* National Institute of Occupational Safety and Health, Cincinnati, 1997.
13. McGrath, J., and Zarb, V. Modapts and its Relationship to the Measurement of Mental Workload in Industry. Research project conducted in partial fulfillment of the requirements of the Graduate Diploma in Ergonomics, School of Human Biosciences, La Trobe University, Melbourne, 1992.
14. Frese, M. Theoretical models of control and health. In *Job Control and Worker Health,* edited by S. L. Sauter, C. L. Cooper, and J. J. Hurrell, pp. 107–128. Wiley, Chichester, U.K., 1989.
15. Hockey, G. R., et al. Assessing the impact of computer workload on operator stress: The role of system controllability. *Ergonomics* 32: 1401–1418, 1989.
16. Spector, P. E. A control theory of the job stress process. In *Theories of Organizational Stress,* edited by C. L. Cooper, pp. 153–169. Oxford University Press, Oxford, 1998.

17. Carayon, P., and Zijlstra, F. Relationship between job control, work pressure and strain: Studies in the USA and in the Netherlands. *Work Stress* 13: 32–48, 1999.
18. Cox, T., and Griffiths, A. The nature and measurement of work stress: Theory and Practice. In *Evaluation of Human Work: A Practical Ergonomics Methodology,* Ed. 2, edited by J. R. Wilson and E. N. Corlett, pp. 783–803. Taylor and Francis, London, 1995.
19. Salvendy, G., and Smith, M. J. (eds.). *Machine Pacing and Occupational Stress*. Taylor and Francis, London, 1981.
20. Johansson, G., Aronsson, G., and Lindstrom, B. O. Social psychological and neuroendocrine stress reactions in highly mechanised work. *Ergonomics* 21: 583–599. 1978.
21. Johansson, G. Psychoneuroendocrine correlates of unpaced and paced performance. In *Machine Pacing and Occupational Stress*, edited by G. Salvendy and M. J. Smith, pp. 277–286. Taylor and Francis, London, 1981.
22. Shikdar, A. A., and Das, B. A field study of worker productivity improvements. *Appl. Ergonomics* 26: 21–27, 1995.
23. Sullivan, B. Personal communication. Brian Sullivan Management Consultant Pty Ltd., Melbourne, 1995.
24. Sen, T. K. Participative group techniques. In *Handbook of Human Factors,* edited by G. Salvendy, pp. 453–469. Wiley, New York, 1987.
25. Wilson, J. R. Ergonomics and participation. In *Evaluation of Human Work: A Practical Ergonomics Methodology,* Ed. 2, edited by J. R.Wilson, and E. N. Corlett, pp. 1071–1096. Taylor and Francis, London, 1995.
26. Bertone, S., et al. *Developing Effective Consultative Practices: Case Studies of Consultation at Work.* South Pacific Publishing, Melbourne, 1998.
27. Marmot, M. Work and other factors influencing coronary health and sickness absence. *Work Stress* 8: 191–201, 1994.
28. Blewett, V., and Shaw, A. OHS best practice column: Integrating OHS through self-managed teams. *J. Occup. Health Safety Aust. N.Z.* 11: 15–19, 1995.
29. Parker, S., and Wall, T. *Job and Work Design: Organizing Work to Promote Well-Being and Effectiveness.* Sage, Thousand Oaks, Calif., 1998.
30. O'Hanlon, J. F. Stress in short-cycle repetitive work: General theory and empirical test. In *Machine Pacing and Occupational Stress*, edited by G. Salvendy and M. J. Smith, pp. 213–222. Taylor and Francis, London, 1981.
31. Sauter, S., et al. Psychosocial and organizational factors. In *Encyclopaedia of Occupational Health and Safety,* Vol. 1, pp. 34.1–34.77, edited by J. M. Stellman. International Labor Office, Geneva, 1997.
32. Ivancevich, J. M., and Ganster, D. C. (eds.). *Job Stress: From Theory to Suggestion.* Haworth Press, New York, 1987.
33. Jex, S. M. *Stress and Job Performance: Theory, Research, and Implications for Managerial Practice.* Sage, Calif., 1998.
34. O'Bryan, S. J., Macdonald, W. A., and Evans, O. M. A comparison of some workload analysis techniques. In *Proceedings of the 27th Annual Conference of the Ergonomics Society of Australia*, pp. 139–147. Ergonomics Society of Australia, Canberra, 1991.
35. Sendapperuma, L., Macdonald, W. A., and Hoffmann, E. R. P.M.T.S: Are they applicable to visual inspection tasks? In *Proceedings of the 27th Annual Conference of*

the Ergonomics Society of Australia, pp. 269–275. Ergonomics Society of Australia, Canberra, 1991.

36. Hoffmann, E. R. Predetermined motion time systems for estimation of task times: Capabilities, limitations and possible alternatives. In *Proceedings of a Seminar Conducted by the Victorian Branch of the Ergonomics Society of Australia*, edited by M. A. Regan. Ergonomics Society of Australia, Canberra, 1992.
37. Hoffmann, E. R., Macdonald, W. A., and Almond, G. C. Quantification of the cognitive difficulty of mail sorting. *Int. J. Ind. Ergonomics* 11: 83–98, 1993.
38. Addison, M., and Macdonald, W. A. Use of subjective and objective techniques in identifying injury risk in a light repetitive task—A case study. *Conference of the Australia and New Zealand Modapts Association.* Melbourne, 1993.
39. Macdonald, W., et al. *An Evaluation of Current Practice in Setting Work Rates.* Report to National Occupational Health and Safety Commission. Canberra, 1999.
40. Hart, S. G., and Staveland, L. E. Development of NASA-TLX (Task Load Index): Results of empirical and theoretical research. In *Human Mental Workload*, edited by P. A. Hancock and N. Meshkati, pp. 139–183. North-Holland, Amsterdam, 1988.
41. Huey, M. B., and Wickens, C. D. (eds.). *Workload Transition: Implications for Individual and Team Performance.* National Academy Press, Washington, D.C., 1993.
42. Tsang, P., and Wilson, G. F. Mental workload. In *Handbook of Human Factors and Ergonomics*, edited by G. Salvendy, pp. 417–449. Wiley, New York, 1997.
43. So, C., and Mert-Iljin, V. Measuring Mental Workload in an Occupational Setting. Research project conducted in partial fulfillment of the requirements of the Graduate Diploma in Ergonomics, School of Human Biosciences, La Trobe University, Melbourne, 1990.
44. Macdonald, W. A. Train controllers, interface design and mental workload. In *People in Control,* edited by J. M. Noyes and M. L. Bransby, pp. 239–258. IEE Press, Stevenage, U.K., 2001.
45. Snook, S. H., and Ciriello, V. M. The design of manual handling tasks: Revised tables for maximum acceptable weights and forces. *Ergonomics* 34: 1197–1213, 1991.
46. University of Michigan. 3D Static Strength Prediction Program (Version 4.0). University of Michigan Office of Technology Transfer, Ann Arbor, 1998.
47. Kroemer, K. H. E., and Grandjean, E. *Fitting the Task to the Human,* Ed. 5. Taylor and Francis, London, 1997.
48. Corlett, E. N. The evaluation of posture and its effects. In *Evaluation of Human Work: A Practical Ergonomics Methodology,* Ed. 2, edited by J. R.Wilson, and E. N.Corlett, pp. 662–713. Taylor and Francis, London, 1995.
49. Hackman, J. R., and Oldham, G. R. Development of the Job Diagnostic Survey. *J. Appl. Psychol.* 60: 159–170, 1975.
50. Fried, Y. Meta-analytic comparison of the Job Diagnostic Survey and Job Characteristics Inventory as correlates of work satisfaction and performance. *J. Appl. Psychol.* 76: 690–697, 1991.
51. Kelloway, E. K., and Barling, J. Job characteristics, role stress and mental health. *J. Occup. Psychol.* 64: 291–304, 1991.
52. Spector, P. E., and Jex, S. M. Relations of job characteristics from multiple data sources with employee affect, absence, turnover intentions, and health. *J. Appl. Psychol.* 76: 46–53, 1991.

53. Forester, C., and Macdonald, W. A. Evaluation of the human-computer interface used by switchboard operators. *J. Occup. Health Safety Aust. N.Z.* 10: 343–351, 1994.
54. Upsdell, T. Occupational Burnout, Stress, Mental Workload, and Job Satisfaction among Rehabilitation Counsellors. Research project conducted in partial fulfillment of the requirements of the Graduate Diploma in Ergonomics, School of Human Biosciences, La Trobe University, Melbourne, 1994.
55. Mackay, C. J., et al. An inventory for the measurement of self-reported stress and arousal. *Br. J. Soc. Clin. Psychol.* 17: 283–284, 1978.
56. Gotts, G., and Cox, T. *Stress and Arousal Checklist: A Manual for its Administration, Scoring, and Interpretation.* Swinburne Press, Melbourne, 1990.
57. Van Katwyk, P. T., et al. Using the Job-related Affective Well-being Scale (JAWS) to investigate affective responses to work stressors. *J. Occup. Health Psychol.* 5: 219–230, 2000.
58. Johansson, G. Psychophysiological stress reactions in the sawmill: A pilot study. In *Ergonomics in Sawmills and Woodworking Industries*, edited by B. Ager. National Board of Occupational Safety and Health, Stockholm, 1975.
59. Proctor, R. W., and Van Zandt, T. *Human Factors in Simple and Complex Systems.* Allyn and Bacon, Boston, 1994.
60. Matthews, G., et al. *Human Performance: Cognition, Stress and Individual Differences.* Psychology Press, Hove, U.K., 2000.
61. Kanawaty, G. (ed.). *Introduction To Work Study,* Ed. 4. International Labor Office, Geneva, 1992.

Section III

Case Studies

Chapter 8

PROFESSIONAL WORKERS AND STRESS

John McCormick

The literature on stress and burnout has acknowledged some similarities in the stress experiences of human, caring, or service professionals (1–5), such as medical doctors, dentists, nurses, social workers, and teachers. Moreover, it is a matter of concern that some seriously dysfunctional behaviors, associated with stress, have been identified in some professions. For example, alcohol and substance abuse have been associated with medical practitioners, psychologists, and social workers (6–8) and a high suicide rate with dentists and physicians (9–11). There are at least four reasonable, putative explanations for similar stress experiences among disparate professional groups. First, similar personality types may be drawn to service professions; certainly, the importance of individual differences has long been acknowledged in the stress and burnout literature (12–14). Second, there are likely to be similarities in these professions because of the centrality of the client-professional relationship (1, 3, 11).[1] Third, there may be common, structural similarities related to the nature of professionalism (15, 16). Finally, these professions may be affected by common environmental elements. In this chapter I discuss aspects of the last three explanations and then present a theoretical model developed for the teaching profession in a large education system that may have relevance for other professionals working within similar organizational structures.

THE NATURE OF PROFESSIONS

A considerable amount has been written about the characteristics of professions (e.g., 16–18), and it is beyond the scope of this chapter to discuss them in any

[1] Many professionals would not be happy with the use of the term "client." Typically, physicians do not think of their patients as clients and teachers do not think of their students as clients. However, as one of the intentions of this chapter is to point to some similarities among some professionals, I have adopted this more generic term.

substantial way. However, they need some acknowledgment so as to contextualize the discussion that follows. Bottery has identified "at least seventeen" characteristics (17, pp. 88–89), a number of which are salient to this chapter:

- the profession is represented by a single professional body;
- the profession administers disciplinary matters related to professional behavior;
- the profession controls entry to the profession;
- the profession maintains a monopoly position;
- members of the profession enjoy considerable financial remuneration;
- members of the profession enjoy high status within the community;
- members of the profession have a high degree of autonomy.

Also implicit in professionalism is the notion of service. For example, physicians and dentists serve their patients, and teachers serve their students. One could argue that it is at least partly on the basis of service to the community that the professional characteristics listed above are tolerated by society.

THE CENTRALITY OF THE CLIENT-PROFESSIONAL RELATIONSHIP

The concept of a vocation, or calling, has long been associated with professional work, suggesting that work in the service professions requires some degree of unselfish "giving," which is, nevertheless, reinforced by some societal rewards. Some of these rewards have already been mentioned, for example, high status and financial remuneration. However, for professionals, there are also likely to be anticipated psychic rewards associated with what may be considered altruistic, professional activities. Most likely, that many enter the service professions because they are motivated to serve and expect to derive satisfaction from contact with those whom they serve. However, the client-professional relationship may not always be positive; clients' demands can increase workload and affect a professional's outside life (19). An extreme negative example is violence. Patients' violence and threat of violence have been reported in the medical professions (9, 20). Violence perpetrated by students against teachers has also been reported (21, 22). When violence occurs, it is an obvious stressor and may cause severe psychological dysfunction (21). However, there may be other, more subtle, stressful aspects of the client-professional relationship.

One of the dimensions of successful professional practice is providing a service that makes a difference to the client and elicits subsequent client satisfaction. Beginning physicians have reported expectations of successful contact with their patients and associated satisfaction (9). However, the reality is that medical doctors are faced with some inevitable "failures," including patients' suffering and dying (9). Moreover, physicians may see a patient only when there is a problem and the patient is fearful. This, by itself, has the potential to induce distress in the physician (9). Many human service professionals would seem to be faced with some inevitable failure. Teachers, for example, will not successfully engage all students in learning, and the needs of some clients of social workers will not be met. Pines (4) and Friedman (3) have associated burnout with people who work with people, whose real-life work experiences are inconsistent with their high ideals, and who have a sense of being externally controlled. Thus, it is desirable for service professionals to be aware of their own limitations and environmental constraints, so that the inevitable failures do not affect their psychological well-being.

Dentists appear to have somewhat problematic relationships with their patients. Although they generally solve patients' immediate problems and do not have to deal with life-and-death situations, the association of dentistry with pain is still problematic, even with technical advances. According to Hilliard-Lysen and Riemer, "Dentists may be as afraid of their patients as their patients are of them. No one wants to go to the dentist. Given patient avoidance, dentists may feel rejection. Brooding before a hostile patient comes in, or before a particular procedure which they may dread was not uncommon among the interviewees" (10, p. 341). In a similar vein, some psychiatrists may be exposed to stress related to their patients' negative perceptions of them (23).

Empirical literature dealing with the job satisfaction of teachers has consistently identified a classroom focus, working with young people, and making a difference in their lives as a prime source of satisfaction (24–27). However, herein lies the paradox of the client-professional relationship: "Teachers gain immense satisfaction from positive outcomes in the classroom. . . . At the same time, teachers experience considerable frustration and stress in the classroom with disruptive and poorly motivated students" (28, pp. 33–34). Dealing with other human beings is inevitably problematic. Professionals can invest themselves in the task of improving outcomes for their clients for, at times, a very poor affective return.

Aside from the affective responses of their clients, there is another potential form of stress in the professional-client relationship. Because of the centrality of the professional-client interaction, some professionals can be expected to define their professional competence in terms of how well they manage that relationship. For example, teachers' sense of professional adequacy is likely to be related to how competently they deal with student misbehavior (29, 30). So there is the potential for a doubly negative experience: the absence of a powerful source of job satisfaction and the presence of strong stressors. If a sufficiently large number of professional-client interactions are negative, the concomitant stress may be predicted to dilute satisfaction with being a professional, perhaps leading to diminished quality of interactions with clients, poorer responses from clients, lower satisfaction, and so on. One might also reasonably predict, over time, the use of fewer problem-solving coping behaviors and more of a palliative nature. Although it is simplistic to portray palliative coping as always inferior (31), problem-solving approaches are likely to be more effective for much occupational distress (32).

PROFESSIONS AND SOCIETY

It is beyond the scope of this single chapter to provide an extensive discussion of conceptions of "profession." Indeed, theoretical conceptions have been and still are contested (33–35). Eliot Freidson (34) has contended that the modern conception of professionalism does not have universal application, but rather should be viewed in the context of Anglo-American societies. Put more strongly, professions are bound to society.

It is important to emphasize that professions are not closed systems and that they have changed over time. At the same time, some writers have posited that professions, to varying degrees, attempt market closure (36). As Collins has pointed out, "Instead of seeing occupations as having fixed positions on a market, we see that occupations themselves can become status groups in the realm of work. . . . Those which are especially successful are the ones which we have come to call 'the professions'" (36, p. 25). It follows, of course, that there can be "turf wars" between some professions as they compete for clients (36). For example, Abbott (33) has described how psychiatrists in the 19th century "moved in on" a number of problematic social areas, such as juvenile delinquency, placing the profession in direct competition with lawyers, clergymen, psychologists, and social workers. In fact, the birth of psychiatry as a profession came about when medical practitioners challenged legal practitioners for the control of "madmen" (33). The status of psychiatrists grew quickly, only to decline when the profession was unable to deliver the promised solutions to society (33). It is important to appreciate that professions do not hold indefinite tenure in society, and certainly not without making adaptations; even the fortunes of the traditional professions have waxed and waned.

PROFESSIONALS AND BUREAUCRACY

Arguably, the medical profession serves as a prototype for traditional professions (16). The traditional professional may be envisaged as an autonomous individual who controls her or his own work, answerable only to the professional body. However, such a professional is unlikely to exist in countries with post-industrial economies (16). Even if a physician is in private practice, there are inevitable intrusions into professional practice by government bureaucracies. Magee and Hojat (37) have suggested that some physicians in the United States think the health care system interferes with their professional autonomy, resulting in a lack of control over their work and concomitant dissatisfaction.

Comparisons with the medical and legal professions have commonly resulted in other, newer, professions being considered semi-professions (17, 18). However, it would seem more logical to conceptualize all professions as lying on a continuum rather than in hierarchical categories.

Weber's analysis (38) of the ideal-type bureaucracy focused on bureaucracies as administrative systems based on technically rational bases of power. Domination is at the heart of bureaucratic theory. Bureaucratic structures are means by which organizational members' autonomy is limited, and their work is controlled through hierarchical relationships between superiors and subordinates (15, 39). Importantly, the formal power wielded by a player in an ideal bureaucracy is embedded in the position that the player holds rather than in his or her personal characteristics (15). Of course, in reality there is no ideal bureaucracy, and Weber's typology is most useful as a theoretical baseline for comparisons. Arguably, bureaucracy is best thought of in terms of degrees of approximation to the Weber model.

Scott (15) has conceptualized a professional organization structure. In simple terms, the professional organization structure exists because the work of the organization's members is complex and non-routine. Individuals need to have the latitude to make decisions about how the work is carried out. This is a characteristic of professional work. Scott made an important distinction between two types of professional organizations: autonomous and heteronomous. An autonomous organization is one in which the administrative structures exist to support the professional activity within the organization. Examples of this form are the traditional university and the hospital: in both cases, the CEO of the organization is a member of the profession, and the professionals largely organize themselves within organizational units. Heteronomous organizations, on the other hand, are those in which the professionals are supervised by the administrators, and "employees in these settings are subject to administrative controls, and their discretion is clearly circumscribed. Unlike their autonomous counterparts, they are subject to routine supervision. This type of professional organization is exemplified by many public agencies—libraries, secondary schools, social welfare agencies" (15, p. 254). This would seem to correspond to a profession versus semi-profession typology. However, one can argue that in any organization there is likely to be tension between bureaucratic and professionalism structures in terms of who controls the work. Autonomous and heteronomous organizations are both compromises, to varying degrees between bureaucracy and professionalism. As argued earlier, however, it is unlikely that such a clean dichotomy adequately describes the nature of professional work in formal organizations. The main justification for this statement is the almost inevitable clash of professional and bureaucratic goals. For example, while the goals of both hospital clinicians and hospital administrators may be oriented to the quality of care for each patient, the goals of the hospital administrator may be shaped more by budgetary constraints.

A relatively early study of stress in a large bureaucratic organization by Zalesnick and colleagues (40) identified some relevant bureaucratic effects, including ritualistic attachment to rules, depersonalization of work, alienation, and apathy. The study also found what was then quite surprising, but is now well-accepted. There had been an assumption that managers at elevated levels of the bureaucracy would experience greater occupational stress than their subordinates, because of managers' greater responsibilities, pressure of making important decisions, and so on. In fact, the reverse was found. I have found similar results in a sample of teachers (41). This can be explained in terms of perceived low control over work being a stressor (42). The greater the organizational authority, the greater is the scope for controlling one's own work. As mentioned earlier, an important characteristic of bureaucracy is the circumscribing and control of employees' work. When one considers the selected characteristics of a profession listed above, it is likely that perceived lack of control over work could be particularly stressful for professionals.

Arnetz (9) has argued that business management principles have been adopted within the health care sectors. One aspect of this shift has been the amalgamation of small enterprises into larger ones. This increase in organizational complexity, as distinct from task complexity, has led to greater bureaucratization and control of physicians' work. "As a consequence, the role of the physician is changing into one of a typical employee in the framework of large bureaucratic organizations" (9, p. 204). Arguably, this trend of increasing privatization of hospital and general practice has also occurred in Australia (43), evoking concern from the Australian Medical Association. One way of conceptualizing this shift is in terms of the frustrated, traditional professional enmeshed in the workings of bureaucracy. However, this may not be the most useful model to adopt.

Another model describes work as deprofessionalized as a consequence of increased bureaucratization (1, 44, 45). Here, the worker is "less of a professional," in terms of a number of descriptors, yet the work itself may be even more technically complex than in the past. Thus, there may be less to distinguish the traditional professions from the so-called semi-professions, when members of the former work within large formal organizations. The argument is that some professionals—for example, hospital physicians and legal practitioners within large firms—are likely to experience similar stressors from working in bureaucratic settings to those experienced by previously considered semi-professionals, such as nurses, social workers, and teachers (17, 18). Even so, there may be an issue of control over work even in small formal organizations. For example, Hilliard-Lysen and Riemer (10) found that dentists who were employees in a practice could be frustrated by a lack of autonomy.

PROFESSIONALS AND CHANGING SOCIAL ENVIRONMENTS

In a sense, much of what I have discussed to this point may be related to changes in service professionals' environments. However, in addition, one can argue that wider societal changes have affected professional work. There are two key aspects to this: changes in the status of the professions, and societal changes that affect the nature of professionals' work.

One of the most notable changes in industrialized societies is the generally increased level of education for most citizens. There is no longer the same gap between the well-educated professional and the "person in the street." A well-educated client may be more inclined to question the professional's decisions. At the same time, better education allows some professions to challenge the monopolies of others (16). For example, in Australia, there has been a move for nurses to prescribe drugs under certain circumstances, and chiropractors have also made inroads into traditional physicians' work. Another consequence of this move to a more egalitarian distribution of educational resources is a general decline in the status of the professions. Not only is the modern population relatively well-educated, but there are more professionals. Even medical doctors have been affected. As Arnetz has pointed out, "Extrinsic stressors of the medical profession are many and growing. Not only is the role of the physician questioned but a real or threatened surplus of physicians has resulted in a relative decrease in salaries. The physician's role is increasingly 'demystified'" (9, p. 206).

This is a more obvious issue for the teaching profession. It is difficult for teachers to attain high status, as many of the services they offer are certainly not rare in a well-educated community. Moreover, media criticism and lack of respect in society are important stressors for teachers (28). Farber drew a similar link with burnout, suggesting that "traditions and values in the greater society, including the chronic undervaluation of work involving the care of children and, similarly, the continual denigration of work primarily performed by women, serve to promote the conditions that make teachers feel overworked and unappreciated" (2, p. 676). A double negative for some teachers may be not only the lowered social status but also their perception that society is responsible for much of the occupational stress they experience. I have earlier reported one teacher's response to the question, "What aspects of your job do you find the source of most stress?: Changes in expectations, changes in principles, changes in morals with kids these days, changes in family backgrounds, the stress it's bringing to children's behaviour" (46, p. 50). The difficult nature of teaching in recent times may further undermine the status of the profession as it may attract less academically able entrants to the profession. Relative status can also be a source of stress. For example, stress related to perceived status relative to physicians has been identified as problematic for dentists (10, 11).

THE "ATTRIBUTION OF RESPONSIBILITY FOR STRESS" MODEL

My colleagues and I have developed and empirically tested the attribution of responsibility for stress (ARS) model (e.g., 41, 46). The model has relevance to this chapter because of its application to the specific context of a large, bureaucratic education system. Arguably, the model has currency for other professionals such as social workers, nurses, and physicians working within bureaucratic formal organizations.

Education systems are readily conceptualized, in organizational terms, as loosely coupled (47-49). However, it is probably more useful to think of these systems as composed of subsystems that can be loose or tight. The looseness-tightness refers to the extent of control that authorities within a system have over the activities of subsystems. So, for example, within a high school, one would generally not expect a principal to exert tight control over the day-to-day classroom activities of a teacher. Within a wider school system, head office is likely to exert even less control over the day-to-day activities within a school. It would seem logical that within a bureaucracy, professional activities should be only loosely coupled, allowing the professional to make appropriate decisions about professional issues. Notwithstanding, one may also expect tension between bureaucratic and professional goals.

A consequence of the loosely coupled nature of school systems is that teachers may develop organizational schemas, and knowledge structures (50), more consistent with loose coupling than with formal organizational charts. That is, they will not think of themselves as embedded within schools that are within a school system that is enmeshed within the wider society; rather, they may develop schemas that place these entities at varying distances from the self. So, in a high school, a teacher will be conceptually closer to her department than to the school as an organization, and the latter will be closer than the school authority or bureaucracy, and so on.

Attribution theory is primarily concerned with individuals' explanations for life events and acknowledges that past experiences and schemas may play a part in attributions (51, 52). Of course, a teacher may experience rare events that are particularly distressful and that generate attributions. They may also have relatively stable and consistent stressful experiences, over time, for which they develop attribution schemas that attribute responsibility for aspects of their occupational stress.

While it is important to acknowledge that stress can be positive (eustress) (53), occupational stress is generally negative (distress). This is an important aspect of the ARS model, as it introduces the notion of success or failure. It is common parlance to talk of successfully coping, or failing to cope, with stress. Being responsible for one's own stress may be associated with a sense of failure. Considerable attention has been paid to attributions for success and failure in attribution theory (e.g., 54), and an important phenomenon, the self-serving or hedonic bias, has been identified (51, 54–57). In simple terms, the self-serving bias is a tendency to take credit for successes and externalize blame for failures. In terms of teachers' occupational stress, the self-serving bias predicts that they attribute responsibility for successful coping (i.e., low stress) to self and attribute failure to cope (i.e., high stress) beyond self.

The two main components of the ARS model are the schemas that place organizational entities at varying distances from self and the self-serving bias that predicts attribution of responsibility for stress to those entities. Moreover, the model suggests that teachers attribute greater responsibility to those entities that are further from self. For example, greater responsibility will be attributed to a distant bureaucracy (the school authority) than to a nearer subsystem (the school), as the latter could involve some self-responsibility. The ARS model has been supported empirically in a number of studies (e.g., 41, 46, 58).

It is logical to consider whether or not the attribution patterns predicted by the ARS model are desirable. On one level, they may be considered functional for the individual, as the externalization process may be predicted to protect self-esteem. However, the externalization could be dysfunctional if the individual feels powerless, controlled, and alienated, and consequently less likely to employ problem-solving coping strategies. It is difficult to conceive how the attribution patterns would be desirable from an organizational perspective, as they are unlikely to be associated with high morale and commitment to organizational goals. For example, systemwide, innovative curriculum changes may be less likely to be embraced and properly implemented by teachers who perceive head office as a distant, bureaucratic, major source of occupational stress. Indeed, the same argument makes sense for day-to-day interactions. Local, organizational dysfunctions are less likely to be openly communicated to distant, head offices that are seen as controlling, major sources of stress. Similar examples may be drawn for other professionals working within health systems, community services, and large legal firms, among others. Moreover, negative outcomes may not be related only to change.

CONCLUSION

I have argued in this chapter that a number of the service professions have begun to converge in terms of some aspects of professionalism. The profession–semi-profession typology may no longer be the most useful, particularly when considering occupational stress. Rather, there have been similar changes in a number of professions corresponding to changes in the wider society. Included in these is a move within formal organizations that employ professionals to greater bureaucratization and a concomitant decrease in professional autonomy. At the same time, considerable similarities can be explained in terms of dealing with other human beings in a service mode. These aspects of professional work can be associated with occupational stress.

The client-professional relationship is central to professionals' work. Professional work that involves interaction with people is arguably inherently difficult and almost certain to involve failure and disappointment. Unrealistic, idealistic expectations have been associated with stress and burnout (2, 4). Because unrealistic, idealistic expectations are formed before exposure to harsh realities, it would seem that this is an issue that should be addressed during professional preparation courses or early in individuals' careers. Of course, this should not be simply a matter-of-fact presentation of negative aspects of professional experience. Rather, it should be incorporated into a course dealing with occupational stress specific to the profession, and the educational purpose of the information must be made clear. The aim should be to temper the idealistic flame with realism, not snuff it out.

In one sense, bureaucracy is antithetical to professionalism; however, when professional work takes place in large formal organizations, such as health or education systems, organizational structure requires an amalgam of the two. Bureaucracy inevitably will limit professionals' autonomy and likely result in occupational stress. However, the ARS model suggests that this process may involve attribution schemas that incorporate organizational distancing. One approach to decrease the perceived stress is to reduce the conceptual distance between the professional workers and the bureaucratic structure. This could occur by making clear to the professionals that the organizational goals are aligned with professional goals and by making clear the linkages between bureaucratic and professional activities. Hence, it could be very worthwhile for large organizations to have educational programs—particularly during induction programs, but also at other times—that clearly demonstrate the symbiotic nature of work at the local level and work carried out in the head office. The emphasis should be interconnectedness between the individual and head office, rather than the alienation that may be associated with a lack of personal identification.

The decline in status of professions is unlikely to be reversed, but hopefully can be arrested. This decline is likely to play less of a role in occupational stress for professionals if they do not perceive deterioration after joining the profession.

REFERENCES

1. Chan, K. B., et al. Work stress among six professional groups: The Singapore experience. *Soc. Sci. Med.* 50: 1415–1432, 2000.
2. Farber, B. A. Treatment strategies for different types of teacher burnout. *In Session: Psychother. Pract.* 56: 675–689, 2000.
3. Friedman, I. A. Burnout in teachers: Shattered dreams of impeccable professional performance. *In Session: Psychother. Pract.* 56: 595–606, 2000.
4. Pines, A. M. Burnout. In *Handbook of Stress: Theoretical and Clinical Aspects*, Ed. 2, edited by L. Goldberger and S. Breznitz, pp. 386–402. Free Press, New York, 1993.
5. Sutherland, V. J., and Cooper, C. L. *Understanding Stress: A Psychological Perspective for Health Professionals*. Chapman and Hall, London, 1990.
6. Brooke, D. The addicted doctor: Caring professionals? *Br. J. Psychiatry* 166: 149–153, 1995.
7. Reamer, F. G. The impaired social worker. *Soc. Work* 37: 165–170, 1992.
8. Sherman, M. D., and Thelen, M. H. Distress and professional impairment among psychologists in clinical practice. *Prof. Psychol.* 29: 79–85, 1998.

9. Arnetz, B. B. Psychosocial challenges facing physicians today. *Soc. Sci. Med.* 52: 203–213, 2001.
10. Hilliard-Lysen, J., and Riemer, J. W. Occupational stress and suicide among dentists. *Deviant Behav. Interdisciplinary J.* 9: 333–346, 1988.
11. Stack, S. Suicide risk among dentists: A multivariate analysis. *Deviant Behav. Interdisciplinary J.* 17: 107–117, 1996.
12. Cox, T. *Stress*. Macmillan Education, London, 1978.
13. Hamid, P. N., and Chan, W. T. Locus of control and occupational stress in Chinese professionals. *Psychol. Rep.* 82: 75–79, 1998.
14. Parkes, K. R. Personality and coping as moderators of work stress processes: Models, methods and measures. *Work Stress* 8: 110–129, 1994.
15. Scott, W. R. *Organizations: Rational, Natural, and Open Systems*, Ed. 3. Prentice-Hall, Englewood Cliffs, N.J., 1992.
16. Shapiro, M. Professions in the post-industrial labour market. In *Contemporary Perspectives on Social Work, the Human Services: Challenges and Change*, edited by I. O'Connor, P. Smyth, and J. Warburton, pp. 102–115. Longman, Melbourne, 2000.
17. Bottery, M. The future of teachers' professionalism. *Aspects Educ.* 48: 86–103, 1993.
18. Goode, W. J. The theoretical limits of professionalization. In *The Semi-professions and Their Organization: Teachers, Nurses/Social Workers*, edited by A. Etzioni, pp. 266–313. Free Press, New York, 1969.
19. Schattner, P. L., and Coman, G. J. The stress of metropolitan general practice. *Med. J. Aust.* 169: 133–137, 1998.
20. Arnetz, J. E., Arnetz, B. B., and Petterson, I. Violence in the nursing profession: Occupational and lifestyle risk factors in Swedish nurses. *Work Stress* 10: 119–127, 1996.
21. Bloch, A. M. Combat neurosis in inner-city schools. *Am. J. Psychiatry* 135: 1189-1192, 1978.
22. Gold, Y., and Roth, R. A. *Teachers Managing Stress*. Falmer Press, London, 1993.
23. Thomsen, S., et al. Feelings of professional fulfilment and exhaustion in mental health personnel: The importance of organizational and individual factors. *Psychother. Psychosom.* 68: 157–164, 1999.
24. Blase, J. J., and Greenfield, W. D. An interactive/cyclical theory of teacher performance. *Administrator's Notebook* 29: 1–4, 1981.
25. Farrugia, C. Career choice and sources of occupational satisfaction and frustration among teachers in Malta. *Comp. Educ.* 22: 221–231, 1986.
26. Lortie, D. *School Teacher*. University of Chicago Press, Chicago, 1975.
27. Nias, J. Teacher satisfaction and dissatisfaction: Herzberg's "two-factor" hypothesis revisited. *Br. J. Sociol. Educ.* 2: 235–246, 1981.
28. McCormick, J., and Solman, R. The externalized nature of teachers' occupational stress and its association with job satisfaction. *Work Stress* 6: 33–44, 1992.
29. Hart, P. M., Wearing, A. J., and Conn, M. Conventional wisdom is a poor predictor of the relationship between discipline policy, student misbehavior and teacher stress. *Br. J. Educ. Psychol.* 65: 27–48, 1995.
30. McCormick, J., and Solman, R. Teachers' attributions of responsibility for occupational stress and satisfaction: An organizational perspective. *Educ. Stud.* 18: 201–222, 1992.

31. Rice, P. L. *Stress and Health,* Ed. 3, Brooks/Cole, Pacific Grove, Calif., 1999.
32. Ogus, E. D. Burnout and coping strategies: A comparative study of ward nurses. In *Occupational Stress: A Handbook*, edited by R. Crandall and P. L. Perrewe, pp. 249–261. Taylor and Francis, Washington, D.C., 1995.
33. Abbott, A. *The System of Professions: An Essay on the Division of Expert Labor.* University of Chicago Press, Chicago, 1988.
34. Freidson, E. The theory of professions: State of the art. In *The Sociology of the Professions: Lawyers, Doctors, and Others*, edited by R. Dingwall and P. Lewis, pp. 19–37. St. Martin's Press, New York, 1983.
35. Macdonald, K. M. *The Sociology of the Professions*. Sage, London, 1995.
36. Collins, R. Market closure and the conflict theory of the professions. In *Theory and History: Rethinking the Study of the Professions*, edited by M. Burrage and R. Torstendahl, pp. 24–43. Sage, London, 1990.
37. Magee, M., and Hojat, M. Impact of health care system on physicians' discontent. *J. Community Health* 26: 357–365, 2001.
38. Weber, M. *The Theory of Social and Economic Organization*, edited by A. M. Henderson and T. Parsons. Free Press, New York, 1964.
39. Bendix, R. *Work and Authority in Industry: Ideologies of Management in the Course of Industrialization.* Wiley, New York, 1956.
40. Zalesnick, A., Kets de Vries, M. F. R., and Howard, J. Stress reactions in organizations: Syndromes, causes and consequences. *Behav. Sci.* 22: 151–162, 1977.
41. McCormick, J. Occupational stress of teachers: Biographical differences in a large school system. *J. Educ. Adm.* 35: 18–36, 1997.
42. Spector, P. E. Perceived control by employees: A meta-analysis of studies concerning autonomy and participation at work. *Hum. Relations* 39: 1005–1016, 1986.
43. Collyer, F., and White, K. *Corporate Control of Health Care in Australia: Discussion Paper No. 42.* The Australia Institute, Canberra, 2001.
44. Arches, J. Social structure, burnout, and job satisfaction. *Soc. Work* 36: 202–206, 1991.
45. Hoff, T. J. Same profession, different people: Stratification, structure, and physicians' employment choices. *Sociol. Forum* 13: 133–156, 1998.
46. McCormick, J. Some aspects of teachers' perceptions of society, educational change and their occupational stress. In *Change, Challenge, and Creative Leadership,* edited by B. Conners and T. d'Arbon, pp. 46–52. Australian Council for Educational Administration, Melbourne, 1997.
47. Logan, C. S., Ellett, C. D., and Licata, J. W. Structural coupling, robustness and effectiveness of schools. *J. Educ. Adm.* 31: 19–32, 1993.
48. Orton, J., and Weick, K. E. Loosely coupled systems: A reconceptualisation. *Acad. Manage. Rev.* 15: 203–223, 1990.
49. Weick, K. E. Educational organizations as loosely coupled systems. *Adm. Sci. Q.* 21: 1–19, 1976.
50. Lord, R. G., and Foti, R. J. Schema theories, information processing, and organizational behavior. In *The Thinking Organization,* edited by H. P. Sims, D. A. Gioa, and associates, pp. 20–48. Jossey-Bass, San Francisco, 1986.
51. Forsterling, F. *Attribution Theory in Clinical Psychology.* Wiley, Chichester, U.K., 1988.
52. Jaspers, J., Hewstone, M., and Fincham, F. Attribution theory and research: The state of the art. In *Attribution Theory and Research: Conceptual Development and Social*

Dimensions, edited by J. Jaspers, F. Fincham, and M. Hewstone, pp. 3–36. Academic Press, London, 1983.

53. Selye, H. *The Stress of Life.* McGraw-Hill, New York, 1976.
54. Weiner, B. An attributional theory of achievement motivation and emotion. *Psychol. Rev.* 92: 548–573, 1985.
55. Anderson, C. A. Attributions as decisions: A two stage information processing model. In *New Models, New Extensions of Attribution Theory,* edited by S. L. Zelen, pp. 12–54. Springer-Verlag, New York , 1991.
56. Weary, G., Stanley, M. A., and Harvey, J. H. *Attribution.* Springer-Verlag, New York, 1989.
57. Kashima, Y., and Triandis, H. C. The self-serving bias in attributions as a coping strategy. *J. Cross-Cultural Psychol.* 17: 83–97, 1986.
58. McCormick, J. An attribution model of teachers' occupational stress and job satisfaction in a large education system. *Work Stress* 11: 17–32, 1997.

Chapter 9

STRESS AMONG BLUE-COLLAR WORKERS

Chris L. Peterson

This chapter examines some of the background and research on stress among blue-collar workers and presents blue-collar stress as belonging to work of a particular class and culture. An analysis of results for blue-collar workers from the Australian Workplace Industrial Relations Survey of 1995 allows an examination of the major determinants of stress. As the analysis shows, changes in work practices are particularly strong predictors of stress for blue-collar workers, as they are for other occupational groups (see Chapter 2).

There is a very large literature on the causes and effects of stress at work. This literature has had a relatively limited focus on the effects of work stress on blue-collar workers, and few studies have focused on differences in the effects of stress on a range of occupational groups, including blue-collar workers.

"Blue-collar work" refers to the work done by laborers, tradespersons, and related employees (1). It can also include assembly and related work. In Australia, as internationally, there has been a decline in blue-collar work. For example, between 1990 and 1995, Australia saw a decrease in the proportion of the population engaged in trade, laboring, and related work, and this "is consistent with the ongoing general decline in unskilled jobs in Australia" (1, p. 43). This decline was mostly reflected in manufacturing industries and in the hospitality industry, including accommodation. In fact, the average decrease over that period was about 12 percent.

The ASCO scales (2) are used widely in Australia to define differences in occupation. While "blue-collar" refers to an occupational category for both women and men, other terms have been used specifically to refer to the same kind of work performed by women. "Pink-collar," for example, has been used to refer to women's assembly and related work (see 3).

CHARACTERISTICS OF BLUE-COLLAR WORK

According to Rifkin (4), many of the major reengineering breakthroughs have occurred in the automobile industry. Concurrently "post-Fordist restructuring is resulting in massive layoffs of blue-collar workers on the assembly line" (4, p. 129). Following the lead of the Japanese in the early 1990s, the United States was hoping to reengineer its automobile production to become more competitive; the aim of automobile manufacturers is to replace labor with technology. According to Rifkin, "despite the fact that labor costs are less than 10 to 15 percent of total costs, they represent a larger percentage of sales than do profits, and are easily reducible with the substitution of new information technologies" (4, p. 130). This can also mean avoiding the problems associated with the human characteristics of a workforce, such as turnover and absenteeism.

Employment in the steel industry has been dramatically affected by the upsurge of computerized mini-mills: to produce a ton of steel, these processes require only one-twelfth of the human labor required by integrated steel mills. The new production processes, together with major restructuring of management processes, are now being used in the steel industry. Rifkin (4) maintains that in countries such as Germany, where highly skilled machinists are regarded as a national treasure, the automated processes are bound to have a profound psychological effect. According to Rifkin (4), the rubber industry has been one of the most highly affected by new automated processes. Also affected has been mining: in the United States in 1992, 45,000 mining workers lost their jobs due to technological displacement. This displacement has also taken place in electronics, with General Electric reducing its workforce by more than 50 percent over nearly 15 years, from the early 1980s. The textile industry is still relatively labor intensive, but the introduction of computerized cloth laying and cutting, as well as microelectronic sewing machines, has led to production efficiencies, changed skill levels, and significantly reduced labor.

Rifkin also notes that millions of blue-collar workers have found themselves trapped between technological eras and marginalized. He argues that "by the mid decades of the [twenty-first] century, the blue collar worker will have passed from history, a casualty of the Third Industrial Revolution and the relentless march towards greater technological efficiency" (4, p. 140).

According to Burdess (5), blue-collar and other jobs obviously differ in the level of income. In Australia, "the highest paid 20 per cent . . . receive nearly 50 per cent of total income; the lowest paid 20 per cent receive less than 5 per cent. This is the most unequal distribution of any of the 20 industrial countries surveyed by the United Nations" (5, p. 179). He points out that the psychological effects of jobs differ for the different social classes. First, people in lower level jobs experience less control at work, and this has the effect of increasing powerlessness in other aspects of life. Second, the "lack of fulfillment experienced by people in working-class jobs results in their attempting to achieve fulfillment through consumption" (5, p. 180). In Burdess's study, managers reported being able to overcome problems, while semi-skilled workers reported the greatest degree of fatalism. In addition, the high rates of injury and illness among blue-collar workers (6) led them to expect their worklife to be unhealthy and unrewarding.

A number of writers, including Quinlan (7), have presented the "blame the worker" hypothesis as an explanation of negative health consequences of work. As Burdess maintained, "traditionally, employers have placed the blame for work-related illness squarely on the shoulders of workers themselves, using notions such as the accident-prone worker, the careless worker, the reckless worker and the malingering worker" (5, p. 174). Burdett refers to the work by Hopkins and Palser (8), who refuted management's claims that the cause of half of the New South Wales coal mining accidents was the workers themselves.

Stress at work has become an important issue in Australia. In Chapter 2 I noted the activities of the Australian Council of Trade Unions (ACTU) in 1998, in mounting a national stress campaign. This was in response to a much more dramatic series of changes that had taken place on the Australian business and industrial landscape over the past few years. Stress had emerged as an important occupational health and safety and industrial relations issue, and while many responded to it as a fad, the events of 1998 heralded stress as a serious problem resulting from the newer economic pressures of globalization and rational economic policies directed at organizing the economy of work.

Stress is not a new concept. As early as 1914, Cannon (9) wrote on the concept of stress, and in 1936, in the journal *Nature,* Hans Selye, a German-born medical practitioner and researcher, published a definitive article on how stress has a role to play in illness (10). The stress response was first described by Selye (11). He referred to the general adaptation syndrome (GAS), which has three stages: (*a*) alarm, where an initial shock precipitates a physiological and often a psychological response; (*b*) resistance, where the body mobilizes its defenses against the effects of the external stressors—at this stage the body's resistance is higher than normal; and (*c*) after a period of time, the body becoming tired and the response to the stressor weak—at this point the person can become quite ill. This process explains the effects of stress on the development of physical and psychological illness. In the stress process, the immune system becomes less effective, and infection and other illness can occur. Psychological ill-health can result also, and much of the process has been explained by Mason (12, 13) and others. The history of the stress concept has been reported by a number of writers (e.g., 14). The major impetus grew out of the initial writings of Cannon (9) and Selye (10, 11).

BLUE-COLLAR WORK AND STRESS

Cooper and Smith (15) argue that blue-collar workers are vulnerable to stress. Fisher maintains that blue-collar workers "have less jurisdiction over their working duties in that, unless they have power because of union or managerial positions on the shopfloor, they carry out those work activities specified by the employers" (16, p. 20). She argues that the changes in automation have altered the stressors from dirt, grime, vibration, and danger to boredom, associated with monitoring automated control processes. And, she continues, there are a number of differences in the type of stress experienced between blue-collar workers and managerial and clerical employees: (*a*) less control over how time is spent; (*b*) fewer opportunities to affect conditions related to the task; (c) fewer opportunities to avoid unpleasant aspects of the job; and (*d*) fewer opportunities to exercise discretion over leaving the job, due to lower wage levels. Fisher finally outlines two arguments relating to the effect of work on the rest of life. The first argument is that the meanings a person gives to work tend to pervade the rest of his or her life; that is, blue-collar workers may be less committed to their jobs than other workers, and the job will be a lesser source of gratification. The second argument is that the state of mind produced at work will have a carry-over effect on home activities; a person feeling depressed all day may spend much of the rest of life in a negative physical and psychological state. According to McLean (17), blue-collar workers have little influence, few opportunities for control, and little support from management and the structure of organizations they work for.

Ganster argues that studies of participation in decision-making explain "about 10–15 percent of the variance of measures in job satisfaction, and perhaps about 5 percent of the variance in self reported mental and physical health outcomes" (18, p. 7). He maintains that many of the cases of participation reported in the literature are modest in scope and degree. Given that they have produced good effects in terms of perceptions of control, however, they should be encouraged. Karasek's foundational work (19, 20) is an example of research that investigates control as an interaction with job demands, although Karasek did not find any statistical interaction. According to Ganster, "there is very little evidence in favour of the proposition that the effects of job demands can be negated by allowing greater employee control" (18, p. 15).

How are blue-collar workers' jobs affected by stress, and how is that stress experienced by different groups? Sutherland and Cooper (21) maintain that blue-collar workers in particular are affected less by the interpersonal aspects of organizational life and more by the physical conditions of work. For blue-collar workers there may be an iterative effect of stress on family and spouse. These authors also maintain that the work stress problems of one partner may lead to mental ill-health consequences in the other partner. Additional problems may result if partners need to be geographically mobile to gain employment. This is especially accentuated when one of the partners needs to be away from home for work reasons for long periods.

In a study of stress management training among blue-collar workers, Thomason and Pond (22) found that the effects of stress management programs were modest, at best, for these workers. Training in stress management and stress management skills had positive effects on state anxiety, somatic symptoms, and blood pressure. Additional training in self-management bolstered the effects of training in stress management skills for blue-collar workers.

I have argued elsewhere that "shift work, changes, monotony, and conflicting work requirements or ambiguous work contribute to stressful reactions" (14, p. 41). Drawing on McLean (17) and Shostack (23), I argued that the fear of losing one's job is a detrimental source of stress for blue-collar workers; although in recent times all employees face this threat, low wages and little to fall back on for support in times of unemployment make job loss a potent stressor for this group. Shostack argues that blue-collar workers have learned to shield themselves from some of the pressures of low incomes: they have learned "to mute and even deny dissatisfactions with stressors that seem out of their hands that they have little hope of reforming" (23, p. 12).

There is much underreporting of the effects of negative work on stress, as is evidenced in the discrepancy between self-reports on stress (6) and official compensation statistics. This is evident in a number of occupational illnesses and injuries (24). Shostack (23) also found regular underreporting of negative work effects. There is ample evidence of the effects of working in physically noxious environments, which contain dust, chemicals, and noise: for example, in Australia, the major compensated illness for men is work-related deafness.

For blue-collar work there is an emphasis on the effects of a number of stressors that are related to poor or low control on the job. Aronsson (25) has argued that a lack of control is an important precursor of stress. Many blue-collar jobs are associated with low status and with accompanying tight work pressures, demands of production schedules, and close supervision. An anomaly arising in Australia during the 1990s was that employees are now expected to take much of the worry of work home with them, even blue-collar workers: that is, their responsibility for the job has increased, but is not commensurate with authority.

A number of studies have been conducted on stress and blue-collar workers. Some of these studies have been exclusively of blue-collar work and factory environments, while others have included blue-collar workers with other groups such as white-collar workers and managers. The studies have variously looked at the major causes of stress, the relationship between control and stress, stressors and job strain, the effects of reward systems on stress, and various health outcomes from stress, including coronary conditions and ischemic heart disease. In a sense, the thrust of the studies is about control, overtly, or a lack of control leading to various ill-health outcomes. In addition, more studies are now looking at jobs with low control and their effects on the rest of life.

Effects of Lack of Control on Blue-Collar Work

Following Aronsson (25), a number of studies of blue-collar work have shown that control is an important factor in stress (see 26). Greif (27) reported on stress and illness in 20 factories over two years. He used a three-dimensional model that looked at stress within and outside the organization, reactions to stress over the short term, including physiological effects, morale, and well-being, and the long-term burden of stress. He found that control and simplified work were the main predictors of somatic and psychic stress. Uncertainty at work has also been associated with increased stress for blue-collar workers. In a study of German blue-collar workers, Semmer and coworkers (28) found that uncertainty and responsibility, environmental stressors, organizational problems with work, and time pressure explained most variations in job strain.

A number of studies have focused on the effects of management control on stress and the negative reactions produced through this for blue-collar workers (see 14). In different cultures this can have some unusual effects. In a study of Malay women, Levidow (29) found that over the last 30 years women have come to accept automation stress and workplace discipline, in contrast to the practice of spirit possession that they previously practiced as a resistance to management control.

Health Effects of Blue-Collar Work

In a study of heart disease among blue-collar workers, Siegrist and Peter (30) combined the results of several studies to investigate predictors of coronary heart disease and risk. They found that high extrinsic effort (manifested by workload and work pressure) and intrinsic effort (as shown by need for control together with low reward) led to neurohormonal activity. Effort and reward imbalance was strongly related to coronary risk and disease, and interventions were required in the workplace. In a later investigation, Peter (31) undertook a longitudinal study of blue-collar workers and found that the balance between effort and reward predicted ischemic heart disease and the prevalence of coronary risk factors. He also found that high effort, both intrinsic and extrinsic, predicted ischemic heart disease risk.

Siegrist and coworkers (32), investigating the relationship between ischemic heart disease and a number of different negative work factors, found that job insecurity, status inconsistencies, need for control, and work pressures predicted the occurrence of this disease. Tsutsumi and coworkers (33) also have reported research into hypertension and blue-collar workers in Japan. Furlan and colleagues (34) undertook a study of shift work and cardiovascular disease; they found that continuous changes in shift work were associated with increased disease.

Tennant (35) undertook a review of the literature on work stress and coronary heart disease and found conclusive evidence of a causal relationship between work stress and cardiovascular disease. Calvert and coworkers (36) investigated ischemic heart disease in several different occupational groups, for males aged 16–60. The highest rate of the disease was recorded for blue-collar groups, among sheriffs, policemen, correctional institution officers, machine operators, and firefighters.

Isaksen (37) investigated the relationship between blue-collar work and mental health, using qualitative methods to discern meanings attached to repetitive work.

Employees were able to identify eight levels of meaning in repetitive work, and Isaksen concludes that meaning ameliorates the stressful experience of work.

Substance abuse has been related to stress and absenteeism for blue-collar workers. However, one study showed there was not a significant relationship between alcohol consumption and absences at work. Vasse and colleagues (38) studied blue-collar workers for associations between alcohol consumption, stress, and sickness absence. They found that not drinking increased absence risk in comparison to moderate drinking. The relationship between stressor and alcohol, and stressor and sickness absence, was moderated by stress. The study failed to find a negative relationship between excessive alcohol consumption and sickness absence.

Effects of Stressors and Extra-Organizational Factors on Stress

Women in nontraditional blue-collar jobs were compared with women in training to see whether those who enter blue-collar work are predisposed to making role transitions successfully or whether they alter their coping styles (39). The women in training were found to have stronger problem- and emotion-focused coping styles than women in nontraditional blue-collar jobs.

Pay systems have also been shown to have an effect on stress, although these tend to be less potent forms of stressors than a lack of control. Shirom and colleagues (40) found that a performance-based and contingent pay system was related to a higher rate of depression and somatic conditions, but it was not related to anxiety. Monotonous work acted as a mediator.

Unionization can have important effects on the stress of blue-collar workers. Shirom and Kirmeyer (41) found that higher union performance was associated with lower reported stress in blue-collar workers. However, union members had greater interrole conflict and ambiguity than nonmembers, but similar levels of somatic complaints and overload.

Ways of coping with job stress have been researched for blue-collar workers. For example, Kanai and Wababayashi (42) studied "workaholism" among blue-collar workers and the extent to which it was a way of dealing with stress for employees who work in highly structured environments. They found that for younger workers overload increased enjoyment, but for older workers enjoyment was impaired.

Effects on the Rest of Life

Other studies have focused on the effects of stressful work events on the rest of life. Ewan and coworkers (43) showed that stress-related conditions need to have medical backing in order for affected workers to gain substantial support from the rest of the community. In the study, the repetitive strain injury experienced by women employed in a chicken-processing plant and a telecommunications organization had strong effects on homelife, relationships, and capacity for housework, and led to distress, poor self-esteem, and a reduced involvement in leisure activities. The authors make the point that the women encountered a lack of belief in their condition by others, uncertain prognosis, and ambiguity about repetitive strain injury, together with a sociopolitical atmosphere within which they negotiated roles and adaptations. It is a common experience for many workers that stress-related conditions need to be seen as legitimate, and therefore carry a medical diagnosis, if workers are to receive support from the community, including support from significant others such as spouses and family members.

METHODS IN THE STUDY OF BLUE-COLLAR WORK STRESS

The data set used in this study is described in detail in Chapter 2. It comes from the 1995 Australian Workplace Industrial Relations Survey (AWIRS95) from the federal Department of Industrial Relations in Australia.There has been no subsequent national data collection of this size, although a similar data collection is planned. In all, 19,155 employees were included in the survey of 2001 workplaces nationally. Different survey results in the set are reported by Moorhead and coworkers (1).

The survey gives the opportunity to report on the causes of stress, and in particular the extent to which perceived workplace changes occurring in the 12 months prior to the study contributed to stress in a national sample of blue-collar workers. One of the interests in the study was the extent to which blue-collar workers had been affected by changes in the way work was done during the past decade. In addition, it was of interest to see the extent to which predictors of stress were different for blue-collar workers than for the national sample of workers (reported in Chapter 2).

The first hypothesis for the study is that work intensification and increases in effort are expected to be significant predictors of stress for blue-collar workers. It has already been shown that workers in blue-collar types of jobs are subject to increases in the amount of effort required on the job (see 32). The second hypothesis is derived from the study reported in Chapter 2, which showed that work-change variables are likely to be better predictors of stress than static work variables. In the study reported in Chapter 2, work-change variables proved to be more potent predictors of stress for all occupational groups. It is therefore expected that for blue-collar workers, as for the national sample of all workers, work-change variables will be the strongest predictors of stress.

The study uses a block recursive regression model (Figure 9.1). Three different blocks of variables are entered separately, producing an estimate of total effects as regression coefficients. This allows calculation of not only direct effects (controlling for the effects of all other variables) but indirect effects, which

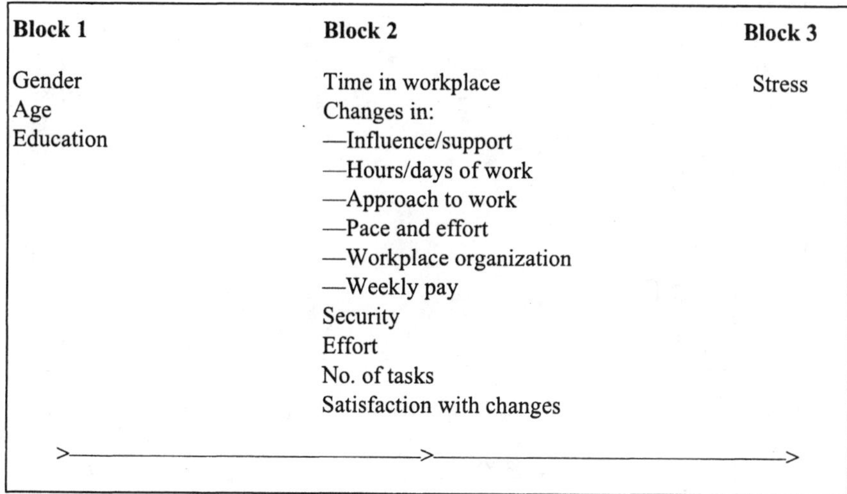

Figure 9.1 Block recursive model.

measure the influence of mediating variables. Total effects are the summation of direct and indirect effects (see Chapter 2).

Descriptive statistics and ANOVA are presented, together with a block recursive regression equation. In the regression equation, the dependent variable *stress* is scored on a scale of 1 to 100 so that partial regression coefficient effects can be calculated as percentages, for ease of interpretation. (For a fuller description of the method, see the methods section in Chapter 2).

The factor analysis derived for the study reported in Chapter 2 is repeated here for the study of blue-collar workers (Table 9.1). Four different factors emerged using a Varimax rotation, which produced the strongest factor solution. The first factor, *influence and support,* refers to a change in control; the scale achieved a moderate to strong reliability (Cronbach's alpha = .73) and a .31 inter-item correlation. The second factor, *number of hours and days during the week,* contains items related to overall working hours; Cronbach's alpha is .79, and the inter-item correlation is .21. The third factor is *type of work and approach to doing work;* the scale has a reliability of .78 and an average inter-item correlation of .54. The fourth factor is *work pace and effort;* Cronbach's alpha is .60, and inter-item correlation is .43.

RESULTS

Of the 8,352, individuals in the blue-collar group (laborer and related, plant and machine operators, tradespersons and apprentices), 28.6 percent (2,386) were women and 71.4 percent (5,966) were men. The gender difference reflects the

Table 9.1

Factor analysis of changes at work

	I	II	III	IV	Average inter-item correlation	Reliability (Cronbach's alpha)
I Influence and support						
1. Change in say in decisions	.75	–.09	–.04	.10		
2. Change in use of ideas	.73	–.08	–.08	–.18		
3. Change in promotion opportunity	.68	–.12	–.02	–.05		
4. Change in satisfaction	.74	–.05	.03	–.08		
5. Change in family balance satisfaction	.51	.26	.06	.25		
6. Change in amount of training	.48	–.05	–.12	–.06	.31	.73
II Number of hours and days of work						
1. Change in hours	–.01	.89	.05	.20		
2. Change in hours per day	.03	.80	.08	.26		
3. Change in number of days per week	–.01	.70	.03	–.09	.21	.79
III Type of work and approach to doing work						
1. Change in type of work	.14	–.10	.77	–.06		
2. Change in how you do your job	.09	–.06	.81	–.19	.54	.78
IV Work pace and effort						
1. Change in effort	–.17	.07	.13	.80		
2. Change in pace	.02	.13	.16	.79	.43	.60

Note: Factor loadings were obtained using Varimax rotation with unities in the main diagonal. Eigenvalues (percent explained variance) are 3.26 (21.73%), 2.35 (15.64%), 1.6 (10.75%), 1.08 (7.17%).

national distribution towards men in these occupations. This represents a much lower proportion of women compared to the national sample of all occupational groups (in the total study, 44.8 percent were women and 55.2 percent were men). There were small and not significant differences between women and men in the degree of stress perceived, with women reporting slightly higher stress (mean scores, 50.1 for men, 47.8 for women). Mean scores differed significantly between blue-collar (49.5), white-collar (56.8), and managerial/professional (69.3) employees, and the differences between each group were significant ($F = 298.65$, $df = 2$, $P = .00$) (Scheffe post hoc test).

The average length of time in the one job was 7.21 years, longer than that for the total AWIRS sample which was 6.28 years (see Chapter 2). A higher proportion of blue-collar workers (37.7 percent) felt insecure than either white-collar (30.8 percent) or managerial/professional (27.2 percent) employees ($F = 49.12$, $df = 2$; $P = .00$) (Table 9.2). In addition, blue-collar workers experienced fewer changes in workplace organization (52.1 percent cf. 59.5 percent for white-collar and 61.7 percent for managerial/professional employees), indicating more workplace stability ($F = 45.59$, $df = 2$, $P = .00$). Pay had increased least for the blue-collar workers (54.7 percent) and most for managerial/professional employees (68.2 percent) ($F = 85.81$, $df = 2$, $P = .00$).

There were few differences in increase in number of tasks between blue-collar (81.2 percent) and white-collar (82.2 percent) workers, but managerial/professional employees (90.4 percent) had a substantially higher increase in number of different tasks to perform ($F = 98.61$, $df = 2$, $P = .00$). While a substantial proportion of blue-collar workers (85.9 percent) reported that they had to put a lot of effort into the job, this was significantly less than for white-collar (88.5 percent) and particularly managerial/professional (92.2 percent) employees ($F = 41.97$, $df = 2$, $P = .00$). However, there were no significant differences between groups in employees' beliefs about how the changes affected their welfare.

Significant differences were evident in the effects of changes during the past 12 months on influence and support at work (Table 9.3). There had been fewer increases for blue-collar workers (1.96) and most increases for managerial/professional employees (1.91) ($F = 12.27$, $df = 2$, $P = .00$). Again, groups differed greatly in terms of increases in number of hours and days per week. Blue-collar workers reported fewest increases (2.05) and managerial/professional employees reported most (2.25) ($F = 300.22$, $df = 2$, $P = .00$). There were fewer changes in approaches to doing work for blue-collar workers (1.63) than for managers/professionals (1.49) ($F = 126.88$, $df = 2$, $P = .00$). Finally, while reporting large changes in workpace and effort, blue-collar workers reported the lowest increases during the past 12 months (2.43, cf. 2.49 for white-collar workers and 2.54 for managerial/professional workers) ($F = 57.70$, $df = 2$, $P = .00$).

Differences in determinants of stress were not so great between blue-collar workers and the total sample reported in Chapter 2 (Table 9.4). As blue-collar

Table 9.2

Differences between blue-collar and other groups for selected variables

	Blue-collar		White-collar		Manager/prof.	
	No.	%	No.	%	No.	%
Job security						
Feel secure	1,449	38.7	3,991	44.3	2,060	46.7
Neither here nor there	885	23.6	2,250	24.9	1,154	26.1
Feel insecure	1,413	37.7	2,778	30.8	1,201	27.2
Total	3,747	100.0	9,884	100.0	4,651	100.0
Change in workplace organization						
No	1,924	47.9	3,848	40.5	1,744	38.3
Yes	2,091	52.1	5,658	59.5	2,804	61.7
Total	4,015	100.0	9,506	100.0	4,548	100.0
Change in pay						
Gone up	2,254	54.7	5,764	60.0	3,137	68.2
Stayed the same	1,598	38.8	3,239	33.7	1,295	28.1
Gone down	266	6.2	601	6.3	170	3.7
Total	4,118	100.0	9,604	100.0	4,602	100.0
Lots of different tasks						
Agree	3,349	81.2	7,937	82.2	4,156	90.4
Neither agree nor disagree	425	10.3	983	10.2	291	6.3
Disagree	348	8.4	736	7.6	149	3.2
Total	4,122	100.0	9,656	100.0	4,596	100.0
Effort into the job						
Disagree	90	2.2	167	1.7	50	1.1
Neither here nor there	493	11.9	947	9.8	307	6.7
Agree	3,563	85.9	8,569	88.5	4,229	92.2
Total	4,146	100.0	9,683	100.0	4,586	100.0
Better due to changes						
Better off	1,122	30.3	2,764	31.4	1,530	35.7
About the same	1,734	46.9	3,884	44.2	1,669	38.9
Worse off	844	22.8	2,141	24.4	1,091	25.4
Total	3,700	100.0	8,789	100.0	4,290	100.0

Table 9.3

Differences in selective work factors for blue-collar, white-collar, and managerial/professional employees—one-way ANOVA

Work factors[a]	Blue-collar	White-collar	Manager/prof.	*F*	*df*	*p*
Changes in influence and support	1.96	1.94	1.91	12.27	2	.00
Changes in number of hours and days of work	2.05	2.11	2.25	300.22	2	.00
Changes in type of work and approach to doing work	1.63	1.54	1.49	126.88	2	.00
Change in workplace and effort	2.43	2.49	2.54	57.70	2	.00
Job security	1.99	1.87	1.81	49.21	2	.00
Change in workplace organization	1.52	1.60	1.62	45.59	2	.00
Change in pay	1.52	1.46	1.36	85.81	2	.00
Lots of different tasks	1.27	1.25	1.13	98.61	2	.00
Effort into the job	2.84	2.87	2.91	41.97	2	.00
Better due to changes	1.92	1.93	1.90	2.64	2	N.S.

[a]All variables are coded as high score for negative effect (e.g., a high score on job security is feeling insecure).

workers became older, their stress increased (standardized regression coefficient [beta] = .07), with an increase of almost one point of stress for each year (unstandardized regression coefficient [*b* score] = .89). For the dummy education variables, employees with a secondary education had a significantly lower level of stress than those with year 10 or 11 education (the omitted category) (beta = –.06), and those with certificate-level education had significantly more stress (.04).

Those who had been longest in the one job experienced more stress than those with less job experience: there was 0.27 percent more stress for each additional year (beta = .06). However, the major factors to predict stress were the

Table 9.4

Regression results for determinants of stressfulness of the job (dependent variable = stress)[a]

Independent variables (entered in blocks)	Total effects[b]	
	b	beta
Block 1		
Women (cf. men)	–.168	–.00
Age	.89	.07**
Primary	–1.47	–.01
Secondary	–3.30	–.06**
Certificate	5.40	.04*
Tertiary	.28	.01
Adjusted *R*-squared		.01
Block 2		
Length of time in the one job	.27	.06**
Changes in influence and support	12.04	.19**
Changes in hours and days	4.65	.06**
Changes in type of work	–3.52	–.06**
Changes in pace and effort	7.78	.14**
Change in workplace organization/management	1.53	.03
Change in weekly pay	.82	.02
Security	3.09	.10**
Effort	4.60	.07**
Number of tasks	–2.27	–.05**
Satisfaction with changes	5.43	.15**
Adjusted *R*-squared		.18

[a]The stress scale has been recalculated between 0 and 100.
[b]*b* is the partial regression coefficient; beta, the standardized regression coefficient.
**$P < .01$; *$P < .05$

work-change variables. Changes in the past 12 months in influence and support had the most effect (.19), with reductions in influence and support on the job during the past 12 months accounting for a more than 12 percent increase in stress. Increases in pace and effort during the past 12 months meant an increase in stress of almost 8 percent (.14). The two other work-change variables (changes in number of hours and days of work, and changes in type of work and approach to doing work) accounted for a moderate increase in stress. The difference between no change and an increase in hours and days worked predicted a nearly 5 percent change in stress (.06), and the difference between no change and an increase in the types of work and approaches to doing work predicted a change of 3.5 percent in the stress score (–.06).

Generally the change variables were stronger determinants of stress than work variables measured at one point in time. However, a shift in job security, from being neither secure nor insecure to feeling insecure, accounted for a more than 3 percent increase in the stress score (adjusted *R*-squared = .10). The effect of having to expend a lot of effort on the job, however, was only half as strong as a predictor of stress as having a change in effort and pace. The difference between being neither here nor there about the amount of effort expended on the job and expending a lot of effort accounted for a more than 4.5 percent increase in the stress score (beta = .07). Together with the effects of a change in pace and effort, this supports the hypothesis that increased effort on the job is a significant predictor of stress.

One of the largest effects on stress was employees' satisfaction with changes on the job: feeling dissatisfied compared to feeling neutral about the changes led to a nearly 5.5 percent increase in the stress score (beta = .15). Finally, the effect of the number of job tasks was small to moderate (–.05), with too many tasks predicting increases in stress.

In all, the results provide some evidence for the verification of the second hypothesis—that work-change variables are strong predictors of stress, stronger than static work variables. However, because different variables were being measured for change factors and static factors, this finding is open to further investigation.

The model accounts for only 18 percent of variance (adjusted *R*-squared = .18), and as such it represents a relatively small proportion of the explanation for work stress. In the absence of home-related and other life variables, the contribution of this wide range of work and biographical variables represents a small, but not insignificant, explanation of work factors that can be controlled to affect stress. What it does signify also is that more research needs to be carried out on the effects of extra-work variables on stress.

DISCUSSION

Overall, the results of the Australian national study showed that during the mid-1990s, some major changes had taken place in blue-collar work in Australia. Blue-collar employment was on the decline. At the same time, as measured for a 12-month period prior to the study, workpace and effort had increased to a marked degree; this was evidenced by reports that effort on the job was extremely high. This finding is supported by a number of studies that have cited work intensification as part of the major changes taking place in Australian industry (see 1), changes that signaled the beginning of a process of dismantling the award structure of many blue-collar jobs, instituted by the new federal Liberal government's workplace relations minister.

In addition, there had been some increase in hours worked and substantial changes in workplace organization and approaches to doing work. The moderate stress reported by blue-collar workers in the national survey was considerably less than that reported by managers, but as Chapter 2 shows, there were specific reasons for the increases in managerial and professional stress, factors that had less of an effect on blue-collar workers. Yet blue-collar workers retained their moderate levels of stress as reported in a number of studies during the preceding two decades (see 14, 44–46).

As the results show, while large changes were occurring for blue-collar work, changes did not occur to the same degree as for white-collar workers, and particularly for managers/professionals. For example, blue-collar employees felt less secure in their work, particularly compared with managers/professionals. And fewer blue-collar workers than white-collar and managerial/professional employees had received increases in pay in the preceding 12 months. However, blue-collar work experienced workplace reorganization to a lesser degree than the other occupational categories.

Blue-collar workers also had less of an increase in the number of different tasks than managerial/professional employees. While they reported a large effort expended on the job, it was not to the degree reported by white-collar and managerial/professional workers. Blue-collar workers reported less beneficial changes than did other occupational groups—for example, they had less increase in influence and control. But at the same time they felt they had fewer increases in number of hours and days worked, particularly compared with managerial/professional employees. And they had fewer changes in approaches to doing work, and the lowest increase in workpace and effort, even though that increase was large. These findings lend weight to the hypothesis presented in Chapter 2 that rational economic management and its attendant work intensification has had its largest negative effect for managerial/professional workers. In that sense, blue-collar workers may have gained some protection from the effects of work changes occurring in the 1990s, more so than other groups, and this may help to account for the lower work stress scores for this group of workers.

I have reported earlier some major differences in the causes of stress between blue-collar workers and other occupational groups (these include the strength of effect of a lack of consideration by management, and role conflict: for white-collar and managerial employees, poor relationships were the major cause of stress, followed by a lack of consideration by management and a lack of skill utilization) (14). However, the national sample has shown that causes of blue-collar stress are similar to those for all occupational groups in the study. This suggests that all workers appear to be subject to the effects of particular work intensification factors (see 1) and that changes were occurring across the board, with a lesser effect on blue-collar workers.

The regression analyses in this study tested a particular model for blue-collar workers: the extent to which changes in work practices were predictors of stress.

As with the sample of all workers reported in Chapter 2, as blue-collar workers became older they were more likely to report higher stress. Also as in the national sample, a higher education gave a protection against the experience of stress; however, for blue-collar workers, having a certificate or tertiary level of education was likely to lead to higher stress.

There were few differences in the effects on stress of too many different tasks between blue-collar workers and the whole sample (see Chapter 2). In both cases, having too many tasks is a moderate predictor of stress. Blue-collar workers experienced fewer increases in the number of different tasks than did white-collar and managerial/professional employees, however. This is an aspect of work intensification that appears to be as important to blue-collar workers as to managerial/professional workers, and it should raise some questions about the direction of excessive multi-skilling and its effect on workers and, potentially, on productivity.

As in the sample of all Australian workers (Chapter 2), the major predictor of stress for blue-collar workers was a reduction in support and influence (which is related to control). Aronsson (25), Jackson (47), Karasek (19, 20), and I (14) have all shown the importance of a lack of control for blue-collar workers, as it is for other groups of employees. In this study I have shown that influence and support have increased less for blue-collar workers than for other groups. However, loss of control and influence appears to be a particularly potent stressor, which may mean that employees become particularly frustrated when that level erodes. For blue-collar workers, this substantiates earlier research on the effects of diminished control. Of interest also is that diminished control and influence as a cause of stress is as important to blue-collar workers as to the composite of all other occupational groups (Chapter 2).

CONCLUSION

The picture for blue-collar workers is a landscape of change—increased technological change and automation, which are affecting the numbers of blue-collar workers employed more than the numbers of white-collar workers and managers and professionals. As Rifkin (4) has argued, we may be entering an era of rapid decline and eventual evaporation of blue-collar work, albeit over a few generations.

In the 1980s, blue-collar work was consistently reported as more stressful than the work of higher occupational groups. As I argued in Chapter 2, economic rationalism and rationalistic management, and the downsizing that has severely reduced middle management, have likely caused white-collar workers, and particularly managers and professions, to suffer higher levels of stress than in the past. This is not to say that blue-collar work is less stressful than in the past. It may be that increased automation and technological development have produced other stressors, but ones that have not increased blue-collar stress levels to the degree that stress for some other groups has increased.

The arguments of Shostack (23) should not be neglected. For blue-collar workers, with often low pay and a class background that present some difficulties in coping (48), the effects of stressful work on the rest of their working lives may be magnified, and the ability to deal with that stress somewhat compromised. So the stress experienced in blue-collar work may well still have dramatic effects on family and personal relations.

In Australia in the 1990s, blue-collar work may have undergone fewer specific negative work-intensification changes—albeit measured as a snapshot, based on self-report over 12 months—than white-collar workers and managers and professionals. Another snapshot may have revealed quite a different picture, but unfortunately, a repeat of the AWIRS study has yet to be commissioned. For example, a comparison between the 1990 and 1995 AWIRS studies revealed structural changes that would be further detrimental to blue-collar work. These included a large decline in the number of workplaces covered by unions and a large increase in retrenchments, mostly in the non-unionized workplaces. Further evidence thus confirms that the structural support for blue-collar work was on the decline. This may have been evident in the large degree of insecurity expressed by blue-collar workers compared with white-collar and managerial/professional employees.

Technological change may bring some benefits, notwithstanding the cost in the level of employment in blue-collar work. And rational economic management may most strongly affect managers, professionals, and white-collar workers, and perhaps in some sense blue-collar work is partially guarded from its full impact on stress. However, the effects of work-related stress on the quality of domestic and personal lives is important for blue-collar workers, as is the ability of the organizations they work for, and of the unions, to protect their workforces against the negative implications of the stress they experience. Central to this is the question of influence, control, and support at work.

REFERENCES

1. Moorhead, A., et al. *Changes at Work: The 1995 Australian Workplace Industrial Relations Survey*. Longman, South Melbourne, 1997.
2. Najman, J. Health and poverty: Past, present and prospects for the future. *Soc. Sci. Med.* 36(2): 157–166, 1993.
3. Ham, L. Women's Work, Women's Health: A Study of Occupational Stress in Gender-Segregated Sectors of Industry. Ph.D dissertation, Department of Sociology, La Trobe University, Melbourne, 1992.
4. Rifkin, J. *The End of Work: Technology, Jobs, and Your Future*. Putnam's, New York, 1996.
5. Burdess, N. Class and health. In *Health in Australia: Sociological Concepts and Issues*, edited by C. Grbich, pp. 163–187. Prentice-Hall, Sydney, 1996.

6. Driscol, T., and Mayhew, C. Extent and cost of occupational injury and illness. In *Occupational Health and Safety in Australia: Industry, Public Sector, and Small Business*, edited by C. Mayhew and C. Peterson, pp. 28–51. Allen and Unwin, St. Leonards, 1999.
7. Quinlan, M. Psychological and sociological approaches to the study of occupational illness: A critical review. *Aust. N. Z. J. Sociol.* 24(2): 189–207, 1988.
8. Hopkins, A., and Palser, J. The causes of coal mining accidents. *Ind. Relations J.* 18(1): 24–49, 1987.
9. Cannon, W. B. The interrelationships of emotions as suggested by recent physiological researchers. *Am. J. Psychol.* 25: 256–282, 1914.
10. Selye, H. A syndrome produced by diverse nocturnal agents. *Nature* 138: 32, 1936.
11. Selye, H. *The Stress of Life*. McGraw Hill, New York, 1956.
12. Mason, J. W. The scope of psychoendocrine research on the pituitary-adrenal cortical system. *Psychosom. Med.* 30: 565–575, 1968.
13. Mason, J. W. A review of psychoendocrine research in the sympathetic-adrenal medullary system. *Psychosom. Med.* 30: 631–653, 1968.
14. Peterson, C. L. *Stress at Work: A Sociological Perspective*. Baywood, Amityville, N.Y., 1999.
15. Cooper, C. L., and Smith, M. J. Introduction: Blue-collar workers are "at risk." In *Job Stress and Blue Collar Work,* edited by C. L. Cooper and M. J. Smith, pp. 1–4. Wiley, Chichester, U.K., 1985.
16. Fisher, S. Control and blue collar work. In *Job Stress and Blue Collar Work,* edited by C. L. Cooper and M. J. Smith, pp. 19–48. Wiley, Chichester, U.K., 1985.
17. McLean, A. *Work Stress*, Addison Wesley, Reading, Mass., 1979.
18. Ganster, D. C. Work control and well being: A review of research in the workplace. In *Job Control and Worker Health,* edited by S. L. Sauter, J. J. Hurrell, and C. L. Cooper, pp. 3–23. Wiley, Chichester, U.K., 1989.
19. Karasek, R. A. Job demands, job decision latitude and mental strain: Implications for job redesign. *Adm. Sci. Q.* 24: 285–308, 1979.
20. Karasek, R. A. Job socialization and job strain: The implications of two related psychosocial mechanisms for job design. In *Working Life: A Social Science Contribution to Work Reform*, edited by B. Gardell and G, Johansson, pp. 75–94. Wiley, New York, 1981.
21. Sutherland, V. J., and Cooper, C. L. Sources of work stress. In *Occupational Stress: Issues and Developments in Research*, edited by J. J. Hurrell Jr., et al., pp. 3–40. Taylor and Francis, London, 1988.
22. Thomason, J. A., and Pond, S. B., III. Effects of instruction on stress management skills and self-management skills among blue-collar employees. In *Job Stress Interventions*, edited by L. R. Murphy et al., pp. 7–20. American Psychological Association, London, 1995.
23. Shostack, A. B. Blue collar worker alienation. In *Job Stress and Blue Collar Work*, edited by C. L. Cooper and M. J. Smith, pp. 7–18. Wiley, Chichester, U.K., 1985.
24. Mayhew, C., and Peterson, C. (eds.). *Occupational Health and Safety in Australia: Industry, Public Sector, and Small Business*. Allen and Unwin, St. Leonards, 1999.
25. Aronsson, G. Dimensions of control as related to work organization, stress, and health. *Int. J. Health Serv.* 19(3): 459–468, 1989.

26. Peterson, C. L. Work factors and stress: A critical review. *Int. J. Health Serv.* 24(3): 495–519, 1994.
27. Greif, S. Stress and gesundheit: Ein bericht uber forschungen zur belastung am arbeitsplatz. (Stress and health: A report on research about workplace stress and injury). *Z. Sozialisations Forschung Zur Und Erziehungs Soziologie* 3: 41–58, 1983.
28. Semmer, N., Zapf, D., and Greif, S. Shared job strain: A new approach for assessing the validity of job stress measurements. *J. Occup. Organisational Psychol.* 69(3): 293–310, 1996.
29. Levidow, L. Women who make the chips. *Science as Culture* 2(10): 103–124, 1991.
30. Siegrist, J., and Peter, R. Job stressors and coping characteristics in work related disease: Issues of validity. *Work Stress* 8(2): 130–140, 1994.
31. Peter, R. Job stressors, coping characteristics, and the development of coronary heart disease (CHD)—Results from two studies. *Psychologische Beitrage* 37(1–2): 40–45, 1995.
32. Siegrist, J., et al. Low status control, high effort at work and ischaemic heart disease: Prospective evidence from blue collar men. *Soc. Sci. Med.* 31(10): 1127–1134, 1990.
33. Tsutsumi, A., et al. Association between job strain and prevalence of hypertension: A cross sectional analysis in a Japanese working population with a wide range of occupations: The Jichi Medical School cohort study. *Occup. Environ. Med.* 58(6): 367–373, 2001.
34. Furlan, R., et al. Modifications of cardiac autonomic profile associated with a shift schedule of work. *Circulation* 102(16): 1912–1916, 2000.
35. Tennant C. Work stress and coronary heart disease. *J. Cardiovasc. Risk* 7(4): 273–276, 2000.
36. Calvert, G. M., Merling, J. W., and Burnett, C. A. Ischaemic heart disease mortality and occupation among 16- to 60-year-old males. *J. Occup. Environ. Med.* 41(11): 960–966, 1999.
37. Isaksen, J. Constructing meaning despite the drudgery of repetitive work. *J. Humanistic Psychol.* 40(3): 84–107, 2000.
38. Vasse, R. M., Nijhuis, F. J. N., and Kok, G. Associations between work stress, alcohol consumption and sickness absence. *Addiction* 93(2): 231–241, 1998.
39. Nash, H. C., and Chrisler, J. C. Personality characteristics and coping styles of women working in and in training for nontraditional blue-collar jobs. *Psychol. Rep.* 87(3, Pt. 2): 1115–1122, 2000.
40. Shirom, A., Westman, M., and Melamed, S. The effects of pay systems on blue-collar employees' emotional distress: The mediating effects of objective and subjective monotony. *Hum. Relations* 52(8): 1077–1097, 1999.
41. Shirom, A., and Kirmeyer, S. The effects of unions on blue-collar role stresses and somatic strains. *J. Organ. Behav.* 9(1): 29–42, 1988.
42. Kanai, A., and Wakabayashi, M. Workaholism among Japanese blue-collar employees *Int. J. Stress Manage.* 8(2): 129–145, 2001.
43. Ewan, C., Lowy, E., and Reid, J. The effects of repetitive strain injury on sufferers' roles and identity. *Sociol. Health Illness* 13(2): 168–192, 1991.
44. Caplan, R. D., et al. *Job Demands and Worker Health.* Survey Research Centre, Institute for Social Research, University of Michigan, Ann Arbor, 1980.

45. Kohn, M. L., et al. Position in the class structure and psychological functioning in the United States, Japan, and Poland. *Am. J. Sociol.* 95(4): 964–1008, 1990.
46. Otto, R. Patterns of Stress, Symptom Awareness and Medical-Help Seeking among Women and Men in Selected Occupations. Ph.D. dissertation, La Trobe University, Bundoora Campus, Melbourne, 1976.
47. Jackson, S. E. Participation and decision making as a strategy for reducing job-related strain. *J. Appl. Psychol.* 68: 3–19, 1983.
48. Mechanic, D. Social structure and personal adaptation: Some neglected dimensions. In *Coping and Adaptation*, edited by G. V. Coelho, D. A. Hamburg, and J. E. Adams, pp. 32–44. Basic Books, New York, 1974.

Chapter 10

EXPLORATION OF THE LINKS BETWEEN WORKPLACE STRESS AND PRECARIOUS EMPLOYMENT

Claire Mayhew

As the research literature has indicated, a number of causes lead to the development of work-related stress, and the symptoms of stress are concentrated in specific types of jobs and at particular hierarchical levels. The high risk for stress, however, is not solely due to job tasks and on-the-job exposures. In this chapter I argue that precarious employment is a significant but usually overlooked contributor to levels of distress.

BACKGROUND: DISTRIBUTION, CAUSES, CONSEQUENCES, AND PREVENTION OF STRESS

Definitions of what constitutes stress vary. Some stress in life is essential to living and working, but when levels of arousal are excessive and/or prolonged, harmful "distress" results. In his pathbreaking work, Selye (1) separated human responses into an alarm phase, resistance, and finally exhaustion or collapse. Arguably, it is imperative that "at-risk" groups of workers and individuals are identified early in the development of stress pathways so that appropriate interventions can be implemented.

International evidence for the prevalence of stress is compelling. In Europe, there has been an increase in the occurrence of stress from slightly more than 25 percent of workers in 1997 to 28 percent in 1998 (2; 3, p. 11). A major random community survey in the United Kingdom (n = 7,069) found that 15 to 20 percent of people were very or extremely stressed, 40 to 45 percent were moderately stressed, and 23 percent had experienced an illness caused by or made worse by work in the previous 12 months (3, p. 11). Similarly, a Yale University study estimated that 29 percent of employees perceived themselves to be "quite a bit" or "extremely" stressed at work (3, p. 12). A Danish survey of more than 1,100 people found "manual workers are much more exposed to psychological stress during their work" (4, p. 16). "High-risk" jobs included skilled blue-collar work, transport, catering, and metal manufacturing (see Chapter 2). Similarly, young workers—those who are more likely to be in subordinate positions in the hierarchy—are at increased risk, particularly if they have been threatened or harassed by their colleagues or superiors (5, p. 23). That is, lower-level workers have a higher incidence of stress, in addition to the range of ill-health indices linked with lower socioeconomic status.

The Australian Workplace Industrial Relations Survey (6) found that 26 percent of employees across Australian workplaces *felt* stressed by their work, 50 percent considered that the stressors had increased over the previous 12 months, and 46 percent cited an increased pace of work. The *occupations* most at risk are professionals (19.7 percent of all successful workers' compensation insurance claims come from this group), clerks (14.2 percent), paraprofessionals (9.8 percent), and managers and administrators (9.2 percent) (7, p. 72, Table 19). The *industry sectors* most affected are finance and insurance (22.8 percent of all claims from this group), education (16.2 percent), government administration and defense (10.4 percent), personal and other services (9 percent), and communication services (4.5 percent) (7, p. 72; see also Chapter 2). Nevertheless, it is widely accepted that compensation claims data greatly underestimate the extent—and costs—of stress conditions (8). If stressful conditions are not ameliorated, burnout may result—as frequently happens among social workers (9). This condition has significant health and personal costs.

Potential Ill-Health Consequences of Stress

Ill-health consequences can include heart disease and hypertension, gastrointestinal conditions including ulcers, and depression and psychological disorders (1, 10). The likely mechanism leading to ill-health is that excessive levels of stress decrease the effectiveness of the immune system. Thus while it is known that excessive stress will at some stage lead to ill-health, the specific illness outcome for each individual is more difficult to predict. An Australian prevalence study based on 9,911 responses found that 72 percent of respondents suffered headaches, 71 percent felt continually tired, and more than half had other ill-health effects (11). Decreased productivity (and hence profitability) consequences are probably inevitable from well-developed distress conditions. There is also a potential for increased work-related injury events as a result of stress, although unambiguous evidence is scant. Similarly, while a number of studies have postulated a link between musculoskeletal disorders and stress, none have unequivocally separated out the cause-effect relationship (12, p. 9). However, the U.K. Whitehall studies found that: "workers who felt they had low levels of control over their jobs were at increased risk of reporting lower back pain" (13).

Subjective and Objective Ways of Measuring Stress

There are both subjective and objective ways to measure stress levels. Objective mechanisms that measure the extent and severity of stress are scant, with most biological assessments being either invasive (e.g., blood samples) or subject to fluctuations for a range of reasons which are not necessarily related to stress levels (e.g., intermittent blood pressure measures). The most accurate *objective* assessments of work-related stress involve physical hormone tests, objective workload measurements, and observations of working conditions that are matched against information from workers (14). Recent Australian research used salivary cortisol level, as it was the most noninvasive but sensitive, robust, and reliable method of measuring stress responses in a sample of bank managers. (Stress activates the pituitary–adrenal cortical system.) The highest levels of salivary cortisol were found late in the evening after work (indicating a failure to "unwind") and on Wednesdays (peak effort mid-week), with elevated steroid levels indicating an increased probability of stress-related disorders (15, pp. 138–140). Salivary cortisol has been used in other physical stress assessments. For example, the Australian Institute of Sport is developing a saliva test to predict when elite athletes are most likely to become ill. Immunoglobulin A (IgA) protects the human body against a number of flu-related viruses, but levels fall because of physical stress, home and work pressures, and diet and hygiene (16, p. 8). However, very few scientific assessments have been done that include observations of actual workplace conditions, workload measurements, and stress outcomes. For these and other reasons, most studies of stress have been based on subjective data.

A significant number of more *subjective* studies of stress have been conducted, often in conjunction with assessments of other variables within research studies. These stress assessments have often been large-scale, based on questionnaire or interview data, and/or based on physical health symptoms. There may also be a close correlation between *feelings* of ill-health caused or linked to stress and later objective ill-health states (see 17).

The General Health Questionnaire (GHQ) can also be used to objectively assess levels of stress through collection of primary subjective data. The GHQ measures current perceived health status and nonpsychotic psychiatric states, and may be a predictor of general future physical health (18, pp. 82–99). The GHQ has preset questions that have numerical scores allocated for each response; these are then totaled to give an overall score. Because the GHQ has proved to be very robust, it is widely used in medical and psychosocial studies and has been repeatedly validated in international studies. However, its use is rare in empirical studies, particularly in social science occupational health and safety (OHS) research. While limitations have been identified with interviewees uncomfortable in "pencil and paper" situations and among blue-collar workers, the GHQ remains a very robust and objective instrument for estimating current stress levels and predicting future outcomes (18, pp. 82–99). In spite of its limitations, the GHQ was recently incorporated in a comprehensive research instrument assessing OHS among long-haul truck drivers (19). Use of such instruments is particularly beneficial in separating out cause and effect relationships in stress pathways.

Causes of Stress-Related Illnesses

One comprehensive study of 7,372 people found that "much of the inverse social gradient in CHD [coronary heart disease] incidence can be attributed to differences in psychosocial work environment" (20, p. 235). Similarly, the Health and Safety Executive (21) identified work environment factors related to stress: workload, scheduling, relationships on the job, job design, employees' role and decision-making, and general management.

The concept of "control" has proved to be of central importance in predicting levels of job stress and ill-health outcomes. The work of Karasek (22, 23) and Aronsson (24) has been pivotal in identifying the interrelationships between the amount of control allowed on the job, work demands, and the development of stress. As Amick and colleagues also found, "Work high in psychological demands and low in level of control has been associated with a variety of deleterious health consequences" (25, p. 54). In a study of San Francisco bus drivers, lack of control over work environment and schedules led to hypertension, back pain, and gastro-intestinal problems and resulted in expenditure of one-third of the bus company budget on casual replacements (26). Stress also commonly follows extensive *shift work*, long hours of labor, and job tasks that require interruption of sleep patterns. Thus fatigue can have a dual effect and both predispose a worker to stress and exacerbate the extent of a preexisting condition. A correlation between work-related injuries and stress following long working hours has also been identified (27). Thus the increasing popularity of 12-hour shifts may result in an increased prevalence of stress, especially among those doing overtime (although many workers *say* they prefer 12-hour shifts).

One severe long-term outcome of stress is coronary heart disease. Marmot and colleagues (20, p. 238) and Syme (28, pp. 156–157, 162) found that low control predicted CHD independently of socioeconomic status. High-demand jobs with low levels of control led to the poorest outcomes; conversely, low demands with a high level of control result in decreased stress risk. The U.K. Whitehall studies found that: "employees with little control over their work environment face a significantly higher risk of heart disease than those with authority to influence their job conditions . . . the way work is organized dramatically affects employee health" (13, p. 24). Although the data are patchy, a causal pathway between stress and CHD has been suggested for two risk factors: low levels of control and shift work (29).

- *Low job control* was consistently associated with increased CHD risk and is probably a causal risk factor. In the Whitehall II study, the odds ratios for low job control were reported to be 2.38 for self-reported and 1.56 for externally assessed (30, p. 68).
- *Shift work* is also likely to be a causal risk factor in the stress-CHD pathway. The mechanism operates through disturbances to the circadian rhythm, fatigue, and elevated levels of serum triglycerides, and shift work also accentuates other risk factors for CHD. Including all work and lifestyle risk factors, shift work may entail up to a 40 percent increase in CHD risk. Shift workers have a relative risk for CHD of between 1.38 and 1.4 in comparison to day workers (31, p. 260; 32, p. 190). This increased level of risk is important, as approximately 20 percent of all workers now do one form of shift work or another.

While indicative, the research study findings were not unanimous for two other identified risk factors:

- *High job demands* predict poor health outcomes. Theorell (33, p. 387) estimated *job strain* had an odds ratio of 1.4. Overall, the relative risk of CHD resulting from job strain may be around 1.09. However, not all studies agree that high demand is a causal risk factor.
- *Effort-reward imbalance* was associated with a 2.15-fold higher risk of CHD in the Whitehall II study and was concentrated among those from lower grades where job control was restricted (30, p. 68). Again, however, the relationship was not unanimous across studies.

In the future, work experiences are likely to be polarized into two groups: (*a*) those with high demands and a high level of control over work, and (*b*) those with low demands and low levels of control. Theorell predicts that "differences in health between these two groups are in the process of becoming even wider" (33, p. 382).

Particular *styles of management* can also result in stress. McCarthy and colleagues (34) identified some inappropriate and coercive management styles that may inadvertently be encouraged when organizations are being restructured. Mullen (35) linked quasi-military management styles with work-related stress and occupational violence, and Babiak (36) identified organizational situations in which "industrial psychopaths" could curry favor and be promoted. Vane acknowledged five organizational factors that contributed to distress: the absence of supportive leadership, poor goal congruence, excessive work demands, the absence of role clarity, and a lack of participative decision-making (37, pp. 274–275). Restructuring, involuntary redundancies, increases in workload, organizational and technological changes, widespread downsizing, job insecurity, lack of training, long hours, poor OHS, and political/economic changes can also lead to stress (11, p. 27). Distress is particularly likely to follow prolonged pressure, aggressive behavior, organizational change, lack of leadership, decreased consultation, and increased uncertainty (38). Finally, among minority groups, discrimination is a stronger predictor of ill-health stress outcomes than are traditional job stresses (3).

Occupational *violence* and *sexual harassment* frequently result in distress (39, pp. 19, 25). Hence the increasing incidence of violence at work is likely to result in a minor epidemic of disabling stress in the near future (40). Chappell and Di Martino (41) have written the most comprehensive international assessment of the incidence and severity of occupational violence. Suffice it to note here that patterns vary across nation states, because levels of exposure and risk factors (such as firearm access) are diverse. In Australia, up to 50 percent of workers have been abused and one in ten physically attacked; most "at risk" were front-line workers in health and community care (5). Among customer service telephonists, stress was most common in 18- to 24-year-olds, who were less experienced and vulnerable to abrasive customers (the average customer service telephonist received five to ten "angry" calls a day) (5). Further, any already stressful work situation can be exacerbated if workers are unable to control the risks of violence—for example, when schoolteachers cannot physically constrain or expel students. Risks are also mediated by gender and employment status, with those employed under precarious arrangements—such as casuals working in the hospitality industry—facing increasing threats of violence (42). Thus, if the incidence of occupational violence increases as expected, stress-related ill-health consequences will inevitably multiply.

Costs of Stress-Related Illness

Stress results in substantial costs for employers and the community as a whole. The economic losses include poor morale, diminished motivation, decreased production, and increased absenteeism, turnover, and injuries (3). These costs are increasing over time as the incidence of distress rises. For example, in 1996 the average cost was $A32,000 for the 1,841 successful stress-related claims from Australian Commonwealth employees (8). In 1995–96 in New South Wales, each incident cost an average of $17,101 (43). An exponential increase in costs was identified in Western Australia: "doubling each year in workers compensation claims for work-related stress . . . the cost per claim for males ($15,178) is much higher than for females ($11,828). The costs per claim are well above the corresponding average for all types of injury ($6,322)" (44, p. 536). However, the *full* costs usually remain hidden. The Industry Commission (now Productivity Commission) in Australia estimated that of all work-related injuries and illness, individuals bore at least 30 percent of the costs, employers around 30 percent, and the community (i.e., the taxpayer) at least 40 percent—with long-term disabilities more expensive than short-term conditions or fatalities (45, 98, 102). It is of relevance here to note that stress conditions often require considerable lengths of time to resolve.

In the United Kingdom, stress costs more than £100 million each year through lost working time and is the second largest category of occupational ill-health after musculoskeletal disorders (46). Fully 53 percent of the 700 human resource and personnel directors in the U.K. Industrial Society stated that stress levels had increased over the last three years: "Workplace stress is now a problem in nine out of 10 organizations" (47, p. 4). European research also indicates that stress is likely to affect greater numbers of workers in the future, with more costs off-loaded to society at large: "work related stress is due to increase and affect more workers. Stress produces a variety of impacts . . . costs tend to be offloaded or shifted to society at large, which has to pay for the costs of disability, unemployment and early retirement" (48, p. 62). Notably, those who are precariously employed— particularly the self-employed and contractors—are unlikely to have workers' compensation insurance coverage in many places. As a result, many will offload the expenses of their work-related stress disorder to taxpayer-funded medical and social security systems. This is an important and growing—but rarely recognized—phenomenon as the basis to employment undergoes a rapid shift towards widespread precariousness.

Interventions to Reduce the Incidence and Costs of Stress

Parkes and Sparkes (49) separated preventive interventions into two types: *socio-technical* (which focused on widespread workplace change) and *psychosocial* (which focused on individuals). Overall, workplace-focused (rather than individually focused) interventions appear to be most effective in decreasing the incidence and severity of work-related stress. However, the evidence is fragmentary and usually limited to single occupational groups facing specific stressors. The most effective interventions include workload reductions, enhanced communication during periods of uncertainty, and avoidance of the introduction of multiple simultaneous changes. Such primary prevention efforts can reduce sickness absence by up to 50 percent (50, pp. 35–36). Unfortunately, preventive efforts remain "disproportionately concentrated on reducing the effects of stress, rather than reducing the presence of stressors at work" (50, p. 1).

These findings are supported by research from a range of industry sectors and employment situations. A study commissioned by the Australian Maritime Safety Authority identified interventions that reduced stress for isolated workers. Recommendations included improved communications between home and ship, support services to minimize "away from home" stressors, and enhanced exercise at sea (51). (These stress-reduction initiatives can be applied to other groups of isolated workers.) Netterstrom's study of bus drivers in Denmark found that the introduction of workplace-wide democracy resulted in a two-thirds decrease in absenteeism and significant cost savings (reported in 50). In a corrective services department with a high incidence of stress, job redesign, enrichment of psychosocial health services, and education and improved communication resulted in a 50 percent reduction in stress claims and saved $A2 million in workers' compensation costs (52). Similarly, a Commonwealth government organization provided volunteer mediators to intervene early in stress situations before they escalated. The result was again a marked decrease in long-term claims and long-term absenteeism—that is, not a decrease in incidence but a decrease in severity (8).

Social support also mediates the impact of stress. The relationship between social support and health has been thoroughly examined over the last two decades and is well documented (e.g., 53). Suffice it to note here that people with weak social support are more vulnerable to a wide range of disease agents. Again, the likely etiological factor is diminished functioning of the immune system (54, p. 467). Thus the provision of support at work should have an intervening effect on levels of stress.

STRESS AND PRECARIOUS EMPLOYMENT

Over the past two decades, the labor markets of most industrialized countries have undergone profound changes. There has been a decline in permanent full-time employment and a rapid increase in the number and proportion of those employed casually, part-time, as subcontractors and contractors, as micro-small business operators, or as short-term employees (55). Economists, lawyers, and industrial relations specialists have spent much effort investigating the productivity and economic benefits (or otherwise) of labor market restructuring, but a range of OHS consequences awaits further investigation. The stress-related consequences from precarious employment have not yet been widely scientifically evaluated, although there are early indicators of increased fatigue, depression, and headaches (56, p. 160). Quinlan has also done significant preliminary work.

A number of insights about the precariously employed have been gained from studies of the health consequences of threatened redundancy, threats to future financial security, and unemployment. Aronsson (24, p. 449) notes that women, because of their weaker labor market position, find it more difficult to refuse poor working conditions and are therefore at increased risk. Workers who have lost their jobs but continue as self-employed in the same industry sector are at increased risk as they compete through working long hours for low returns (57). Increased ill-health also results when individuals remain in jobs they should have left, for example, after the physical wear and tear becomes too demanding (56).

For the precariously employed, the balance between work demands, level of control, and economic security are central for stress prevention. While economic stress—or anticipated economic stress—is of core importance to those who are precariously employed, a variety of factors are interrelated. For example, financially stressed workers are more likely to work longer hours if that results in greater income and renewed contracts, or if penalties are due when contract deadlines are not met. Arguably, precariously employed workers whose income flow is uncertain are also more likely to be desperate to secure additional income for future survival. Thus, if additional and long hours of work are on offer, the contract may be willingly accepted, irrespective of short-term negative health consequences.

Table 10.1 shows hours worked per week by 2,731 precariously employed workers. These data were collated from face-to-face interviews during ten different Australian OHS studies that my colleagues and I have conducted over the past decade (19, 59–67). The study findings are briefly summarized below and have been discussed in detail elsewhere (see 58). Since not all interviewees answered the question on working hours, and some provided two separate answers (such as when they normally worked 40 hours per week but in the past week had been on the job for 70 hours), line totals in Table 10.1 do not always add to 100 percent.

The most recent study evaluated OHS risk factors among 300 long-haul transport drivers (19). We found that economic stress was the underlying cause of long hours, fatigue, excessive stress, and poor OHS indices. Precariously employed owner/drivers were found to be at higher risk than employee drivers. The 1998 study of 304 young casual workers in a multi-national fast food chain found that a stringent OHS management system could be an effective mechanism to improve OHS outcomes, levels of knowledge, and risk assessment skills (59). Unusually for the precariously employed, hours of labor were tightly controlled to reduce overheads. The 1997–98 clothing manufacturing study involved comparison of OHS indices between 100 factory-based and 100 precariously employed outworkers (60). Overall, we found that outworkers worked very long hours and had an injury incidence around three times that of factory-based workers. The 1997 "Interventions" study evaluated the relative impact of three different OHS preventive interventions: an intensive mail campaign, on-site visits by an OHS inspector, and a regulatory change (61). Long hours of labor were again the norm for the precariously employed. The 1996–97 "Barriers" study assessed comprehension of three major OHS areas: manual handling, hazardous substances, and legislation (62). Again, long working hours were almost the norm for the economically precarious micro-small business owner/managers. The 1995–96 outsourcing study compared OHS indices between employees and outsourced workers in four industry sectors (63). We found that the primary determinant of injury risk was industry sector/job task, but precarious employment was an important subsidiary risk factor. Again, the outsourced workers spent longer on the job than did employees. The 1996 indigenous worker study was designed to provide baseline data on OHS among indigenous Australian workers (64). Precarious employment and negative OHS outcomes were common, with very few interviewees owning their own business. In the 1994–95 self-employed builder study we interviewed 600 small-scale builders in Australia and the United

Table 10.1

Hours worked per week by 2,731 precariously employed Australian workers

Study topic (reference) and no. interviewed	Percent of interviewees by hours worked						
	1–15	16–24	25–34	35–39	40	41–48	49+
Truck drivers (19)							
n = 300		6	0.3	0.3	2.7	2.7	93.7
Young casual (59)							
n = 304	26	23	16.8	31.9	3.9		
Clothing manufacturing (60)							
In factory	1	0	2	54	37	5	1
Outworkers	3	2	3	10	6	13	61
n = 200							
Interventions (61)							
n = 331	0.9	0.6	0.9	1.5	6.3	14.8	74.6
Barriers (62)							
n = 248	0	0.4	0.4	0.8	4.8	19.3	73.8
Subcontracting/outsourcing (63)							
Employees	1.9	5.8	9.7	13.6	27.2	13.6	28.1
Outsourced	0	2	2	2	9.8	21.6	62.7
n = 205							
Indigenous (64)							
n = 257				77			23
Builders (65)							
Queensland							
n = 500	0.6	0.4	0.8	1.2	8	19	70
U.K.							
n = 100	0	0	1	4	12	27	66
Taxi drivers (66)							
n = 100	4	7	8	4			77
Builders and transport (67)							
Builders							
n = 66							100
Transport							
n = 71							100

Kingdom (65). A high level of chronic morbidity, poor OHS knowledge, low levels of legislative understanding, and long hours of labor were widespread. The 1993 study of violence among taxi drivers found this was a high-risk industry with 12-hour shifts the norm (66). The 1992 study of self-employed truck drivers and builders involved comparisons between workers' compensation, hospital and ambulance service data, and interviews with medics and all self-employed builders and truck drivers in a rural town (67). All interviewees worked long hours. We also found that the different data sources picked up on quite different, largely non-overlapping, features of injury.

The most striking feature of the data in Table 10.1 is that 67.2 percent of the 2,731 precariously employed workers were on the job for more than 40 hours a week, and 56.9 percent for more than 49 hours. In fact, the most precariously employed workers *normally* spent long hours on the job each week. Owner/operators (19), the self-employed (66, 67), contractors (63, 65), micro-small business owner/managers (61, 62), and home-based workers (60) evidenced far longer working hours. Generally, only *employees* worked less than 40 hours per week—for example, casual fast-food workers (59), *factory-based* clothing manufacture employees (60), and employees interviewed in the subcontracting/outsourcing (63) and indigenous studies (64). This pattern of responses supports the hypothesis that people whose future income flow is insecure will labor long hours when work is available.

As noted earlier, long hours of work and fatigue (and shift work) are common precursors of stress. However, the cause-effect pathway in the development of stress must be clarified. Long hours may be either an *independent* variable determining the level of stress outcomes or a *dependent by-product* from other stressors such as economic insecurity, or stress indices and long hours may merely be *correlated* and ultimately determined by another *independent variable*. Separating out a clear cause-effect relationship is very difficult. Nevertheless, the research literature discussed earlier clearly points to lack of control as the most likely *independent variable* determining levels of stress and ill-health consequences (20, 22–24, 28, 30, 32, 56, 57, 68). Of note, a causal relationship between stress and CHD was recently accepted by the WHO for two risk factors: low job control and shift work (29).

Precariously employed workers lack control over the extent and length of their employment, their pay and economic security, and their work process. The result of this lack of control and insecurity is extended hours of work when jobs are available, the shaving of wages or profit margins to ensure continued income flow at some level, endemic fatigue when long hours of labor are on offer or required, and ongoing anxiety. For the most precariously employed, distress is probably inevitable. That is, long hours of work can be both a mechanism to reduce economic insecurity and anxiety and a cause of stress; hence the relationship between fatigue and stress is two-way, or dialectical. The *independent* variable is the level of precariousness of labor and income.

In the most recent research study included in Table 10.1, we used the General Health Questionnaire to estimate levels of stress among a population of 300 long-haul truck drivers (19). (See the earlier discussion of the GHQ.) The GHQ was attempted by 290 of 300 interviewed long-haul drivers, with the lowest score recorded at 0 and the highest at 33. Past studies have indicated that a score of around 8.59 is relatively normal, and a score greater than 14 is so clinically significant that the person probably requires urgent treatment (69). Drivers regularly scored above the 8.59 baseline, with 15.7 percent of the interviewed population having a tally above the clinically significant figure of 14. Variations in truck drivers' GHQ scores on the basis of employment status (owner/driver, employed in a small fleet, or an employee in a large trucking organization), highway on which they were driving, and other factors were examined in-depth and have been reported elsewhere (60, pp. 77–88). Independent and dependent variables were identified during the analysis. We found that *economic stress was the core underlying variable;* drivers on the most competitive routes and under the greatest economic stress had the highest GHQ scores. Conversely, truck drivers under least financial stress and working on the most economically rewarding contracts had the lowest levels of stress. Notably, the most precariously employed truck drivers—the owner/drivers—had the highest GHQ scores. Economic stress was the *independent variable.* While long working hours and fatigue were correlated with higher GHQ stress scores, we found that they were *dependent variables.* That is, the GHQ proved to be a very useful tool for more objectively estimating levels of stress—and for clarifying cause-effect relationships in the stress pathway—among a group of precariously employed (and precariously paid) blue-collar workers.

CONCLUSION

Excessive levels of stress lead to significant personal, employer and taxpayer-funded economic losses. While many cases of stress are closely correlated with lack of control and fatigue following shift work, others follow occupational violence incidents, work overload, job insecurity, and precarious employment. The proportion of the working population suffering ill-health as a result of excessive stress is almost certainly growing. For example, workers' compensation claims data in Australia indicate a substantial increase in stress claims in recent years. These data, however, are unlikely to accurately reflect the true prevalence of stress, as those who are precariously employed are quite unlikely to lodge claims. This exclusion results essentially from lack of coverage of many groups of precariously employed workers, especially the self-employed, contractors, and independent owner/operators, under the various Australian workers' compensation insurance systems. Further, those casually employed workers who *are* covered may be too frightened to lodge a claim in case this prejudices future work contracts.

Loss of control has been identified as a key determinant of stress, although all the causal links have not been fully enumerated. Arguably, a factor of central importance is economic stress. Economic vulnerability is likely to be felt most strongly by those who are precariously employed and/or have insecure income. The qualitative and quantitative data from the various OHS empirical studies that my colleagues and I have conducted among precariously employed workers indicate that enhanced competitive pressures have direct negative flow-on effects on working hours and OHS generally. The use of the GHQ instrument in the latest long-haul transport study unequivocally demonstrated that extreme stress could also follow. Indeed, long hours of labor and endemic fatigue are now the norm for most Australian long-haul truck drivers. Notably, this is an industry sector characterized by increasing levels of precarious employment through widespread outsourcing to owner/drivers.

In this chapter I have argued that evidence from across a range of industry sectors clearly indicates that precariously employed workers carry a disproportionately high burden of injury, ill-health, and economically induced stress. Their general OHS vulnerability is only partially due to characteristics inherent in particular occupational and industry sectors.

While separating out cause-effect relationships is difficult, it is now clear that intense and unremitting economic pressure can lead to excessive hours of work and endemic fatigue, as well as a range of ill-health consequences including severe stress. Precariously employed workers lack control over the extent and length of their employment, income, and work process. To reduce levels of economic anxiety, extended hours of labor are worked when job contracts are available, and minimal wages or profit margins are accepted as the price for survival. By accepting a reduction in their working conditions and remuneration, precariously employed workers at least ensure *some* control over their future income flow. Distress is, however, almost inevitable—although the extent and severity are unlikely ever to appear in workers' compensation data banks, as these precariously employed workers are normally excluded from such social support systems. (This exclusion will further exacerbate levels of distress if a severe injury or illness occurs.)

The underlying cause of stress among the precariously employed is the insecure nature of their employment; the most at-risk jobs are those filled by casuals, part-timers, contractors and subcontractors, micro-small business owner/managers, or short-term employees. Broader and more proactive forms of stress prevention are required than currently exist, including a focus on the holistic work environment and its economic underpinnings. Individually focused approaches appear to be quite insufficient to remedy the causes of stress among precariously employed workers—even those strategies that address lack of control.

In sum, a dual vulnerability is apparent. A number of at-risk jobs have been identified in which workers have little control over their work. When these jobs are also under economic pressure, the probability of stress and other negative

OHS consequences is multiplied. Recent research data unequivocally indicate that the extension of precarious employment results in an intensification of economic pressure that in turn exacerbates both the incidence and severity of stress-induced ill-health conditions.

REFERENCES

1. Selye, H. *The Stress of Life.* McGraw Hill, New York, 1956.
2. More than one worker in four feels stressed by work. *Euro Review* 1: 6–8, 1997.
3. Hoel, H., Sparks, K., and Cooper, C. *The Cost of Violence/Stress at Work and the Benefits of a Violence/Stress-Free Working Environment.* Report commissioned by the International Labour Organization. University of Manchester, Manchester, U.K., 2001.
4. Psychological stress at work can threaten physical health. *Janus: Health and Safety at Work* 25: 16, 1997.
5. Dean, A. Stress epidemic: The age of rage. *Bulletin*, June 9, 1998, pp. 20-23.
6. Moorehead, A., et al. *Changes at Work: The Second Australian Workplace Industrial Relations Survey.* Longman, Melbourne, 1997.
7. National Occupational Health and Safety Commission. *Compendium of Workers' Compensation Statistics 1995/96.* AusInfo, Canberra, 1998.
8. Peterson, C. Dealing with stress-related disorders in the public sector. In *Occupational Health and Safety in Australia: Industry, Public Sector, and Small Business*, edited by C. Mayhew and C. Peterson, pp. 174–186. Allen and Unwin, Sydney, 1999.
9. Greenglass, E., and Burke, R. The impact of social support on the development of burnout in teachers: Examination of a model. *Work Stress* 11(3): 267–278, 1997.
10. Peterson, C. *Stress at Work: A Sociological Perspective.* Baywood, Amityville, N.Y., 1999.
11. ACTU. Occupational Health and Safety Unit. *A Report on the 1997 ACTU National Survey on Stress at Work.* Melbourne, 1998.
12. Shelerud, R. Epidemiology of occupational low back pain. *Occup. Med. State of the Art Reviews* 13(1): 1–22, 1998.
13. Sullivan, T. Workplace stress: Taking it to heart. *OHS Canada*, October 1998, pp. 24-25.
14. Measurements of stress levels. *Euro Review* 1: 11, 1997.
15. Bassett, J., Spillane, R., and Hocking, B. Cortisol excretion and illness reporting: A psycho-physiological study of business executives at home and at work. *J. Occup. Health Safety* 14(2): 135–141, 1998.
16. Ferrari, J. Aiding survival of the fittest. *Weekend Australian*, October 10-11, 1998, p. 8.
17. Lazarus, R. S. *Psychological Stress and Coping Process.* McGraw Hill, New York, 1966.
18. Goldberg, D. *The Detection of Psychiatric Illness by Questionnaire.* Oxford University Press, London, 1972.
19. Mayhew, C., and Quinlan, M. *Occupational Health and Safety amongst 300 Long Distance Truck Drivers: Results of an Interview-Based Survey.* Research report conducted as part of the Motor Accident Authority of New South Wales Safety Inquiry into the Long Haul Trucking Industry. Industrial Relations Research Centre, University of New South Wales, Sydney, 2001.

20. Marmot, M., et al. Contribution of job control and other risk factors to social variations in coronary heart disease incidence. *Lancet* 350: 235–239, 1997.
21. Health and Safety Executive. *Stress at Work: A Guide for Employers.* HSE Books, London, 1995.
22. Karasek, R. A. Job demands, job decision latitude and mental strain: Implications for job redesign. *Adm. Sci. Q.* 24: 285–308, 1979.
23. Karasek, R. A. Job socialization and job strain: The implications of two related psychosocial mechanisms for job design in working life. In *A Social Science Contribution to Work Reform,* edited by B. Gardell and G. Johansson, pp. 75–94. Wiley, New York, 1981.
24. Aronsson, G. Contingent workers and health and safety. *Work Employment Society* 13(3): 439–460, 1999.
25. Amick, B., et al. Relationship of job strain and iso-strain to health status in a cohort of women in the United States. *Scand. J. Work Environ. Health* 24(1): 54–61, 1998.
26. Syme, S. L. Visiting lecture at the National Occupational Health and Safety Commission, Sydney, October 27, 1998.
27. Savery, L., and Luks, A. Long Hours at Work: Are They Dangerous and Do People Consent to Them? Unpublished paper. School of Management, Curtin University of Technology, Western Australia, 2000.
28. Syme, S. L. Community participation, empowerment, and health: Development of a wellness guide for California. In *Wellness Lecture Series.* California Wellness Foundation and University of California, 1997.
29. Mayhew, C. *The Contribution of Stress to CHD.* Paper commissioned as part of the World Health Organization Global Burden of Disease project. WHO, Geneva, 2001.
30. Bosma, H., et al. Two alternative job stress models and the risk of coronary heart disease, *Am. J. Public Health* 88(1): 68–74, 1998.
31. Tenkanen, L., et al. Shiftwork, occupation and coronary heart disease over 6 years of follow-up in the Helsinki heart study. *Scand. J. Work Environ. Health* 23: 257–265, 1997.
32. Nurminen, M., and Karjalainen, A. Epidemiologic estimate of the proportion of fatalities related to occupational factors in Finland. *Scand. J. Work Environ. Health* 27(3): 161–213, 2001.
33. Theorell, T. Measuring psychosocial factors in working life. *Working Life Research and Development News.* Newsletter No. 5. National Institute for Working Life, Stockholm, 1998.
34. McCarthy, P., Sheehan, M., and Kearns, D. *Managerial Styles and Their Effects on Employees' Health and Well-Being in Organisations Undergoing Restructuring.* Report to NOHSC. Canberra, 1995.
35. Mullen, E. Workplace violence: cause for concern or the construction of a new category of fear? *J. Ind. Relations* 39(1): 21–32, 1997.
36. Babiak, P. When psychopaths go to work: A case study of an industrial psychopath. *Appl. Psychol. Int. Rev.* 44(2): 171–188, 1995.
37. Vane, T. Challenges in applying the risk management approach to the prevention of occupational stress. In *Capitalising Occupational Hygiene.* Conference Proceedings of 17th annual conference, Canberra, December 5-9, 1998.
38. WorkSafe Western Australia. *Work-Related Stress: Different Meanings to Different People.* Perth, 2001.

39. Department of Labour. *Stress and Fatigue: Their Impact on Health and Safety in the Workplace, Occupational Safety and Health Service.* New Zealand, 1998.
40. Mayhew, C. Occupational violence: The latest OHS epidemic? *J. Occup. Health Safety, Aust. N.Z.* 16(5): 371–375, 2000.
41. Chappell, D., and Di Martino, V. *Violence at Work.* International Labor Office, Geneva, 2000.
42. Mayhew, C. Occupational violence in industrialised countries: Types, incidence patterns, and "at risk" groups of workers. In *Violence at Work: Causes, Patterns, and Prevention*, edited by M. Gill, V. Bowie, and B. FisherWillan, pp. 21–40. Cullompton, U.K., 2002.
43. WorkCover New South Wales. Analysis of mental disorder claims. In *Workers Compensation Statistics New South Wales 1995/96.* Catalogue No. 525/96. Sydney, 1997.
44. Terry, A. Work-related stress: Legislation as a prevention strategy. *J. Occup. Health Safety* 12(5): 535–546, 1996.
45. Industry Commission. *Work, Health, and Safety: Inquiry into Occupational Health and Safety,* Vols. 1 and 2. Report No. 47. AGPS, Canberra, 1995.
46. Health and Safety Executive. Health and Safety Commission Chair Says That Tackling Stress is Dogged by Misunderstanding. Press release C019:97. London, June 20, 1997.
47. Stress in action. In *Hazards 1996.* Hazards Publications, Sheffield, U.K., 1996.
48. van Waarden, F., et al. *Prospects for Safe and Sound Jobs: The Impact of Future Trends on Costs and Benefits of Occupational Health and Safety.* Dutch Ministry of Social Affairs and Employment and the Netherlands School for Social and Economic Policy Research, The Hague, Netherlands, 1997.
49. Parkes, K., and Sparkes, T. *Organizational Interventions to Reduce Work Stress: Are They Effective? A Review of the Literature,* pp. 43–46. Health and Safety Executive and Oxford University, London, 1998.
50. Kompier, M., and Cooper, C. (eds.). *Preventing Stress, Improving Productivity: European Case Studies in the Workplace.* Routledge, London, 1999.
51. Parker, A., et al. *A Survey of the Health, Stress, and Fatigue of Australian Seafarers.* Australian Maritime Safety Authority, Canberra, 1997.
52. Dollard, M., Forgan, R., and Winefield, A. Five-year evaluation of a work stress intervention program. *J. Occup. Health Safety* 14(2): 159–165, 1998.
53. Cohen, S., and Syme, S. L. (eds.). *Social Support and Health.* Academic Press, London, 1985.
54. Syme, S. L. Rethinking disease: Where do we go from here? *Ann. Epidemiol.,* 1996, pp. 463-468.
55. Quinlan, M., and Mayhew, C. *Evidence versus Ideology: Lifting the Blindfold on OHS in Precarious Employment.* Working Paper Series No. 138. School of Industrial Relations and Organisational Behaviour, University of New South Wales, Sydney, 2001.
56. Aronsson, G., and Goransson, S. Permanent employment but not in a preferred occupation: Psychological and medical aspects, research implications. *J. Occup. Health Psychol.* 4(2): 152–163, 1999.
57. Aronsson, G. Influence of worklife on public health. *Scand. J. Work Environ. Health* 25(6): 597–604, 1999.
58. Mayhew, C. The growing OHS challenges in small business: Old problems and emerging risks. *Safety Science Monitor* 6(1): 26-37.

59. National Occupational Health and Safety Commission. *Occupational Health and Safety Issues for Young Workers in the Fast Food Industry,* by C. Mayhew et al., NOHSC, with the Division of Workplace Health and Safety (Queensland) and the WorkCover Authority of New South Wales. AusInfo, Canberra, 2000.
60. Mayhew, C., and Quinlan, M. The effects of outsourcing on occupational health and safety: A comparative study of factory-based workers and outworkers in the Australian clothing industry. *Int. J. Health Serv.* 29(1): 83–107, 1999.
61. Mayhew, C., et al. *An Evaluation of the Impact of Targeted Interventions on the OHS Behaviours of Small Business Building Industry Owners/Managers/Contractors.* Workplace Health and Safety Program and National Occupational Health and Safety Commission. AGPS, Canberra, 1997.
62. Mayhew, C. *Barriers to Implementation of Known OHS Solutions in Small Business.* National Occupational Health and Safety Commission and Division of Workplace Health and Safety. AGPS, Canberra, 1997.
63. Mayhew, C., Quinlan, M., and Bennett, L. *The Effects of Subcontracting/ Outsourcing on Occupational Health and Safety.* Industrial Relations Research Centre Monograph. University of New South Wales, Sydney, 1996.
64. Mayhew, C., and Vickerman, L. Aboriginal and Torres Strait Islander occupational health and safety: A pilot study. *Aust. Aboriginal Stud.* 2: 61–68, 1996.
65. Mayhew, C. *An Evaluation of the Impact of Robens Style Legislation on the OHS, Decision-Making of Australian and United Kingdom Builders with Less than Five Employees,* report to Work Safe Australia, Sydney, 1995.
66. Mayhew, C. Occupational violence: A case study of the taxi industry. In *Occupational Health and Safety in Australia: Industry, Public Sector, and Small Business*, edited by C. Mayhew and C. Peterson, pp. 127–139. Allen and Unwin, Sydney, 1999.
67. Mayhew, C. Identifying patterns of injury in small business: Piecing together the data jigsaw. In *Occupational Health and Safety in Australia: Industry, Public Sector, and Small Business*, edited by C. Mayhew, and C. Peterson, pp. 105–115. Allen and Unwin, Sydney, 1999.
68. Aronsson, G. Dimensions of control as related to work organization, stress and health. *Int. J. Health Serv.* 19(3): 459–468, 1989.
69. Bohle, P. School of Industrial Relations and Organisational Behaviour, University of New South Wales. Personal communication, April 26, 2000.

Section IV

Stress, Older Workers, and Outside Work Experiences

Chapter 11

WORK STRESS AND CAREGIVER STRESS

Yvonne Wells and David de Vaus

Over the past two decades, substantial attention has been given to the interface between work and family and the extent to which workers balance their work and family roles (see 1). The bulk of the research on the interaction between work and family roles has focused on workers with responsibility for young children. More recently, however, researchers have given increasing attention to the impact of caregiving responsibilities among older workers. Early work focused attention on tensions experienced by middle-aged women, who were described as the "sandwich generation" (2, 3) and "women in the middle" (4). These terms designate women who are caught by the conflicting demands of multiple roles. Some women are in the middle generation, with both dependent children and living parents who require assistance. Others are caught between the traditional value of family care and the new value of employment and careers for women.

There is still relatively little agreement on how these two pivotal life foci—work and family caregiving—interact (5). Previous studies of the interaction between work and family caregiving have tended either to compare the hours of care provided and the well-being of working and nonworking caregivers or to compare the work performance of caregiving and noncaregiving employees. Few studies have compared caregiving and noncaregiving workers for outcomes such as work stress, job satisfaction, and well-being.

The aim of this chapter is to explore the interface between work and caregiving responsibilities of older working men and women. In particular, it addresses six issues. First, to what extent do older workers with caregiving responsibilities experience greater work stress than those without such responsibilities? Second, is there evidence that older workers with caregiving responsibilities have a more positive attitude to work than those without such responsibilities? Third, what is the joint impact of caregiving and work on the well-being of older workers? Fourth, do positive attitudes to work make a difference? Fifth, why might caregivers find work more stressful than noncaregivers? And sixth, does combining work and caregiving roles affect men and women differently?

MODELS OF THE RELATIONSHIP BETWEEN WORK STRESS AND CAREGIVING

The consequences of occupying particular role combinations has long been a central concern in psychosocial research. Early perspectives proposed that the domains of work and family are inherently distinct and disconnected and that involvement in one domain does not necessarily affect upon the other (6). This *separate spheres* view has been criticized and several alternative models advanced. The work-family *spillover model* proposes that both negative and positive moods may "spill over" from one domain to another and that this may occur in either direction. Hence, stresses and rewards experienced at work may affect the experience of family caregiving, and vice versa (6).

The *role conflict (or scarcity) theory* focuses on negative emotions. Role conflict arises when the demand from two or more roles is such that adequate performance of one role jeopardizes adequate performance of others (7). Two types of role strain have been identified. Role demand overload is defined as having so many demands related to one's roles that satisfactory performance is improbable, while perceived role inadequacy refers to a person's perception that he or she cannot meet his or her own standards of adequate role performance (8).

The role conflict approach has been challenged by the *role accumulation (or role enhancement) hypothesis,* which proposes that the beneficial aspects of occupying multiple roles usually outweigh the stressful aspects. Multiple roles may provide a sense of mastery and well-being and augment one's energy by increasing sources of identity, self-esteem, and privileges (9, 10). There may also be a mental health advantage in diversifying investment by taking on additional roles rather than being strongly invested in any single role. Experiencing stress in one domain may be offset by fulfillment in another domain. However, cause and effect are not clear, and mentally healthier people may take on more voluntary roles because they have the capacity to do so (11).

The *role expansion hypothesis* assumes that individuals can expand role sets without concomitant increases in role strain and distress, but that this depends on the extent to which the individual feels committed to each role (12). Individuals may become stressed when they have to perform an additional role to which they feel uncommitted, whereas their energy and time can be abundant when they are strongly committed to that role (10).

While role theory has generally been applied to child care, most of the work on care for older people has used a *stress and coping perspective* (5, 9). This model emphasizes the interactive, dynamic nature of the caregiving experience as a stress process. The model incorporates individuals' backgrounds, stressors, stress-related mediators (such as appraisal, coping strategies, and social support), and outcomes (13). In this paradigm, the severity of the felt stress depends on how demanding both the work and the caregiving roles are for the employee (14). More positively, rewards derived from either the job or the caregiving relationship may provide a buffer to cope with these demands (15).

ANALYSES OF DATA FROM THE HEALTHY RETIREMENT PROJECT—EXTENDED

Little work on the interface between work stress and caregiving has been carried out in Australia. Turvey and Thomson (16) studied caregivers' ability to remain in paid employment, and Howe and Schofield (17) examined the consequences of employment among adult daughter caregivers. Neither of these studies examined work stress per se. The analyses reported here use the models presented above to compare working caregivers with noncaregivers, with a particular emphasis on work stress.

The Healthy Retirement Project (HRP) was conceived jointly by the Lincoln Gerontology Centre and the Council on the Ageing (Victoria), prompted partly by dissatisfaction with existing programs on preparation for the retirement transition and partly by lack of good, up-to-date, local knowledge of retirement. Much of the existing research on retirement pre-dated the dramatic work-force changes of the past 10–15 years and was cross-sectional rather than prospective. The HRP was designed to inform an innovative pilot intervention program being developed by the Council on the Ageing (Victoria) and was funded by the Victorian Health Promotion Foundation.

The original sample in this project (n = 7,022) was extended for the analyses presented here (HRP-E) to include individuals recruited for two smaller, parallel studies of older employees born in Italy (n = 107) and Poland (n = 160). The sample is highly diverse and includes employees aged 50 and over recruited through a variety of sources, including 35 workplaces, five superannuation funds, ten trade unions, seven ethno-specific clubs and organizations, and media appeals. Respondents with missing data on key variables (n = 196) were excluded from the analysis, leaving a total of 7,093 participants.

Aspects of the models on the interface between work stress and caregiving stress (as presented above) may be addressed using data from the Healthy Retirement Project. The analyses reported here focus on a comparison of the experiences of working caregivers and noncaregivers, with an emphasis on work stress. We first carried out a simple descriptive analysis of the sample of working caregivers, then conducted bivariate and (to control for important covariates) multivariate analyses. Multivariate analyses with dichotomous outcomes (i.e., work stress, health, and happiness) employed hierarchical logistic regression; multivariate analyses with continuous outcomes (i.e., job satisfaction, work ethic) employed linear regression. We used loglinear analysis with model selection to assess more complex interactions between categorical variables (i.e., between gender, work stress, and caregiver status in predicting health or happiness).

RESULTS

Who Are the Working Caregivers?

The major independent variable, caregiving status, was measured through the item "Do you have the main responsibility in caring for someone who has a long-term illness, disability, or other problem?" Respondents indicated whether they were caring for a spouse, parent, adult child, or other person and could check more than one alternative.

Just over 10 percent of the sample (n = 734; 10.5 percent) defined themselves as caregivers, which is consistent with estimates of the prevalence of caregiving responsibilities among employees (18). The biggest group of caregivers provided care for parents (n = 350, 5.0 percent), followed by spouse caregivers (n = 227, 3.2 percent), parents caring for disabled children (n = 136, 1.9 percent), and caregivers for other people (n = 75, 1.1 percent). A few people (n = 49) were caring for more than one person.

Among the caregivers, 347 were men and 387 were women. Nearly half of both the men (47.3 percent) and women (48.1 percent) were caring for a parent or parent-in-law. More than one-third (35.0 percent) of the male caregivers were caring for a spouse, compared with 27.5 percent of the female caregivers. More women than men were involved in caring for a child (20.6 percent vs. 16.0 percent) or for other relatives and friends (12.7 percent vs. 8.0 percent). Among the whole sample, women were more likely than men to view themselves as caregivers (12.8 percent vs. 9.0 percent). Individuals in the middle age group (55 to 59) were more likely to view themselves as caregivers than either younger or older respondents (11.9 percent, vs. 9.8 percent of 50- to 54-year-olds and 11.2 percent of those aged 60 or over). Of the women aged 55 to 59, 14.1 percent saw themselves as caregivers. These women were most likely to be caring for a child or a parent. However, men over 60 were the group most likely to be caring for a spouse.

Most of these working caregivers were married or had a partner (82.1 percent), about one-third also had financially dependent children (32.5 percent), almost one-quarter (23.6 percent) also found time for voluntary work, and a substantial minority (11.8 percent) were involved in child care outside the family home.

The working hours of caregivers differed substantially from those of noncaregivers. Caregivers were more likely to work fewer than 30 hours per week (21.8 percent vs. 17.0 percent) and less likely to work more than 40 hours per week (23.4 percent vs. 28.0 percent). Caregivers were also more likely than noncaregivers to be in low-status jobs, such as sales, service, personal care, and semi-skilled or unskilled work (59.4 percent vs. 54.8 percent).

Do Caregivers Report Higher Work Stress Than Noncaregivers?

Surprisingly, few studies have compared the work stress of caregivers and noncaregivers. The spillover model suggests that stress experienced in caregiving could result in higher work stress. In a recent study of working women with parent-care responsibilities, Atienza and Stephens (19) found that work stress was associated with caregiving stress, and spillover of negative emotions in both directions was commonly reported. However, positive spillover also was noted by about two-thirds of the women, especially enjoyment of positive mood in one role because of positive experiences in the other (20).

Many studies have emphasized pervasive negative effects of caregiving on work performance and, by implication, work stress. Substantial proportions of caregivers sometimes take leave from their jobs or have to rearrange work schedules to accommodate caregiving duties, such as accompanying older relatives to medical appointments (21–26). Studies in the United States and Australia indicate that about 80 percent of caregivers in employment have to make some kind of accommodation in their work-life (5, 17).

Caregiving may also cause work stress through interruptions, distractions, or impaired concentration (27). More than two-thirds of caregivers report making or receiving phone calls at work related to elder care (24). Work performance may be affected by caregiving anxiety, upset, or fatigue (21, 22, 28).

In the current study, we measured work stress by the item "my job involves a lot of stress," with four response categories ranging from "very true" to "not at all true." This measure was highly skewed: 32 percent of the sample responded "very true." Hence, the item was treated as dichotomous, and we used binary logistic regression to predict the likelihood of experiencing work stress. Respondents were classified as either "work stressed" (i.e., strongly agreed, n = 2,294) or "not work stressed" (n = 4,799).

Caregivers were no more likely than noncaregivers to report high work stress: 34.8 percent of caregivers and 32.2 percent of noncaregivers were in the work-stressed group. However, as already indicated, there were important sociodemographic and work-related differences between the caregivers and noncaregivers. We repeated the analysis of the difference between caregivers and noncaregivers on work stress using multivariate methods and controlling one at a time for working hours, job status, gender, and age group. The results of these analyses are presented in Table 11.1. Odds ratios may be interpreted as the relative probability of the outcome for different levels of the independent variable. An odds ratio of greater than 1.0 indicates that the category of interest is more likely than the reference category to be associated with the outcome, and the size of the ratio indicates the extent of the difference. Hence, caregivers were about 12 percent more likely than noncaregivers to report high job stress. The oldest group of workers, those aged over 60, were only about 70 percent as likely as those aged

50 to 55 to report high job stress. High job stress increased dramatically with the hours worked and was higher for people in high-status occupations.

Working hours functioned as a "suppressor variable": having controlled for working hours, caregivers were significantly (about 20 percent) more likely than noncaregivers to report high job stress. Table 11.2 illustrates the difference between caregivers and noncaregivers in the probability of being work stressed for different work hours. Being a caregiver increased the risk that the job would be experienced as highly stressful. This effect was not particularly strong in comparison with other predictors of work stress (especially work hours and job status). This is not surprising, given that work hours and job status are concepts that are close to work stress, while caregiving status belongs to a different conceptual domain and caregiving stress per se was not measured. This result supports the hypothesis that there is negative spillover from caregiving stress to work. The separate spheres model was not supported.

Table 11.1

Analysis of job stress by caregiver status alone and with control variables

Independent variable (reference group)	Wald statistic (*df*)	Odds ratio	95% confidence interval
Caregiver status (noncaregivers)	4.78 (1)	1.12	0.96–1.32
Gender (male)	0.13 (1)	0.98	0.89–1.09
Caregiver status (noncaregivers)	3.03 (1)	1.15	0.98–1.35
Age group (<55)	21.83 (2)	1.00	
55–59		0.87*	0.77–0.98
60+		0.67***	0.57–0.80
Caregiver status (noncaregivers)	2.25 (1)	1.13	0.96–1.33
Work hours (<15)	283.57 (4)	1.00	
15–29		4.01***	2.60–6.20
30–39		4.60***	3.04–6.98
40		6.60***	4.231–10.01
>40		10.30***	6.79–15.65
Caregiver status (noncaregivers)	5.35 (1)	1.21*	1.03–1.43
Job status (low)	101.34 (1)	1.69***	1.52–1.87
Caregiver status (noncaregivers)	3.55 (1)	1.17	0.99–1.38

$*P < .05$; $**P < .01$; $***P < .001$

Table 11.2

Workers work-stressed, by caregiver status for different work hours, percent

Work hours	Noncaregivers	Caregivers
<30	19.7%	23.5%
30–39	26.9	30.7
40	35.0	35.5
>40	45.0	51.7

Do Caregivers Have a More Positive Attitude to Work Than Noncaregivers?

The spillover hypothesis suggests that positive emotions experienced in the caregiving sphere might be manifested in higher work satisfaction among caregivers than among noncaregivers. We could not locate any previous studies that compare caregivers with noncaregivers on positive feelings about work. However, there is evidence that caregivers benefit from being employed. Work is a welcome relief for caregivers and provides a balance to the caring role (17, 21, 29, 30). Nearly one-third of respondents in Scharlach's study (31) claimed that their job had no negative effects on their caregiving and listed benefits such as improved finances, emotional support from coworkers, and a better relationship with the care recipient.

While the bulk of research documents the costs of caregiving for work performance, some authors have noted that caregiving may provide employees with extra experiences and skills that are advantageous in the workplace. These advantages include greater sensitivity to human needs, increased feelings of competence, and enhanced management of difficult situations (31, 32). Such skills may improve caregivers' work productivity and job satisfaction.

The measures used in this study to assess a positive attitude to work included job satisfaction, work ethic, and work commitment. The job satisfaction scale was adapted from the CARNET studies (33) and comprised eight items, each rated on a four-point scale (from "strongly agree" to "strongly disagree"). Coefficient alpha for the scale was .88. Examples of items include "I like my job" and "I feel appreciated." The work ethic scale, adapted from Goodwin (34), comprised eight items, each rated on a four-point scale from "strongly agree" to "strongly disagree." Coefficient alpha for the scale was .78. Examples of items include "work should be the most important part of a person's life" and "hard work makes you a better person." Work commitment was a six-item scale containing items such as "the work I do is one of the most satisfying parts of my life." Coefficient for work commitment was .77. The scale was divided into tertiles (low, medium, and high) for some analyses.

We compared caregivers with noncaregivers on job satisfaction, work ethic, and work commitment, using *t*-tests and multiple regression. Multivariate analyses controlled for gender, age, work hours, and job status (see Table 11.3). Caregivers did not differ from noncaregivers on job satisfaction, work ethic, or work commitment. There was no evidence of positive spillover from caregiving rewards to work satisfaction. Nor did caregivers value work more than noncaregivers. For positive emotions towards caregiving and work, the separate spheres model was supported.

What Is the Joint Impact of Caregiving and Work on the Well-Being of Older Workers?

The role conflict hypothesis proposes that the combination of caregiving and work leads to high strain and hence to deterioration in health and mental health. Similarly, the stress and coping model predicts that work stress and caregiving stress combine additively to predict poor health and mental health. In contrast, the role enhancement hypothesis suggests that combining the positive aspects of caregiving and work leads to greater well-being among caregivers than noncaregivers.

There has been very little research comparing the well-being of caregiving and noncaregiving workers. One such study, by Neal and colleagues (1), examined the stress accumulated from both work and caregiving contexts. On the other hand, there is a plethora of research comparing working with nonworking caregivers, much of which supports the role enhancement model. Among caregivers, those who work report better health and well-being and lower anxiety, strain, burden,

Table 11.3

Relationship between work variables and caregiver status, bivariate and multivariate

	Means (S.D.)		Bivariate,	Multivariate[a]
Outcome	Noncaregivers	Caregivers	*t*, sig.	beta, sig.
Job satisfaction	3.12 (0.54)	3.11 (0.57)	0.43	–0.09
Work ethic	2.98 (0.48)	2.97 (0.51)	0.27	0.01
Work commitment	3.04 (0.51)	3.06 (0.53)	0.89	0.02

[a]Multivariate analyses controlled for gender, age, work hours, and job status (high/low).

and depression (23, 35–41). This is also true among special groups of caregivers, such as those caring for people with AIDS (42) or schizophrenia (43).

However, some of the literature comparing working with nonworking caregivers supports the role conflict model. Employment may worsen caregiver stress if the caregiving workload is high (40, 44–47) and the caregiver feels caught between the two obligations or feels not in control (48, 49). Employment may also add to caregiving stress if work schedules are inflexible, if the job is demanding, stressful, or insecure, or if the social environment at work is conflict-ridden rather than supportive (5, 19, 50–54). Caregivers also experience higher stress if caregiving responsibilities interrupt their work or require taking time off (55, 56).

In the current study, we assessed well-being using measures of happiness and health, each with five response categories. Responses to the item "how often do you feel happy?" ranged from "very frequently" to "never." Self-rated health was rated from "excellent" to "poor." These two items were significantly correlated ($r = .29$, $P < .001$). Responses to both items were heavily skewed. A majority of respondents indicated that they were in excellent or very good health (60.8 percent) and very frequently or frequently happy (78.9 percent). Because these variables could not be used in linear regression, they were dichotomized to allow logistic regression analysis (see Tables 11.4 and 11.5). Participants were consistently more likely to be in very good health and frequently happy if their job satisfaction was high, their work stress was low, and they were not caregivers. The impacts of work stress and caregiving on well-being were additive: there was no interaction effect between caregiver status and work stress in predicting either health or happiness.

These results support the role conflict model: lower well-being was associated with having more than one major life role. The results are also consistent with the stress and coping model, in that stresses were additive and work satisfaction reduced the impact of the two stressors on well-being. The role enhancement model was not supported for these mature workers, since adding the caregiving role did not lead to greater well-being.

Do Positive Attitudes to Work Make a Difference?

The stress and coping model suggests that job satisfaction might act as a buffer against the effects of (*a*) caregiving on job stress and (*b*) both caregiving and job stress on well-being. The role expansion hypothesis suggests that commitment to work may similarly act as a buffer. We could not find any previous studies that assessed either job satisfaction or commitment to work as buffering variables.

A variable acts as a buffer when it partly or totally ameliorates the effect of stress on negative outcomes. For buffering to occur, there must be an interaction effect between the buffer and the stressor. When stress is low, the presence of the buffer should make little difference to the outcome, but when stress is high, the presence of the buffer should result in a better outcome (57). We assessed the

Table 11.4

Analysis of health[a] by caregiver status, work stress, and control variables

Independent variable (reference group)	Wald statistic (*df*)	Odds ratio	95 % confidence interval
Gender (male)	20.63 (1)	1.30***	1.16–1.45
Age group (<55)	0.78 (2)	1.00	
55–59		0.97	0.86–1.08
60+		0.94	0.80–1.11
Work hours (<15)	15.69 (4)	1.00	
15–29		0.86	0.66–1.12
30–39		1.03	0.80–1.32
40		1.04	0.79–1.36
>40		1.23	0.94–1.61
Job status (low)	9.50 (1)	1.19**	1.06–1.32
Work stress (low)	28.32 (1)	0.75***	0.70–0.83
Job satisfaction	82.75 (1)	1.54***	1.41–1.70
Caregiver status (noncaregivers)	11.34 (1)	0.76**	0.65–0.89

[a]1 = good, fair, or poor; 2 = very good or excellent.
*$P < .05$; **$P < .01$; ***$P < .001$

capacity of job satisfaction, work ethic, and work commitment to act as buffers against caregiving and job stress.

There was very little evidence that any of these positive attitudes to work could act as a buffer. Instead, positive attitudes to work affected outcomes directly. Regardless of whether or not people were caregivers, several generalizations could be made about the impacts of positive attitudes to work on well-being. First, people with high job satisfaction were less likely to feel work stress and were more likely to be in good health and frequently happy than those whose job satisfaction was low. Second, people who were highly committed to work were similarly more likely to be in good health and frequently happy than those with low work commitment. Third, participants were less likely to be work-stressed if their work commitment was in the middle range, neither too high nor too low. Finally, people whose work ethic was high tended to report high work stress, but their well-being was not affected.

The only significant interaction effect was between work ethic and work stress in predicting health. However, the results were not consistent with a buffering hypothesis. Instead, work stress was least likely to have a detrimental effect on health when people had moderate levels of work ethic, rather than very high or very low levels. The role expansion hypothesis was not supported.

Table 11.5

Analysis of happiness[a] by caregiver status, work stress, and control variables

Independent variable (reference group)	Wald statistic (*df*)	Odds ratio	95 % confidence interval
Gender (male)	7.84 (1)	1.22**	1.06–1.39
Age group (<55)	0.58 (2)	1.00	
55–59		0.98	0.86–1.13
60+		0.92	0.75–1.13
Work hours (<15)	4.59 (4)	1.00	
15–29		1.01	0.72–1.42
30–39		1.13	0.82–1.54
40		1.28	0.92–1.80
>40		1.17	0.84–1.64
Job status (low)	0.00 (1)	1.00	0.87–1.14
Work stress (low)	23.49 (1)	0.73***	0.64–0.83
Job satisfaction	310.51 (1)	2.79***	2.49–3.12
Caregiver status (noncaregivers)	24.18 (1)	0.63***	0.53–0.76

[a]1 = sometimes, rarely, or never; 2 = frequently or very frequently.
*$P < .05$; **$P < .01$; ***$P < .001$

Why Are Caregivers More Likely Than Noncaregivers to Find Work Stressful?

There are several possible explanations as to why caregivers might find work more stressful than noncaregivers. Having to change work schedules, feeling anxious, or having difficulty concentrating at work could all render work more stressful. None of these possibilities can be tested using data from the HRP-E. However, a further possibility can be tested: that work is stressful for caregivers because caregivers are more pressured than noncaregivers in out-of-work time. To our knowledge, no prior studies have assessed this possibility. The criteria used here for testing the hypothesis (i.e., mediation) are consistent with those of Baron and Kenny (58). Two items indicating pressure in nonwork hours were "I don't have enough spare time" (vs. "I have just about the right amount of/too much of spare time") and "apart from the time when you are at work, how often do you do things that you really enjoy?" (responses on a five-point scale from "very frequently" to "never").

Caregivers were more likely than noncaregivers to not have enough spare time (69.0 percent vs. 63.7 percent). This was especially true of caregivers involved in parent care, 72.3 percent of whom had insufficient spare time. Caregivers were also less likely than noncaregivers to be able to do frequently things that

Table 11.6

Analysis of mediation of the relationship between caregiver status and work stress[a]

Independent variable (reference group)	Wald statistic (*df*)	Odds ratio	95 % confidence interval
Analysis 1. Caregiver status (alone)			
Caregiver status (noncaregivers)	4.78 (1)	1.21*	1.02–1.43
Analysis 2. Mediators (entered together)			
Not having enough spare time	28.06 (1)	1.37***	1.22–1.53
Not frequently enjoying activities	21.92 (1)	1.30***	1.16–1.44
Analysis 3. Caregiver status entered with mediators			
Caregiver status (noncaregivers)	3.49 (1)	1.18	0.99–1.39
Not having enough spare time	27.39 (1)	1.36***	1.21–1.53
Not frequently enjoying activities	21.21 (1)	1.29***	1.16–1.44

[a]All analyses controlled for gender, age group, working hours, and job status.
*$P < .05$; **$P < .01$; ***$P < .001$

they enjoyed (57.5 percent vs. 65.3 percent). Not having enough spare time and not frequently enjoying nonwork activities both predicted work stress. The relationship between carer status and work stress was partly mediated by each of the two indicators of stress in out-of-work time and was fully mediated by the combination of these (see Table 11.6). The data support the hypothesis that caregivers experience more stress at work than noncaregivers because they are more pressured in nonwork hours.

To What Extent Does Combining Work and Caregiving Roles Affect Men and Women Differently?

Combining caregiving and work is frequently presented as a gender issue. Care of an ill or disabled family member or friend is disproportionately carried out by women in late midlife, which is also the time in the life course when women's labor force participation peaks (59). Entering employment does not mean that women are forsaking care work. Rather, women with both caregiving and work roles have become more likely to cease caregiving than to leave their jobs (60). Because of social pressures, gender expectations, and lack of alternatives, women are adding to their responsibilities rather than shifting them (59, 61).

Gender differences are frequently noted in studies of the impact of caregiving on work. Caregiving women are more likely than men to report that caregiving interferes with their work (62, 63). Female caregivers are more likely than male caregivers to change their work schedules, take unpaid leave, or use sick days to accommodate their caregiving responsibilities (17, 26, 64–66). Women are also more likely than men to have missed promotional opportunities or to have been excluded from the workforce because of their caregiving (17, 64).

However, employed caregiving men also report significant levels of strain and make numerous family and work accommodations to meet their dual responsibilities (5). Men are more likely than women to report interrupted workdays (64), and one study indicates that more husbands than wives cut back on paid work to assist their spouse (67). Men may actually find it more stressful than do women when caregiving interrupts their work schedules, perhaps because employers are less tolerant when men have to take time off for caregiving (56).

We undertook a series of analyses to test whether men and women react differently to combining work and caregiving roles; we looked for interaction effects involving gender and caregiving status. The first question is whether women are more likely than men to reduce their work hours if they are caregivers. As noted earlier, caregivers tend to work fewer hours than noncaregivers, and women are more likely to be caregivers than men. However, the difference in hours worked by caregivers and noncaregivers was no longer significant when gender was taken into account. Put differently, the hours worked by caregiving men were no different from those of their noncaregiving counterparts, and the same was true for women (see Table 11.7). Neither men nor women cut back significantly on their work hours to accommodate caregiving responsibilities.

Table 11.7

Hours worked by caregiver status for men and women, percent

	Men		Women	
Work hours	Noncaregiving	Caregiving	Noncaregiving	Caregiving
<15	1.4%	2.3%	8.5%	9.8%
15–29	3.4	4.0	24.3	25.8
30–39	38.9	37.0	38.9	39.2
40	17.3	20.1	14.3	13.7
>40	38.9	36.7	14.1	11.6
Total	100.0	100.0	100.0	100.0

The second question we looked at is whether combining work and caregiving is more stressful for women than for men. There was no evidence that caregiving affected either health or happiness differently for men and women (see Table 11.8). Men tended to report lower well-being than women, and caregivers lower well-being than noncaregivers, but there was no significant interaction effect. In the case of work stress, there appears to be more difference between caregivers and noncaregivers among women than among men. However, this interaction effect is not statistically significant (at the $P = .05$ level). Attempts to clarify the findings using multivariate methods yielded conflicting results. While no significant interaction effects were detected for the sample as a whole, on analyzing the data separately for men and women we found that caregiver status contributed significantly to work stress for women but not for men.

We also analyzed the effects of the combination of gender, work stress, and caregiving responsibility on both health and happiness. There was no evidence that the combination of work stress and caregiving stress operated differently on men and women to affect well-being. Women were more likely than men to report high levels of well-being, regardless of whether or not individuals were caregivers and/or in the high work stress group.

DISCUSSION

The main finding from this series of analyses is that caregivers report significantly higher work stress than noncaregivers when work hours are taken into account. Stress from caregiving appears to spill over to the stress experienced at work. However, caregivers did not express higher work satisfaction than noncaregivers, nor did they have higher work ethic or work commitment, indicating a lack of positive spillover. Nor did caregivers value work more than noncaregivers.

Employees were less likely to be healthy or happy if they were caregivers, were highly stressed at work, and derived little satisfaction from work. No stress-buffering effects were found for work satisfaction or work commitment. The

Table 11.8

Negative outcomes by caregiver status for men and women, percent

	Men		Women	
Outcome	Noncaregiving	Caregiving	Noncaregiving	Caregiving
Work-stressed	32.5%	34.0%	31.7%	36.4%
Low health	40.4	47.9	36.0	44.3
Low happiness	22.4	29.1	17.9	28.2

effects of combining work and caregiving did not differ significantly for men and women.

Models of the relationship between work stress and caregiving stress supported by this study were the negative spillover model, the role conflict model, and the stress and coping model. The lack of any buffering effects or positive spillover is disappointing but not surprising, given that the study included no measures of caregiving satisfaction.

We found few gender differences in the intersection between work and caregiving. There was some indication that women might find this combination of roles more stressful than men, but the difference proved elusive. One weakness of the present study is that it did not include a measure of the extent of caregiving responsibilities. It is possible that the men in the study were less involved in caregiving than the women. Studies have found that among adult-child caregivers, men tend to undertake less personally demanding tasks than do women (e.g., 68). However, among caregiving spouses, husbands are responsible for just as many tasks as wives (e.g., 69). Of course, a major difference between adult-child caregivers and spouse caregivers is that most of the latter have retired. The literature on working spouse caregivers is sparse. Caregiving responsibilities may lend weight to the decision to retire, though this has received little attention in the retirement literature. There is room here for further research on gender differences in the capacity to continue to work that takes into account financial and social pressures. We need to know more about how to support both women and men with caregiving roles to remain in paid work, while minimizing work stress and work interference.

It is interesting to speculate why caregivers should be more likely than noncaregivers to rate their work as stressful. The data used here could not be applied to test the hypothesis that this difference was due to caregivers either experiencing more interruptions at work or feeling more anxious than noncaregivers. However, the data did support the notion that caregivers experienced more stress in work time than noncaregivers because they are more pressured in nonwork hours: they are more likely to have insufficient spare time and are less likely to frequently do things they really enjoy.

Caregivers who feel stressed may be assisted by making the workplace less stressful for caregivers and noncaregivers alike (e.g., by making sure that work hours are not unduly extended and that job flexibility is maximized; see also Chapter 12). However, policies to assist working caregivers in particular may need to focus on nonwork hours. The evidence suggests that work stress could be reduced if support were provided to caregivers to use more of their nonwork hours in enjoyable recreation or relaxation. Currently, caregiver day respite programs (e.g., adult day-care centers) usually operate during office hours rather than in the evening or at weekends. Residential respite provided by some nursing homes and hostels is poorly used (70). Undoubtedly, while day respite programs allow some caregivers to work, they do not necessarily support them during their hours off. In Australia, these programs have been offered through the Home and Community Care program, and a change in their operating hours would require a shift in government policy. The Australian government has already recognized the value of both supporting caregivers (71) and encouraging mature workers to remain in the workforce to reduce strain on the public purse (72).

Using data from the Healthy Retirement Project presents both advantages and disadvantages in studying the interface between caregiving and work stress. Advantages include the nature of both the recruitment method and the sample. An advantage of the recruitment method is that the ostensible purpose of the study is not to document the burdens of combining work and caregiving. Hence, caregivers (and in particular, caregivers who feel especially burdened) are no more likely than noncaregivers to respond to an invitation to participate in the study. The importance of including noncaregiving employees, of the sample not being self-selected on the basis of caregiving, and of not being site-specific has been noted elsewhere (73). A further advantage of the HRP is that its participants are occupationally diverse, including both men and women, people in part-time and full-time work, and representatives from the whole range of occupational categories.

Tennstedt and Gonyea (73) also recommend that employment and caregiving not be treated as dichotomous and that studies should include measures of the structure and supportiveness of one's job. As noted above, a disadvantage of our study is that it did not include measures of the extent of caregiving. We knew only whether respondents had caregiving responsibilities and for whom they provided care.

What cannot be taken into account in any study of caregiving employees is the operation of selection effects. It is not known whether the caregivers in the sample differ from those who had already left work to provide care, and whether these differences include stresses experienced in caregiving, at work, or in trying to combine the two roles. Only a prospective research design would allow some disentangling of these effects. However, prospective studies of taking on the caregiving role are rare, as are prospective studies of retirement. A design that included a sufficient number of individuals to permit prospective study of the impacts of taking on caregiving on work stress and on giving up work would be prohibitively expensive.

CONCLUSION

While the issue of working caregivers has attracted a good deal of attention from researchers over the past 15 years, the study reported here has begun to explore an area that has not been well researched in the past. Few previous studies of the intersection between work and caregiving have specifically included work stress as a measure. Nor have more global well-being outcomes often been included.

In our sample, caregivers were more likely to report high work stress than other employees, partly because their nonwork hours were less likely to be relaxing and enjoyable. The study supports the spillover hypothesis of the relationship between work and caregiving, which states that stresses and enjoyment experienced in one sphere may influence the experience of the other. However, work stress did not have a more deleterious effect on caregivers than on their counterparts who were not providing care. Work stress predicted lowered well-being among caregivers and noncaregivers alike.

Employers can assist working caregivers by making sure that the workplace is as supportive and flexible as possible. Recent attempts by Australian trade unions to monitor and reduce work stress may benefit both caregivers and noncaregivers. Governments can assist mature, working caregivers to remain in the workforce by encouraging such initiatives. In addition, government agencies should consider the community supports provided to caregivers who are employed. Respite and other services could be extended to out-of-work hours to support working caregivers' recreational opportunities. Further, more research is needed to explore gender differences in the intersection between work stress and caregiving stress and find ways of supporting caregivers to remain in the workforce. Individuals, workplaces, and the community as a whole may benefit from retaining the strengths of caregivers in the workforce.

REFERENCES

1. Neal, M. B., et al. *Balancing Work and Caregiving for Children, Adults, and Elders.* Sage, Newbury Park, Calif., 1993.
2. Miller, D. A. "Sandwich" generation: Adult children of the aging. *Soc. Work* 26: 419–423, 1981.
3. Shanas, E. Older people and their families: The new pioneers. *J. Marriage Fam.* 42: 9–15, 1980.
4. Brody, E. M. "Women in the middle" and family help to older people. *Gerontologist* 21: 471–480, 1981.
5. Fredriksen-Goldsen, K. I., and Scharlach, A. E. *Families and Work: New Directions in the Twenty-First Century.* Oxford University Press, New York, 2001.
6. Zedeck, S., and Mosier, K. L. Work in the family and employing organization. *Am. Psychol.* 435: 240–251, 1990.
7. Gignac, M. A. M., Kelloway, E. K., and Gottlieb, B. H. Impact of caregiving on employment: A mediational model of work-family conflict. *Can. J. Aging* 15: 525–542, 1996.
8. Scharlach, A. E. Role strain in mother-daughter relationships in later life. *Gerontologist* 27: 627–631, 1987.
9. Biegel, D. E., Sales, E., and Schulz, R. *Family Caregiving in Chronic Illness: Alzheimer's Disease, Cancer, Heart Disease, Mental Illness, and Stroke.* Sage, Newbury Park, Calif., 1991.
10. Dautzenberg, M. G. H., et al. Competing demands of paid work and parent care. *Res. Aging* 22: 165–187, 2000.

11. Doress-Worters, P. B. Adding elder care to women's multiple roles: A critical review of the caregiver stress and multiple roles literatures. *Sex Roles* 31: 597–616, 1994.
12. Marks, S. R. Multiple roles and role strain: Some notes on human energy, time and commitment. *Am. Sociol. Rev.* 42: 921–936, 1977.
13. Folkman, S., et al. Dynamics of a stressful encounter: Cognitive appraisal, coping and outcomes. *J. Pers. Soc. Psychol.* 59: 992–1003, 1986.
14. Chapman, N. J., Ingersoll-Dayton, B., and Neal, M. B. Balancing the multiple roles of work and caregiving for children, adults, and elders. In *Job Stress in a Changing Workforce: Investigating Gender, Diversity, and Family Issues*, edited by G. P. Keita and J. J. Hurrell Jr., pp. 283–300. American Psychological Association, Washington, D.C., 1994.
15. Thoits, P. A. Conceptual, methodological, and theoretical problems in studying social support as a buffer against life stress. *J. Health Soc. Behav.* 23: 145–159, 1982.
16. Turvey, K., and Thomson, C. Caregiving and Employment I: Who Cares, What's Involved? Different Caregiving Relationships and Their Impact on Caregiver Employment. Paper presented at Family Research: Pathways to Policy, 5th Australian Family Research Conference, Brisbane, November 1996.
17. Howe, A., and Schofield, H. Will you need one, or will you be one, in the year 2004? Trends in carer roles and social policy in Australia over the last and next 20 years. In *Towards a National Agenda for Carers: Workshop Papers*, pp. 4–18. Australian Government Publishing Service, Canberra, 1996.
18. Gorey, K. M., Rice, R. W., and Brice, G. C. Prevalence of elder care responsibilities among the work force population: Response bias among a group of cross-sectional surveys. *Res. Aging* 14: 399–418, 1992.
19. Atienza, A. A., and Stephens, M. A. P. Social interactions at work and the well-being of daughters involved in parent care. *J. Appl. Gerontol.* 19: 243–263, 2000.
20. Stephens, M. A. P., Franks, M. M., and Atienza, A. A. Where two roles intersect: Spillover between parent care and employment. *Psychol. Aging* 12: 30–37, 1997.
21. Enright, R. B., and Friss, L. *Employed Caregivers of Brain-Impaired Adults: An Assessment of the Dual Role.* Family Survival Project, San Francisco, 1987.
22. Gibeau, J. L., and Anastas, J. W. Breadwinners and caregivers: Interviews with working women. *J. Gerontol. Soc. Work* 14: 19–40, 1989.
23. Orodenker, S. Z. Family caregiving in a changing society: The effects of employment on caregiver stress. *Fam. Community Health* 12: 58–70, 1990.
24. Scharlach, A. E., and Boyd, S. L. Caregiving and employment: Results of an employee survey. *Gerontologist* 29: 382–387, 1989.
25. Stephens, S. A., and Christianson, J. B. *Informal Care of the Elderly.* Lexington Books, Lexington, Mass., 1986.
26. Stone, R., Cafferata, G. L., and Sangl, J. Caregivers of the frail elderly: A national profile. *Gerontologist* 27: 616–626, 1987.
27. Merrill, D. M. *Caring for Elderly Parents: Juggling Work, Family, and Caregiving in Middle and Working Class Families.* Auburn House, Westport, Conn., 1997.
28. Abel, E. K. Informal care for the disabled elderly: A critique of recent literature. *Res. Aging* 12: 139–157, 1990.
29. Lechner, V. M., and Gupta, C. Employed caregivers: A four-year follow-up. *J. Appl. Gerontol.* 15: 102–115, 1996.

30. Rands, G. Working people who also care for the elderly. *Int. J. Geriatr. Psychiatry* 12: 39–44, 1997.
31. Scharlach, A. E. Caregiving and employment: Competing or complementary roles? *Gerontologist* 34: 378–385, 1994.
32. Lechner, V. M., and Neal, M. B. *Work and Caring for the Elderly: International Perspectives*. Brunner/Mazel, Philadelphia, 1999.
33. CARNET. *Into the Age of Aging: Selected Findings*. CARNET Administrative Centre, Centre for Studies of Aging, University of Toronto, 1996.
34. Goodwin, L. *Do the Poor Want to Work? A Social-Psychological Study of Work Orientations*. Brookings Institution, Washington, D.C., 1972.
35. Jutras, S., and Veilleux, F. Informal caregiving: Correlates of perceived burden. *Can. J. Aging* 10: 40–55, 1991.
36. Pavalko, E. K., and Woodbury, S. Social roles as process: Caregiving careers and women's health. *J. Health Soc. Behav.* 41: 91–105, 2000.
37. Robinson, K. M., and Kaye, J. The relationship between spiritual perspective, social support, and depression in caregiving and noncaregiving wives. *Sch. Inq. Nurs. Pract.* 8: 375–389, 1994.
38. Schultz, C. L., et al. Predictors of anxiety in family caregivers. *Aust. Occup. Ther. J.* 41: 153–161, 1994.
39. Spitze, G., et al. Middle generation roles and the well being of men and women. *J. Gerontol. Soc. Sci.* 49: S107–S116, 1994.
40. Stoller, E. P., and Pugliesi, K. L. Other roles of caregivers: Competing responsibilities or supportive resources. *J. Gerontol. Soc. Sci.* 44: S231–S238, 1989.
41. Tennstedt, S., Cafferata, G. L., and Sullivan, L. Depression among caregivers of impaired elders. *J. Aging Health* 4: 58–76, 1992.
42. Wight, R. G., LeBlanc, A. J., and Aneshensel, C. S. AIDS caregiving and health among midlife and older women. *Health Psychol.* 17: 130–137, 1998.
43. Scazufca, M., and Kuipers, E. Links between expressed emotion and burden of care in relatives of patients with schizophrenia. *Br. J. Psychiatry* 168: 580–587, 1996.
44. Birkel, R., and Jones, C. Comparison of the caregiving networks of dependent elderly individuals who are lucid and those who are demented. *Gerontologist* 29: 114–119, 1989.
45. Montgomery, R. J. V., Gonyea, J. G., and Hooyman, N. R. Caregiving and the experience of subjective and objective burden. *Fam. Relations* 34: 19–25, 1985.
46. Penning, M. J. In the middle: Parental caregiving in the context of other roles. *J. Gerontol. B Psychol. Sci. Soc. Sci.* 53: S188–S197, 1998.
47. Rankin, E. D. Caregiver stress and the elderly: A familial perspective. *J. Gerontol. Soc. Work* 15: 57–73, 1990.
48. Brody, E. M., et al. Work status and parent care: A comparison of four groups of women. *Gerontologist* 27: 201–208, 1987.
49. Duxbury, L., Higgins, C., and Lee, C. Work-family conflict: A comparison by gender, family type, and perceived control. *J. Fam. Issues* 15: 449–466, 1995.
50. Fredriksen, K. I., and Scharlach, A. E. Caregiving and employment: The impact of workplace characteristics on role strain. *J. Gerontol. Soc. Work* 28: 3–22, 1997.
51. Hong, J., and Seltzer, M. M. The psychological consequences of multiple roles: The nonnormative case. *J. Health Soc. Behav.* 36: 386–398, 1996.

52. Mui, A. C. Caregiver strain among black and white daughter caregivers: A role theory perspective. *Gerontologist* 32: 203–212, 1992.
53. Stephens, M. A. P., and Townsend, A. L. Stress of parent care: Positive and negative effects of women's other roles. *Psychol. Aging* 12: 376–386, 1997.
54. Thomas, L. T., and Ganster, D. C. Impact of family-supportive work variables on work-family conflict and strain: A control perspective. *J. Appl. Psychol.* 80: 6–15, 1995.
55. Scharlach, A. E., Sobel, E. L., and Roberts, R. E. Employment and caregiver strain: An integrative model. *Gerontologist* 31: 778–787, 1991.
56. Starrels, M. E., et al. Stress of caring for a parent: Effects of the elder's impairment on an employed adult child. *J. Marriage Fam.* 59: 860–872, 1997.
57. Cohen, S., and Wills, T. A. Stress, social support, and the buffering hypothesis. *Psychol. Bull.* 98: 310–357, 1985.
58. Baron, R. M., and Kenny, D. A. The moderator-mediator variable distinction in social psychological research: Conceptual, strategic and statistical considerations. *J. Pers. Soc. Psychol.* 51: 1173–1182, 1986.
59. Pavalko, E. K., and Artis, J. E. Women's caregiving and paid work: Causal relationships in late midlife. *J. Gerontol. B Psychol. Sci. Soc. Sci.* 4: S170–S179, 1997.
60. Moen, P., Robison, J., and Fields, V. Women's work and caregiving roles: A life course approach. *J. Gerontol.* 49: S176–S186, 1994.
61. Cox, E., and Spalding, B. Women and caring: The need for a new scenario. In *Towards a National Agenda for Carers: Workshop Papers,* pp. 55–67. Australian Government Publishing Service for the Department of Human Services and Health, Canberra, 1996.
62. Fredriksen, K. I. Gender differences in employment and the informal care of adults. *J. Women Aging* 8: 35–53, 1996.
63. Robison, J., Moen, P., and Dempster-McClain, D. Women's caregiving: Changing profiles and pathways. *J. Gerontol. B Psychol. Sci. Soc. Sci.* 6: S362–S373, 1995.
64. Martin-Matthews, A., and Campbell, L. D. Gender roles, employment and informal care. In *Connecting Gender and Ageing: A Sociological Approach*, edited by S. Arber and J. Ginn, pp. 129–143. Open University Press, Buckingham, U.K., 1995.
65. Mutschler, P. H. From executive suite to production line: How employees in different occupations manage elder care responsibilities. *Res. Aging* 16: 7–26, 1994.
66. Stone, R. I., and Short, P. F. Competing demands of employment and informal caregiving to disabled elders. *Med. Care* 28: 513–526, 1990.
67. Jutras, S., and Veilleux, F. Gender roles and care giving to the elderly: An empirical study. *Sex Roles* 25: 1–18, 1991.
68. Montgomery, R. J. V., and Kamo, Y. Parent care by sons and daughters. In *Aging Parents and Adult Children,* edited by J. A. Mancini. Lexington Books, Lexington, Mass., 1989.
69. Barusch, A. S., and Spaid, W. M. Gender differences in caregiving: Why do wives report greater burden? *Gerontologist* 29: 667–676, 1989.
70. Brodaty, H., and Gresham, M. Prescribing residential respite care for dementia—effects, side-effects, indications and dosage. *Int. J. Geriatr. Psychiatry* 7: 357–362, 1992.

71. Bishop, B. *The National Strategy for an Ageing Australia: Attitudes, Lifestyle and Community Support.* Discussion Paper. Commonwealth of Australia, Canberra, 2000.
72. Bishop, B. *The National Strategy for an Ageing Australia: Employment for Mature Age Workers.* Issues paper. Commonwealth of Australia, Canberra, 1999.
73. Tennstedt, S. L., and Gonyea, J. G. An agenda for work and eldercare research: Methodological challenges and future directions. *Res. Aging* 16: 85–108, 1994.

Chapter 12

STRESS AMONG OLDER WORKERS AND RETIREES

David de Vaus and Yvonne Wells

Economic, demographic, legislative, and policy changes have transformed the context in which older people work in and leave the workforce. Despite these major social changes, we know little about the worklife of older workers—especially their experience in the contemporary work environment. We know even less about the transition of older workers from an active worklife into retirement. Since most older workers make this transition sooner or later, the neglect of this normative transition is surprising. Work stress, the theme of this book, is normally taken to mean stress in paid work. However, a number of chapters in this book also address the stresses of unpaid work. Here, we go one step further and explore the stresses in work in the later part of a person's worklife and stresses in the transition from being in work to not working.

We focus on three main questions: first, to what extent do older workers find their work environment stressful, unpleasant, and unwelcoming? Second, to what extent is retirement itself stressful? That is, to what extent is *not* working stressful? Third, do stressed workers continue to be stressed following retirement? These questions are addressed using data from the Australian Healthy Retirement Project (HRP; see Chapter 11). We use two sets of data from this project. The first set is derived from a survey of 7,000 workers aged 50 and over. The second is based on a panel study of retirees who were recruited from the larger sample of older workers. This panel consists of approximately 416 members, depending on the variables and the stage of analysis. The panel members were first interviewed just as they were about to retire, then again, briefly, 6 months after retirement; and again 12 months and 24 months after retirement. Details of these two data sets are provided in Chapter 11.

WORK STRESS AMONG OLDER WORKERS

The contemporary work environment has many elements that could make the workplace highly stressful for older people. Economic restructuring over the past two decades has led to constant change, restructuring, and substantial downsizing. The downsizing is especially evident in the established sectors in which many older workers have been trained and have developed their careers. This has led to a substantial reduction in the number of older people in the workforce, as a result of either forced redundancy or early retirement. In 1997, 77 percent of men and 87 percent of women in Australia had already retired from full-time work five years before reaching pensionable age (1), and 45 percent of all Australians aged 55 to 65 were retired (2). Indeed, the sharp decline in workforce participation rates at around age 55 means that Australia has one of the lowest mature-age labor force participation rates in the OECD (3).

These figures, however, mask a gender difference in work participation among mature workers. While men are leaving the workforce earlier, women are more inclined to remain at work longer than they used to. In 1978, 83 percent of men aged between 55 and 59 were in the workforce. By 2001, this had declined to 68.6 percent. For women in the same age group, the participation rate increased from 30.1 percent in 1978 to 46.5 percent in 2001 (4).

Economic restructuring has been designed to achieve higher productivity. This has involved the use of new technologies that can disadvantage older workers through one of three related processes. First, the technologies reduce the skill advantage of many older workers. Second, there is a widespread belief that older workers are technophobic and cannot learn the new skills demanded by new technologies and processes (3). Third, older workers are generally given less opportunity to obtain in-service retraining to learn new systems and technologies (3).

This work context can make older workers feel unwelcome, insecure and out of place, which in turn, can produce a stressful work environment. The large number of people who take early retirement may reflect the desire of older workers to escape the difficult and stressful world of the contemporary workplace. While early retirement may be an attractive management tool for employers as they strive to meet downsizing targets and to restructure, there are countervailing trends that can make it more difficult to leave the workforce despite the workplace pressures.

Members of the postwar baby boom population are beginning to reach the typical retirement age. For governments, this has become a major policy issue. Early retirement combined with increased longevity means that the average male retiree will be retired for 25 to 28 years. Women who reach the age of 60 can be expected to live for an additional 30 years (5). Not only could this aging of the population lead to increased health costs (this has been debated—it depends on whether the number of years of disability increases), but it also has implications for retirement income policies. When this factor is combined with a declining birth rate, governments have become concerned about the adequacy of the taxation base to support the older retired population.

Some concern has also been expressed about labor shortages in the future if the current early retirement trends and low fertility trends continue (3). Access

Economics (6) has advised that the working-age population currently increases by 170,000 people a year but, if current trends continue, will grow by only 125,000 for the *entire decade* of the 2020s.

These population trends and retirement patterns have led to policy responses designed to encourage labor force participation among older workers and to reduce the cost to government of supporting the health and incomes of an aging population. Tighter targeting of old age pensions has been introduced, and the policy expectation is that older people will be responsible for their own retirement income and care costs. In Australia this targeting has led to the introduction of assets tests for receiving the old age pension and the requirement for greater personal contributions towards the cost of aged care accommodation. It is also leading to policies to encourage older workers to remain in the workforce for longer. The OECD advocates the removal of early retirement incentives (7). Changing the ages at which people can access superannuation and at which women can obtain the old age pension adds to the reasons why older workers may feel they need to keep working. The National Ageing Strategy has made policy proposals to assist in keeping older people in the workforce longer (3).

Anti-discrimination legislation has abolished age-related mandatory retirement in most of Australia's industries, thus enabling older workers to keep working if they wish. While this is to be welcomed, it can have negative effects for some workers. Apart from having to *decide* when to retire, the absence of a set and predictable retirement age can lead to unpleasant informal workplace pressures and devices that force people to retire "voluntarily."

Changing family structures also can contribute to the need to keep working. The consequences of increased divorce rates are now working their way through the population, so that increasing numbers of older people have been divorced. Divorce has substantial economic costs for both men and women (8)—especially women—which can mean that divorced older people cannot afford to retire.

In summary, older workers face two opposing pressures that could create a difficult and stressful workplace. On the one hand, workplace factors are making employment less predictable and increasing the pressure on older workers to retire. On the other hand, broader social, demographic, and policy changes mean that older workers may feel they cannot afford to stop working. They can expect to live for many years after retirement and increasingly are required to provide for themselves in later life. In this context, it is appropriate to explore the way in which older workers actually experience work in the later part of their working life.

Knowing about workplace stress among older workers is valuable for a number of reasons. High levels of stress at any age can be detrimental to health and work performance, and for these reasons alone, knowing and controlling stress in the workplace is important. In addition, high levels of stress in the workplace can affect retirement decisions. As people approach the age at which retirement is possible, high levels of workplace stress can affect decisions and lead to premature retirement. Since retirement becomes a feasible "escape" from a highly stressful workplace, older workers may take this route to early retirement. Premature retirement may have many negative outcomes, including lack of financial security and poor health. Premature retirement that stems from the desire to escape a stressful workplace will be a particular problem where it results in retirement without sufficient planning. Well-being in retirement is linked with the extent to which people have planned financially, socially, and psychologically for this stage of their life. To retire suddenly without adequate preparation will make the successful transition to retirement more difficult (9–11).

PREVIOUS RESEARCH: TWO MODELS

We have already outlined some reasons why older workers might find the contemporary workplace stressful, but little research has directly explored the extent to which older workers do, in fact, find it to be so. However, two models can be deduced from the literature on aging and worker satisfaction.

The "Happy Older Worker" Model

There is considerable research showing that older workers are more satisfied, committed, and motivated than younger workers (12–15). Several reasons have been offered for this pattern. First, older workers are more senior and have the better jobs; second, older workers are a more select group—the unhappy older employees have already left the workforce; third, older workers grew up in a different era, have a different attitude towards work, and are more easily satisfied with their lot than are younger workers (12). If this model is correct and can be applied to work stress, we would expect that *the older workers are, the less work stress they will report.*

The "Role Exit" Model

An alternative model is based on the concept of "anticipatory socialization." To the extent that retirement is predictable, older workers who are close to their anticipated retirement will anticipate their life after retirement and begin the process of "role exit" while they are still working. Ekerdt and DeViney argue that during this role exit: "Workers are engaged in a pre-retirement process of reinterpreting their work situations as they gradually dissociate from a role that has been central to their identity. . . . With the greener grass of retirement in view, the older workers are free to admit doubts about the quality and demands of their jobs" (12). If this model is correct, we would expect that *workers close to retirement will view their workplace in more negative terms (including seeing it as more stressful) than those whose retirement is not imminent.*

RESULTS ON WORK STRESS OF OLDER WORKERS

In this section we address three questions about work stress among older workers. First, to what extent do older workers show evidence of work-related stress? Second, which of the two age-based models of workplace stress gains the most support: do older workers become less stressed and more committed, or do levels of work-related stress increase as workers grow older and approach retirement? And third, to what extent does work stress vary according to factors such as gender, health, and various job characteristics? This analysis is based on data from the HRP survey of 7,000 workers; the general characteristics of this sample are described in Chapter 11.

What Are the Levels of Stress?

One-third of older workers (32.5 percent) indicated a high level of work stress, while a quarter (26.3 percent) said their work was not at all stressful. The remainder (41.3 percent) indicated that their work involved some stress. In addition to reporting their levels of work stress, participants described various aspects of their workplace. Tables 12.1 and 12.2 show how older workers rated a range of other workplace characteristics. Table 12.1 indicates the overwhelmingly positive way in which most workers regarded their workplace. On most indicators, close to 90 percent of the sample rated their workplace in positive terms. Table 12.2 shows the percentage of workers who were highly stressed according to the characteristics of the workplace. Not liking one's job is linked with finding the job highly stressful. Of those who did not like their job, 61.6 percent said their job was highly stressful. In contrast, only 30.2 percent of those who liked their job found it highly stressful. Of those who said that people at work are not friendly, 75 percent found their work very stressful. Enjoying the job and the people at work, feeling appreciated and valued, feeling that they fitted in and that people worked cooperatively together all made the workplace less stressful. The absence of good social relationships, teamwork, and a sense of being valued all contributed significantly to finding work and the workplace stressful.

Does Work Stress Increase with Age?

Are the older workers in this sample less stressed and happier than the younger workers? Or are older workers more stressed and disenchanted than younger ones, as Ekerdt and DeViney (12) would predict? The evidence is clear. The older workers were, the *less* likely they were to report their job as being highly stressful. Of those aged under 55, one-third (34 percent) found their job highly stressful, versus only a quarter of those aged 60 or over (Table 12.3). The same pattern held with other job characteristics. The older workers evaluated their workplace more positively than the younger group. Compared with those under 55, workers aged

Table 12.1

Older workers' ratings of workplace characteristics, percent agreeing with statement

ALL older workers	Very true	Fairly true	Not very true	Not at all true
Like job	42.0%	47.3%	8.2%	2.5%
Enjoy people at work	49.0	46.5	3.9	0.6
People are friendly	52.5	44.7	2.6	0.2
I feel appreciated	24.1	51.6	18.8	5.4
People pull together	21.6	54.1	18.6	3.9
Older workers valued	16.8	41.0	29.3	13.0
Work is a pleasant place	26.7	54.2	15.0	4.1
I fit in	35.2	53.1	9.6	2.1

Source: Healthy Retirement Project, Wave One survey.

Table 12.2

Older workers' work stress and workplace ratings, percent agreeing with statement who find job highly stressful

	Very true	Fairly true	Not very true	Not at all true	Gamma
Like job	30.2%	30.5%	45.8%	61.6%	–0.12***
Enjoy people at work	32.6	30.8	46.1	41.5	–0.05*
People are friendly	30.1	34.3	43.2	75.0	–0.12***
I feel appreciated	28.9	29.9	37.0	56.3	–0.17***
People pull together	32.5	30.8	35.1	45.2	–0.07***
Older workers valued	29.0	28.8	32.9	47.7	–0.17***
Work is a pleasant place	25.4	30.3	43.1	68.0	–0.25***
I fit in	30.2	31.8	39.2	56.6	–0.11***

Source: Healthy Retirement Project, Wave One survey.
$*P < .05$; $**P < .01$; $***P < .001$

Table 12.3

Evaluation of workplace by age group

	<55 yrs	55–59 yrs	60+ yrs	Gamma
Find job highly stressful	34.0%	31.1%	25.3%	0.11***
Like job (very true)	37.9	47.2	55.8	–0.20***
Enjoy people at work (very true)	46.8	52.5	54.5	–0.11***
People are friendly (strongly agree)	50.6	55.2	58.8	–0.11***
I feel appreciated (strongly agree)	21.3	26.2	36.7	–0.17***
People pull together (strongly agree)	20.6	23.5	27.6	–0.08***
Older workers valued (strongly agree)	14.9	18.2	25.8	–0.13***
Work is a pleasant place (strongly agree)	23.9	30.3	36.2	–0.14***
I fit in (strongly agree)	32.7	38.3	44.8	–0.13***

Source: Healthy Retirement Project, Wave One survey.
$^*P < .05$; $^{**}P < .01$; $^{***}P < .001$

60 or over liked their job more and were more likely to enjoy the people at work, to judge their workmates as friendly and their workplace as pleasant, to perceive that older workers were valued, and to feel appreciated and that they fitted in.

While these patterns support the "happy older worker" model (13, 14), they may not be a fair test of Ekerdt and DeViney's "role exit" model. Since retirement can take place at any age, a fairer test of this model requires an examination of worker stress and satisfaction by proximity to anticipated retirement.

Table 12.4 presents data on the levels of job stress according to how far away workers expect their retirement to be. Older workers experienced similar levels of work stress and gave similar workplace ratings, regardless of whether they expected to retire in the next 12 months, 1 to 5 years, or 6 to 10 years. That is, proximity to retirement seems to have no effect on perceptions of work stress or workplace ratings. For example, regardless of whether they expected to retire in the next 12 months, within 1 to 5 years, or within 6 to 10 years, about 39 percent said they liked their job. The same pattern applied to each of the job evaluation characteristics.

How Do Gender, Health, and Job Characteristics Affect Stress?

Gender: Research on work stress and retirement has paid less attention to older women workers and retirees than to comparable men. The results in Table 12.5 add

Table 12.4

Work stress and workplace ratings by time to anticipated retirement

	Next 12 months	1–5 yrs	6–10 yrs
Find job highly stressful	34.2%	31.7%	32.4%
Like job (very true)	38.5	38.5	39.1
Enjoy people at work (very true)	51.2	49.1	46.1
People are friendly (strongly agree)	56.3	55.9	51.9
I feel appreciated (strongly agree)	27.7	23.1	23.1
People pull together (strongly agree)	21.4	21.8	21.2
Older workers valued (strongly agree)	19.3	15.1	15.2
Work is a pleasant place (strongly agree)	29.1	26.1	25.7
I fit in (strongly agree)	38.1	35.9	34.3

Source: Healthy Retirement Project, Wave One survey.

to the little we know about gender differences in stress among older workers. Older women found their work just as stressful as did older men—one-third of both male and female older workers rated their work as highly stressful. On a number of other measures, however, women reported more positive workplace experiences than did men. Women were far more likely than men to enjoy their job (49 percent vs. 36 percent) and the people at work (57 percent vs. 42.5 percent). Women were also a little more likely than men to feel that they fitted in, that people were friendly, and that work was a pleasant place, and to say that older workers were appreciated.

At first sight, the *absence* of any gender difference in work stress is somewhat misleading. Other analyses not reported here have indicated a strong relationship between hours of work and stress—the more hours a person worked, the more stressful they reported the job to be (see Chapter 11). We also know that women in our sample worked fewer hours than men. For example, 33.3 percent of the women worked less than 30 hours a week, compared with only 4.9 percent of the men; and 39.5 percent of the men worked more than 40 hours a week, compared with only 13.6 percent of the women. Accordingly, we expected men to report higher levels of stress than did women. In other words, women workers were reporting higher levels of stress than might have been expected.

To explore this question further we compared the stress levels of men and women who worked similar hours (Table 12.6). This analysis revealed a different picture. When comparing men and women who work similar hours, women were

Table 12.5

Work stress and workplace ratings by gender

	Male	Female	Gamma
Find job highly stressful	32.5%	32.2%	0.04
Like job (very true)	36.4	49.0	–0.23***
Enjoy people at work (very true)	42.5	57.0	–0.27***
People are friendly (strongly agree)	50.4	55.2	–0.09***
I feel appreciated (strongly agree)	22.4	26.2	–0.03
People pull together (strongly agree)	21.6	22.4	–0.01
Older workers valued (strongly agree)	14.1	20.0	–0.12***
Work is a pleasant place (strongly agree)	24.3	29.6	–0.12***
I fit in (strongly agree)	32.6	38.5	–0.13***
Base no. for %	3,759	3,057	

Source: Healthy Retirement Project, Wave One survey.
*$P < .05$; **$P < .01$; ***$P < .001$

Table 12.6

Percent finding work highly stressful by gender and by hours worked per week

Hours per week	Male	Female	Gamma
<15	9.4%	7.4%	–0.02
15–29	16.3	26.2	0.26***
30–39	23.4	32.1	–0.16***
40	32.2	40.0	–0.18***
>40	43.9	51.6	–0.13**

Source: Healthy Retirement Project, Wave One survey.
*$P < .05$; **$P < .01$; ***$P < .001$

considerably *more* stressed than their male counterparts. For example, of those who worked between 30 and 39 hours a week, less than a quarter (23.4 percent) of the men found their job highly stressful, compared with almost one-third (32.1 percent) of the women. Our data do not indicate *why* equivalent hours of work are more stressful for women, but it is probably related to responsibilities beyond the workplace. Although these women are unlikely to have young children to care for, their family and related caring responsibilities may nevertheless affect how they experience their workplace (see Chapter 11).

Health. Personal health can affect the way in which all other aspects of one's life are experienced. As Table 12.7 indicates, workers' health affects their experiences at work. Workers in excellent health are very positive about their workplace. Compared with those in poorer health, healthy workers find their job less stressful, like their job more, find people friendlier, feel more appreciated, and feel they fit in better. It is difficult in a cross-sectional study such as this to clarify the direction

Table 12.7

Work stress and workplace ratings by self-rated health (excellent to poor)

	Excellent	Very good	Good	Fair	Poor	Gamma
Find job highly stressful	30.3%	29.7%	34.4%	42.9%	48.3%	–0.10***
Like job (very true)	51.5	43.1	36.9	32.6	32.8	0.17***
Enjoy people at work (very true)	56.2	50.3	44.1	43.5	38.3	0.14***
People are friendly (strongly agree)	62.2	53.5	47.4	42.3	46.7	0.18***
I feel appreciated (strongly agree)	31.2	24.5	21.2	16.6	10.0	0.13***
People pull together (strongly agree)	28.6	22.1	18.9	17.3	13.3	0.14***
Older workers valued (strongly agree)	23.3	15.9	14.3	14.1	8.3	0.12***
Work is a pleasant place (strongly agree)	34.5	27.6	22.1	20.4	13.6	0.16***
I fit in (strongly agree)	45.7	36.3	29.4	26.0	16.7	0.20***

Source: Healthy Retirement Project, Wave One survey.
$^{*}P < .05$; $^{**}P < .01$; $^{***}P < .001$

of any causal link between health on the one hand and work stress and workplace ratings on the other. Poorer health may be due to high stress levels and a less friendly and supportive work environment. Alternatively, poor health may affect both the extent to which work is experienced as stressful and how the workplace is perceived and experienced. Without knowing the nature of a person's health problems and using a longitudinal design, it is difficult to clarify this matter further.

Physical and Mental Demands of the Job. Job stress was clearly linked to the degree to which jobs required mental concentration. As Table 12.8 shows, of those employees whose job required heavy mental concentration, 45.7 percent found the work highly stressful. Physically demanding jobs appeared less stressful, with only 19.2 percent reporting their physically demanding job as being highly stressful. While a job that was both physically and mentally demanding was the most stressful, it was mental demands that seemed to contribute most to job stress.

Type of Occupation. Perhaps mental stress is the reason why older workers in managerial and professional jobs found their jobs more stressful than did those working in lower white-collar and traditional blue-collar jobs. Table 12.9 indicates the higher stress levels among these upper white-collar workers. The table also shows that it was these workers who found their jobs most mentally demanding and least physically demanding.

IMPACT OF RETIREMENT ON STRESS

To what extent does the *absence* of work result in stress among older people? There are two opposing schools of thought on the impact of retirement on stress levels among retired workers.

Table 12.8

Work stress by mental and physical effort required in job

Level of job stress	Heavy physical effort and mental concentration	Heavy mental concentration	Heavy physical effort	Neither physical effort nor mental concentration
High	58.0%	45.7%	19.2%	14.5%
Some	30.9	42.2	38.6	43.3
Low	11.1	12.2	42.2	42.2

Source: Healthy Retirement Project, Wave One survey.
Gamma = 0.53; $P < .001$

Table 12.9

Work stress by occupational group

	Manager/ admin.	Prof.	Paraprof.	Clerical	Sales	Trade	Machine op.	Laborer	Gamma
Highly stressful	39.9%	38.0%	38.7%	26.6%	33.6%	26.2%	22.2%	15.9%	0.20***
Physically demanding	5.0	4.2	13.2	4.6	27.7	28.3	20.2	49.1	–0.36***
Requires a lot of concentration	57.2	62.7	56.2	53.9	40.4	49.3	43.4	39.3	–0.18***

Source: Healthy Retirement Project, Wave One survey.
$*P < .05$; $**P < .01$; $***P < .001$

"Role Loss" Model

One model sees retirement as a time of loss—loss of a work role, loss of companionship from fellow workers, loss of income, loss of social standing, and loss of self-identity (16–21). By this view, retirement is a transition from having a central, productive, socially valued role to what Burgess (22) has called a "roleless role." Miller (19) portrays retirement as a "socially debilitating loss" and a "degrading withdrawal of all legitimate identity." Loss of the work role through retirement has been equated with loss through unemployment (23) and has been anticipated to have similar negative social and psychological consequences to those of unemployment.

According to this model, these losses produce higher levels of stress among retired workers, which in turn produce more physical disorders, earlier death, and greater social withdrawal (24, 25). Although the reduction of income is a well-known concomitant of retirement, this model views the losses resulting from retirement much more broadly.

It might be argued that the sense of loss will be greater for men than for women, since work is more likely to have been the core of men's adult identity. Women may have had a more marginal workforce attachment due to family and other caring responsibilities. While work is an important part of the life of many women, it is not their only identity, so retirement will be a less complete loss for women than for men (26, 27). However, it is likely that with the greater role of paid work in women's lives, with more women working throughout their lives, and with changes in the structure of families (more divorce, less marriage, smaller families, and higher rates of childlessness), leaving work will increasingly become a major transition and source of potential loss for women workers as well as for men. Indeed, we may find that leaving work becomes an even greater loss for women than for men. In her recent book *The Time Bind,* Hochschild (28) argues that for many women, work has become a source of solace and rewards compared with the constant demands of home life.

This negative conception of retirement does not entertain the possibility that leaving work can provide relief from difficult, demanding, and stressful workplaces and afford new opportunities through leisure, voluntary work, and community participation. The assumption is that since these activities are unpaid, they suffer from the same lack of value and recognition as the unpaid caring and domestic work of women.

Alternatives to the Loss Model

The role loss model of retirement has been challenged by more recent writers and research as too generalized and simplistic. Ekerdt has argued that "the vitality of the notion of retirement harms health is in part due to the availability of vivid anecdotes, the tendency to interpret big events as major causes of illness, the cultural celebration of work, theoretical perspectives in gerontology fostering expectations that retirement is disruptive, and the misinterpretation of research findings" (29). The loss model takes too much for granted. It assumes that work is a positive and meaningful activity and role for most older workers. However, for many people work can be boring, alienating, and a source of considerable stress. In the era of economic restructuring, pressures towards increased productivity, constant change, new technology, downsizing, and the ever present danger of redundancy, work can be a place of very considerable stress, anxiety, and conflict. To the extent that older workers experience these pressures, leaving the workforce in a respectable way by retiring may be a relief from stress rather than a source of stress. For workers who are in good health, who have secured their financial future through pension or superannuation savings and own their own home, retirement offers the potential for a new and positive life phase. A more positive view of retirement is that it can be a period of new opportunities rather than an occasion of loss.

The assumption that retirement is analogous to unemployment is also simplistic. Many people exercise a much greater degree of control over their retirement than they do over being unemployed. In our HRP panel study, 53 percent of retirees had complete say in the timing of their retirement, and a further 18 percent had a great deal of say. Previous research has demonstrated that the more control people have over their transition to retirement, the better they adapt to the transition (10, 30). A further, important difference between retirement and unemployment is that retirement is a much more normative life stage than is unemployment. So long as the retirement transition is "on time," the transition is widely accepted as a socially legitimate part of the life course and the adjustment to retirement is much better (18, 31, 32).

Older workers and retirees are a heterogeneous group (16). To assume a uniform response to retirement is to ignore this heterogeneity. For some people, leaving work will be a release; for others it will be a loss. Some workers will be financially secure, while others will struggle financially. Workers will vary in the degree of control they exercise over the retirement decision. Similarly, any stress of retirement may depend on what people retire *to*. If retirement involves retiring to care for an ill or disabled parent or partner, or if it means spending more time in an unhappy and stressed home environment, we can expect higher retirement stress than among those who retire to a happy and supportive family and community context. Some people retire earlier than they want, while others retire when they want. Some retire before or after the normatively acceptable time, while others retire at the "correct" time.

Research Evidence

The research on stress in retirement supports the second model described above: that is, retirement is not a uniformly stressful transition. Indeed, in the few studies that explicitly consider stress in retirement, about 30 percent of male retirees show signs of significant stress and about two-thirds do not find retirement stressful (16). The more common finding is that, taken overall, retirement is a positive time of life—often an improvement on pre-retirement life (33).

RESULTS ON STRESS IN RETIREES

Given the space limitations, we cannot detail in this chapter the correlates of post-retirement stress; this will be explored in later publications from the Healthy Retirement Project. Here we focus on the extent to which retirees found the post-retirement period difficult and stressful and whether the stress abates over time.

Our analysis is based on the HRP panel study of up to 416 retirees. We use data from up to four waves of the study: the immediate pre-retirement wave, the 6-month questionnaire, and the 12-month and 24-month follow-up interviews. We approach the study of change using both retrospective and prospective methods and by applying both aggregate-level and individual-level analysis.[1]

Retirement is no longer a simple event and is best thought of as a transition. Part of the purpose of the HRP was to track changes in health and well-being across this transition—to identify what changes took place, how quickly they took place, and how stable the changes were. For this reason, we adopted a longitudinal design by which we could track changes of the same set of individuals over time.

Ease or Difficulty of Retirement—Retrospective Evidence

One way of testing whether retirement is stressful is to ask retirees how easy or difficult they have found it to be. We asked respondents 24 months after they retired to recall the extent to which they found things easy or difficult at work before they retired; how easy or difficult things were in the first 6 months after retirement, in the next 6 months, and so forth, up to 24 months after retirement. Figure 12.1 plots the aggregate percentages of retirees indicating that things were easy or difficult at certain points in the retirement transition. The figure shows a very clear pattern. About a quarter of retirees found things difficult at around the time they retired. Whether this simply reflected their normal level of difficulties at work or whether there was a heightened level of difficulties around the retirement event we cannot tell. After retirement there was a steady decline in the percentage of people recalling the time following retirement as difficult. Only 19 percent thought the first 6 months were difficult; 10 percent thought the second 6 months

[1] Aggregate analysis is based on comparing the percentage *of the sample* with particular characteristics across waves. Individual analysis is based on tracking the extent to which individuals change between waves. Since some individuals may become more stressed between waves and others may become less stressed, aggregate-level and analysis may mask the extent of individual change.

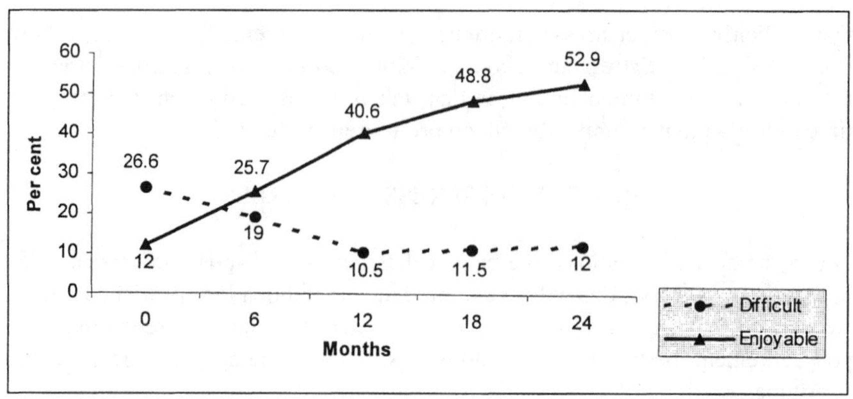

Figure 12.1. Difficulties and enjoyment of retirement by time since retirement. Aggregate figures based on retrospective questions asking about difficulty or enjoyment of specified periods after retirement.

were difficult. Thereafter, the percentage of the sample recalling the 12- to 18-month period and the 18- to 24-month period as difficult stabilized at around 10 to 12 percent.

Over the same period, we see a sharp rise in the percentage of the sample that found things easy. Only 12 percent of people recalled the period just before retirement as easy. However, a quarter of the sample thought of the first 6 months after retirement as easy. Even more (40.6 percent) recalled the 6- to 12-month period as easy. This figure keeps increasing, so that more than 50 percent thought of the 18- to 24-month period as easy. In other words, things got easier the longer people were retired (or at least, they did within the first two years after retiring).

Reduction in Stress: Aggregate Evidence

Table 12.10 indicates the frequency with which retirees reported a range of emotions. While stress is listed as a separate item, many of these items can be construed as symptoms of stress. Each column indicates the percentage of retirees who frequently felt each negative emotion at a given point in the retirement transition. These data did not involve retrospective questioning; rather, retirees reported how they felt at the time of each interview.

A clear and consistent pattern is evident. Just before retirement, respondents reported relatively high levels of these more negative feelings. However, the percentage feeling this way declined very rapidly, so that 6 months after retirement very few retirees reported frequently having these negative feelings. For example, while 21.2 percent of retiring workers reported being frequently irritated at the time they retired, this figure dropped to 3.6 percent within 6 months and remained

Table 12.10

Percent reporting negative feelings by months since retirement

Frequently feeling:	Just before retirement	6 months	12 months	24 months
Annoyed	29.3%	3.9%	9.4%	8.3%
Stressed	27.8	N.A.	5.5	7.6
Worried	21.4	8	9.2	8.8
Irritated	21.2	3.6	5.1	6.0

Source: Healthy Retirement Project, panel sample.

at a low level thereafter. Although respondents were not asked about stress levels at 6 months, the same general pattern occurred with stress. At the time of retiring, 27.8 percent said they frequently felt stressed. After 12 months of retirement this figure dropped dramatically to just 5.5 percent, and after 24 months to 7.6 percent.

Overall, the aggregate change analysis indicates a very sharp and sustained reduction in stress and negative feelings relatively soon after retirement. However, we do not know whether the high levels of stress and other negative emotions just before retirement were due to anxieties about retirement or reflected typical feelings among older workers. Regardless of which interpretation is correct, the evidence demonstrates low levels of these more negative feelings among retirees.

Ease or Difficulty of Retirement: Aggregate Prospective Evidence

A very positive picture of retirement is provided by other evidence in the survey. At each survey wave, we asked retirees how easy or difficult they had found the period since we last spoke to them. Figure 12.2 shows that retirees overwhelmingly assessed each post-retirement period as easy. About 85 percent regarded the first 6 months as easy, and thereafter 70 percent rated each period as easy. On the other hand, a small group of 15 percent rated each period after retirement as difficult.

In addition to asking about the general ease or difficulty of retirement, we inquired about particular aspects of post-retirement life to identify areas of life that retirement seems to benefit and areas for which it produces problems. Figure 12.3 indicates some of the downsides of retirement, showing the percentage of retirees reporting problems 12 months after retirement and again after 24 months. Relatively few people were disappointed with their retirement (6 to 7 percent), had time

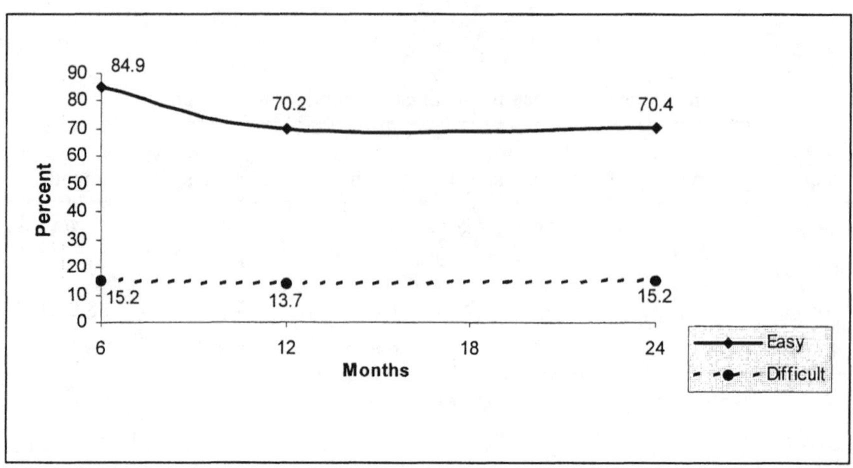

Figure 12.2. Ease or difficulty of retirement at given intervals after retirement. Aggregate data based on data collection at each wave. Questions asked about the period since the previous interview.

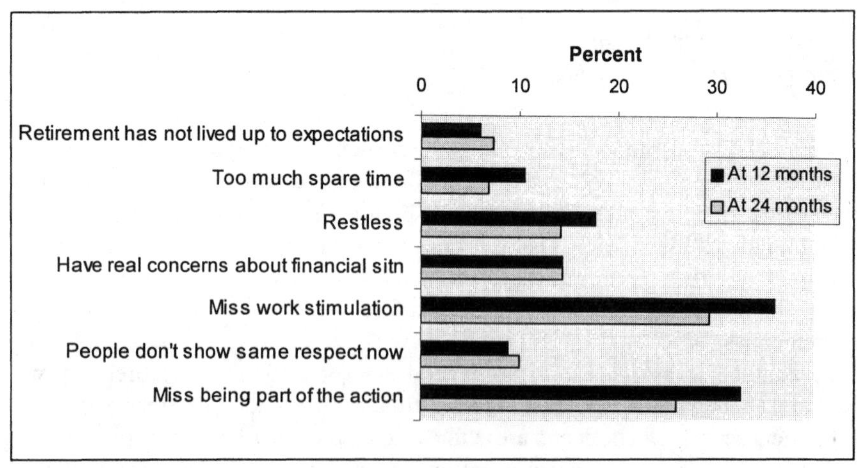

Figure 12.3. Problems following retirement after 12 and 24 months.

on their hands (7 to 11 percent), and felt they had lost the respect of other people (9 to 10 percent). Similarly, relatively few felt restless in retirement (14 to 17 percent), and only 14 percent indicated that they had financial concerns. The level of these concerns was remarkably stable over the 24-month period following retirement. Two areas that retirees reported as a downside of retirement were missing the stimulation of work (30 to 36 percent) and being part of the action (26 to 33 percent).

Figure 12.4 focuses on some benefits of retirement, reporting feelings at the 12-month and 24-month points after retirement. Approximately 90 percent of retirees said they enjoyed being at home a great deal, frequently doing things they really enjoyed, and enjoyed being retired and being busy. These very positive responses recorded at the end of 12 months were sustained until at least 24 months after retirement.

The more remarkable finding emerging from Figures 12.3 and 12.4 is the much greater frequency of reporting benefits than problems in retirement. In addition, patterns established in the first year persisted into the second year. It remains to be seen whether they persist beyond this time.

Reduction in Stress: Individual-Level Evidence

Individual-level analysis can indicate a pattern quite different from that provided by aggregate-level analysis. Given the space considerations, individual analysis is reported here for only a limited set of items: the frequency of negative feelings

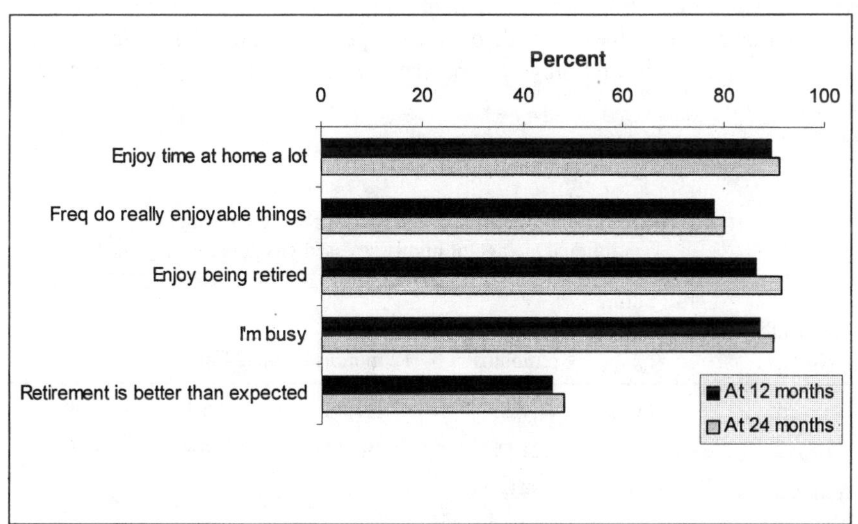

Figure 12.4. Benefits of retiring by time since retirement.

at various times after retirement. Aggregate-level analysis can mask the extent to which individuals change. If over time the same number of individuals become more stressed as become less stressed, these opposite changes would cancel each other out in aggregate-level analysis and thus mask the amount of real change in stress levels.

Table 12.11 shows changes in feeling stressed, anxious, and so forth, over the period of the panel study; it shows the percentage of retirees who frequently felt stressed, worried, annoyed, or irritated. It includes only those who frequently had these negative feelings around the time they retired. (Table 12.12, p. 265, explores those who rarely had these feelings.) Among those who frequently had these negative feelings at retirement time, there is a rapid and sustained improvement following retirement. The first row of Table 12.11 shows changes among those who, prior to retirement, reported frequently feeling stressed. *Of these highly stressed workers,* only 11.1 percent were stressed 12 months later and only 5.1 percent were still stressed 24 months later. Similarly, of those workers who were frequently feeling irritated at the time they retired, only 4.3 percent were still feeling this way 6 months later; after 24 months, none of the 72 individuals who initially were frequently irritated still felt that way.

While these figures show that workers who had these difficulties at the time they retired improved after retirement, they tell only half the story. What happens to those who were managing perfectly well when they retired? Do they continue to do well or do they deteriorate? Table 12.12 presents the changes among those who *rarely or never* experienced these negative feelings when they retired. Of those who initially rarely had these negative feelings, a proportion reported having these feelings *more* often following retirement. For example, *of those that rarely felt stressed* at the time they retired, only 87.3 percent reported still feeling this way 12 months later, and only 76.3 percent never felt stressed 24 months later.

Table 12.11

Improvement in stress and related feelings since retirement, individual change of highly stressed workers

Frequently feeling:	Just before retirement (t_0)	6 months	12 months	24 months	No. at t_0
Stressed	100%	N.A.	11.1%	5.1%	99
Worried	100	21.9%	9.6	6.8	73
Annoyed	100	4.4	1.1	1.1	92
Irritated	100	4.3	1.4	0	72

Source: Healthy Retirement Project, panel sample.

Table 12.12

Decline in stress and related feelings following retirement, individual change of workers who rarely felt stressed

Rarely feeling:	Just before retirement (t_0)	6 months	12 months	24 months	No. at t_0
Stressed	100%	N.A.	87.3%	76.3%	118
Worried	100	75.0%	61.7	56.7	120
Annoyed	100	77.3	55.2	41.4	87
Irritated	100	64.0	60.3	46.6	116

Source: Healthy Retirement Project, panel sample.

The rate of change was even more marked for worrying, irritation, and feeling annoyed. On each of these measures, of those who were relatively carefree around the time they retired, only about half remained as carefree 24 months later.

Overall, the pattern of individual change after retirement indicates that for those who frequently had a range of negative feelings at around retirement time, the frequency of these negative feelings rapidly declined. Virtually all these people improved quickly after retirement and sustained that improvement. On the other hand, those who rarely had these feelings around retirement time showed some evidence of deterioration following retirement. This analysis of individual change indicates that there is change in *both directions* after retirement. Some people do better while others seem to do worse.

Some of this change undoubtedly reflects the statistical phenomenon of regression to the mean—that is, people who score at the extremes on a measure tend to moderate over time: there is a convergence of the extremes. Furthermore, measures such as these inevitably reflect some degree of measurement error. For these reasons, some care should be taken in interpreting the absolute figures in these tables.

The important finding, however, is the different *patterns* of change. Among those who were frequently struggling with negative feelings around retirement time, the decline in these feelings was rapid and very large. Most of the change occurred in the first 6 months and declined to very low levels. That is, those who were not doing so well emotionally when they retired had a very high probability of improving and sustaining that improvement. In contrast, the pattern of change among those who were untroubled when they retired was much smaller and more gradual.

The obvious next question is, *who* improves and who deteriorates after retirement? What factors predict adjustment after retirement? Unfortunately, we must restrict ourselves here to just one question: how well did workers who found work to be highly stressful adjust to retirement? Did the stressed workers become the stressed retirees?

Table 12.13 provides information on the relationship between high job stress and a range of emotions at retirement time. Those experiencing high job stress were more worried, annoyed, irritated, and generally stressed than those whose job was not stressful. Twelve months later, these feelings had declined sharply. For example, while 40 percent of those in highly stressful jobs frequently felt annoyed at around retirement time, only 8.9 percent of this group still frequently felt annoyed 12 months later. Twenty-four months later, the same low levels of feeling annoyed were evident among those who had retired from stressful jobs. The same pattern applies to feelings of worry, irritation, and general stress. This means that the effects of high job stress appear to dissipate rapidly following retirement.

CONCLUSION

Our purpose in this chapter has been to describe how stress and related factors impinge on the work experience of older workers, what role stress plays in the

Table 12.13

Stress experienced at and after retirement by level of job stress

Frequently feeling:	High job stress	Some job stress	Low job stress	Gamma
At retirement				
Worried	33.6%	17.3%	12.0%	0.27***
Annoyed	40.2	28.8	20.9	0.24***
Irritated	31.7	21.5	12.7	0.20***
Stressed	42.1	24.1	8.9	0.40***
12 months after retirement				
Worried	12.1	7.0	8.9	0.06
Annoyed	8.9	8.4	11.9	0.02
Irritated	5.1	4.9	5.0	0.07
Stressed	5.0	7.0	4.0	0.12
24 months after retirement				
Worried	13.1	7.5	5.2	0.10
Annoyed	9.9	6.7	8.3	0.07
Irritated	6.6	5.2	6.3	0.04
Stressed	11.2	6.0	5.2	0.11

Source: Healthy Retirement Project, panel sample.
*$P < .05$; **$P < .01$; ***$P < .001$

transition from the workforce, and how withdrawal from the workforce affects stress and related feelings.

The general picture provided by the sample of 7,000 older workers and the panel of 416 retirees is a positive one. Only a minority of older workers found their work and workplace to be highly stressful. The majority enjoyed their work and their workplace, enjoyed the people, and felt appreciated. However, a significant minority did feel that, in general, older workers were not appreciated in their workplace. Despite this, and despite the uncertainty and change produced by economic restructuring and opposing pressures to continue work, these workers did not appear to experience their work as highly stressful or particularly uncomfortable. In addition, job and workplace characteristics were linked to work stress. High stress was linked to not enjoying the job, finding the workplace unpleasant, and finding people at work not very friendly. Workers who felt appreciated and supported by other people and felt that they fitted in were relatively less stressed.

The oldest workers were the least stressed and rated their workplaces more positively than the younger workers in this sample of workers aged 50 and over. There was no support for the proposition that as workers near retirement they become more negative about work. Older female workers were no more stressed than male workers but would have been more stressed had they worked the same number of hours as the men. Presumably, these women tried to manage the stress of combining work, family, and caring responsibilities by working part time.

Work stress and workplace rating were linked to occupational type and the level of concentration required. It was not physical effort that the older workers found stressful but high levels of sustained concentration. Blue-collar workers found their work less stressful than white-collar workers. The study found that health and stress were linked: healthy workers found their jobs less stressful than those with poor health.

For most retirees, the actual experience of retirement was very positive. There was no support for the "loss model" of retirement. Looking back, most workers felt that all stages of retirement were easy and very few found any stage difficult. Both individual-level and aggregate-level analyses showed a sharp and sustained decline in stress and other negative feelings following retirement. While some people manifested some increase in stress and other negative feelings after retirement, these cases were outweighed by those in which general well-being improved. In addition, the effects of high work stress on feelings such as worry, irritation, annoyance, and general stress rapidly dissipated following retirement.

Further work is required to identify the particular types of people who cope best with retirement and those who struggle. From those who cope best we should be able to learn more about the factors that assist in their successful transition to a less stressful life after leaving the workforce. The findings here are encouraging: they show that for these workers retirement was not the end of their life. Rather, it was the beginning of a new and positive stage of life that could last for a quarter of a century. Identifying the best ways of making the successful transition to this new life stage is clearly an important focus for ongoing research.

REFERENCES

1. Crowley, P., and Cutbush, G. *Ageing Gracefully: An Overview of the Economic Implications of Australia's Ageing Population Profile.* Commonwealth Department of Health and Aged Care, Canberra, 1999.
2. Australian Bureau of Statistics. *Australian Social Trends 1998.* Catalogue No. 4102.0. Canberra, 1998.
3. Bishop, B. *The National Strategy for an Ageing Australia: Employment for Mature Age Workers.* Issues paper. Commonwealth of Australia, Canberra, 1999.
4. Australian Bureau of Statistics. *Year Book, Australia, 2002.* Canberra, 2002.
5. Australian Bureau of Statistics. *Deaths, Australia, 2000.* Canberra, 2001.
6. Access Economics. *Population Ageing and the Economy.* Commonwealth Department of Health and Aged Care, Canberra, 2001.
7. OECD. *Ageing in OECD Countries: A Critical Policy Challenge.* Paris, 1996.
8. McDonald, P. (ed.). *Settling Up: Property and Income Distribution on Divorce in Australia.* Prentice-Hall, Melbourne, 1986.
9. Braithwaite, V. A., and Gibson, D. M. Adjustment to retirement: What we know and what we need to know. *Ageing Soc.* 7: 1–18, 1987.
10. Hardy, M. A., and Quadagno, J. Satisfaction with early retirement: Making choices in the auto industry. *J. Gerontol. B Psychol. Sci. Soc. Sci.* 50B: 217–228, 1995.
11. Villani, P. J., and Roberto, K. A. Retirement decision making: Gender issues and policy implications. *J. Women Aging* 9: 151–163, 1997.
12. Ekerdt, D. J., and DeViney, S. Evidence for a pre-retirement process among older male workers. *J. Gerontol.* 48: S35–S43, 1993.
13. Glenn, N., and Weaver, C. Age, cohort and reported job satisfaction in the United States. In *Current Perspectives on Aging and the Life Course,* edited by Z. S. Blau, Vol. 1, pp. 89–109. JAI Press, Greenwich, Conn., 1985.
14. Kalleberg, A., and Loscocco, K. Aging, values and rewards: Explaining age differences in job satisfaction. *Am. Sociol. Rev.* 48: 78–90, 1983.
15. Rhodes, S. Age related differences in work attitudes and behaviour: A review and conceptual analysis. *Psychol. Bull.* 93: 328–367, 1983.
16. Bosse, R., Spiro, A., III, and Levenson, M. R. Retirement as a stressful life event. In *Clinical Disorders and Stressful Life Events*, edited by T. W. Miller, pp. 325–350. International Universities Press, Madison, Conn., 1997.
17. Harris, L., et al. *Aging in the Eighties: America in Transition.* National Council on Aging, Washington, D.C., 1981.
18. McGoldrick, A. E. Stress, early retirement and health. In *Aging, Stress, and Health,* edited by K. S. Markides and C. L. Cooper, pp. 91–118. Wiley, New York, 1989.
19. Miller, D. R. The study of social relationships: Situation, identity and social interaction. In *Psychology: A Study of Science*, Vol. 5, edited by S. Kick, pp. 315–328. McGraw-Hill, New York, 1965.
20. Streib, G., and Schneider, C. J. *Retirement in American Society: Impact and Process.* Cornell University Press, Ithaca, N.Y., 1971.

21. Thompson, G. B. Work versus leisure roles: An investigation of morale among employed and retired men. *J. Gerontol.* 28: 339–344, 1973.
22. Burgess, E. W. Aging in western culture. In *Aging in Western Societies: A Comparative Study*, edited by E. W. Burgess, pp. 3–27. University of Chicago Press, Chicago, 1960.
23. Moen, P. A life course perspective on retirement, gender and well-being. *J. Occup. Health Psychol.* 1: 131–144, 1996.
24. Adams, O., and Lefebvre, L. Retirement and mortality. *Aging Work* 4: 115–120, 1981.
25. MacBride, A. Retirement as a life crisis? Myth or reality. *Can. Psychiatr. Assoc. J.* 21: 547–556, 1976.
26. Szinovacz, M. Preferred retirement timing and retirement satisfaction in women. *Int. J. Aging Hum. Dev.* 24: 301–317, 1987.
27. Wingrove, C. R., and Slevin, K. F. A sample of professional and managerial women: Success in work and retirement. *J. Women Aging* 3: 95–117, 1991.
28. Hochschild, A. *The Time Bind: When Work Becomes Home and Home Becomes Work.* Holt, New York, 1997.
29. Ekerdt, D. J. Why the notion persists that retirement harms health. *Gerontologist* 27: 454–457, 1987.
30. Quick, H. E., and Moen, P. Gender, employment, and retirement quality: A life course approach to the differential experiences of men and women. *J. Occup. Health Psychol.* 3: 44–64, 1998.
31. Neugarten, B. Retirement in the life course. *Triangle* 29: 119–125, 1990.
32. Palmore, E. B., Fillenbaum, G. G., and George, L. K. . Consequences of retirement. *J. Gerontol.* 39: 109–116, 1984.
33. Matthews, A. M., et al. A crisis assessment technique for the evaluation of life events: Transition to retirement as an example. *Can. J. Ageing* 1: 28–39, 1982.

CONTRIBUTORS

JIM BARRY is a political sociologist and reader at the University of East London. He is currently co-director of the University's Organisation Studies Research Group, based in the East London Business School, and is a member of the European Network on Managerialism and Higher Education. He is involved in two long-term research projects: one into gender and organizations, with particular reference to managerialism in higher education; the other into gender, politics, and urban governance in London and Mumbai (formerly Bombay). He is an associate editor of *Gender, Work, and Organization* and has published on gender and politics, gender and public service, gender and organizations, gender and business ethics, gender and stress, gender and higher education, managerialism and higher education, and lone parenting and employment.

ELISABETH BERG is a docent in sociology at Luleå University of Technology in Sweden, with an appointment as senior visiting research fellow at the University of East London. She has been involved in several research projects into gender and organizations, with particular reference to the public sector, and is a member of the European Network on Managerialism and Higher Education. Her current research interests include gender and managerialism in higher education and the human consequences of recent changes in the public sector for stress and burnout. She has a number of publications, including *Kvinna och chef i offentlig förvaltning* (Women and leader in public service) (Liber, 2000).

JOHN CHANDLER is a principal lecturer and sociologist teaching organizational studies in the East London Business School at the University of East London. His current research interests include gender and managerialism in higher education and the "new careers." He is a co-director of the Organisation Studies Research Group in the East London Business School and is a member of the European Network on Managerialism and Higher Education. He has a number of publications, including *Organisation and Identities* (edited with Jim Barry and Heather Clark; International Thomson, 1994) and *Organization and Management: A Critical Text* (edited with Jim Barry and others; International Thomson, 2000).

DAVID DE VAUS is an associate professor of sociology at La Trobe University, in Melbourne. He has published extensively in the areas of survey research methodology, family sociology, and life course transitions. His main books are *Surveys in Social Research* (Routledge); *Letting Go: Relationships between Adults and Their Parents* (Oxford); *Research Design in Social Research* (Sage),

Australian Family Profiles (AIFS), and *Analysing Social Science Data* (Sage). He is a chief investigator in a VicHealth-funded longitudinal study on the effects of retirement on health and is currently advising the World Health Organization on health-promotion strategies among older people.

JANE FERRIE is a senior research fellow in the Department of Epidemiology and Public Health at University College London. She earned an M.Sc. in health promotion at Leeds Metropolitan University while working on an action research project to reduce rates of sexually transmitted diseases and population AIDS risk in Nicaragua. In 1999 she completed a Ph.D. on the relationship between labor market status and health in the Whitehall II study of white-collar civil servants. She is currently writing papers based on a project examining the contribution of perceived job insecurity to inequalities in health and is contributing to a series of papers on work-related issues in Finland. Her research interests include job insecurity, exit from work, retirement, income, and health inequalities.

WENDY A. MACDONALD is currently ergonomics area coordinator and manager of the Centre for Ergonomics and Human Factors in the Faculty of Health Sciences, La Trobe University, in Melbourne. She has undergraduate and graduate qualifications in psychology and a Ph.D. in human engineering, focusing on the measurement of task demands. Her main areas of research interest are workload analysis and evaluation in relation to work rates, staffing levels, occupational stress, and work-related musculoskeletal disorders, and the analysis and evaluation of driver performance in relation to road safety.

CLAIRE MAYHEW is a visiting fellow in the School of Management at Griffith University and an associate of the Industrial Relations Research Centre at the University of New South Wales, Sydney. She has a Ph.D. in occupational health and safety and has worked in the health care system, as an academic, at the Australian Institute of Criminology. In August 2001 she was seconded to the Task Force on Prevention and Management of Violence in the Health Workplace to conduct a major empirical study of the incidence and severity of the different types of occupational violence experienced by health workers. She has published a number of books and monographs as well as numerous journal articles in the Australian and international scientific press on a range of OHS issues. She has particular interests in OHS among small business and the self-employed, in the prevention of occupational violence, and in the links between violence and stress. In October 2001 she drafted the report "The Contribution of Stress to Coronary Heart Disease" for the WHO Global Burden of Disease project.

JOHN MCCORMICK is a senior lecturer and coordinator of educational administration in the School of Education, University of New South Wales, Sydney. His research involves stress and burnout of teachers working in large education systems and various other aspects of motivation related to teachers' work and students' learning, including leadership and organizational decision-making.

LAWRENCE R. MURPHY, Ph.D., is a research psychologist at the U.S. National Institute for Occupational Safety and Health. He has more than 20 years of experience conducting research in the areas of job stress and stress reduction. His current research involves identifying characteristics of healthy work organizations and examining the health and safety consequences of downsizing.

LEWIS D. PEPPER, M.D., M.P.H., is an assistant professor of environmental health at the Boston University School of Public Health. He has been an occupational medicine physician for 20 years. His current research examines the relationship between the quality of health care provided and the working conditions in primary care clinical practices. He is also the principal investigator of a U.S. Department of Energy Medical Surveillance program for former nuclear weapons workers at the Nevada Test Site.

CHRIS L. PETERSON is a health sociologist and senior research fellow in the Faculty of Medicine, Nursing and Health Sciences, Monash University, Melbourne, Australia. He previously worked at La Trobe University, where he also coordinated the E-Healthcare Education and Research Group. He has worked with members of Worksafe, Australia (now the National Occupational Health and Safety Commission) and the Australian Council of Trade Unions on the national stress campaign. Prior publications include *Stress at Work: A Sociological Perspective* (Baywood, 1999) and books and articles on occupational health and safety management. Dr. Peterson is a chief investigator in a major National Health and Medical Research Council research project on self-management programs for people with chronic illness.

YVONNE WELLS is a psychologist and a research fellow at the Lincoln Gerontology Centre at La Trobe University, in Melbourne, where she has been involved in several major research projects and consultancies. She is the project coordinator for the Healthy Retirement Project, a longitudinal study that focuses on adjustment to retirement, and she is a member of the Evaluation Unit, which monitors the work of the Aged Care Assessment Service. She has had a longstanding interest in family caregiving, and more recent studies include an emphasis on cross-cultural issues. In 2000, she became a Fellow of the Australian Association of Gerontology, in recognition of her outstanding professional contribution to gerontology.

INDEX